# Managing Oracle
# Fusion Applications

**Richard Bingham**

New York   Chicago   San Francisco
Lisbon   London   Madrid   Mexico City   Milan
New Delhi   San Juan   Seoul   Singapore   Sydney   Toronto

*The McGraw·Hill Companies*

Cataloging-in-Publication Data is on file with the Library of Congress

## Managing Oracle Fusion Applications

1 2 3 4 5 6 7 8 9 0   DOC DOC   1 0 9 8 7 6 5 4 3 2 1

ISBN   978-0-07-175033-2
MHID      0-07-175033-9

**Sponsoring Editor**
Wendy Rinaldi

**Editorial Supervisor**
Jody McKenzie

**Project Managers**
Arushi Chawla and
Vasundhara Sawhney,
Cenveo Publisher Services

**Acquisitions Coordinator**
Stephanie Evans

**Technical Editor**
Kai Pigg

**Copy Editor**
Lisa Theobald

**Proofreader**
Claire Splan

**Indexer**
Jack Lewis

**Production Supervisor**
Jean Bodeaux

**Composition**
Cenveo Publisher Services

**Illustration**
Cenveo Publisher Services

**Art Director, Cover**
Jeff Weeks

**Cover Designer**
Pattie Lee

To my wife, Kate, for your total support; to my daughter, Charlotte, for keeping mummy occupied; and to my son, Gabriel, for keeping us all happy.

# About the Author

**Richard Bingham** is a senior principal support engineer currently working on the design and delivery of the tools, processes, and services that make up Oracle Fusion Applications Support. Richard joined Oracle in 1999 and has supported more than ten different application products and thousands of customers.

Between graduating with a BS in Geology and joining Oracle, Richard worked as a developer, an analyst, an implementer, and a system manager (as well as a doorman and a offshore mud-logger!). Richard is also an accredited assessor for the UK Institute of Customer Services, awarding professional customer service certifications to a wide range of organizations.

# About the Technical Editor

**Kai Pigg** is Director in Fusion Apps Functional Architecture, specializing in Customer Software Lifecycle Management. With a background in both IT and accounting, Kai worked with Oracle Applications for more than 20 years in various roles in EMEA and North America, before joining the Fusion Apps Development team.

# Contents at a Glance

# Contents

# Foreword

Fusion Applications takes the concept of an Enterprise Application to a whole new level. Whether you're in the IT department, a systems integrator, a business leader, or an end user, Fusion Applications has more of what you need, less of what you don't, and some of what you didn't even think possible.

Being designed from the ground up on Oracle's latest technologies, it is based entirely on industry open standards, allowing it to fit perfectly alongside existing architectures, infrastructures, and applications. Its thousands of features support a broad range of common business processes, and are based on both innovative, new capabilities as well as the best features from a combination of Oracle's E-Business Suite, PeopleSoft, JD Edwards, and Siebel applications. And when this still isn't enough, it contains an unparalleled capability to adapt to organizational, departmental, or even user-specific needs, allowing it to truly enhance and not just manage complex business operations. The products in Fusion Applications can be deployed in many different ways: one at a time, as a complete suite, in co-existence with other Oracle Application suites, or integrated with third-party applications. In addition to standard OnPremise licensing, Oracle offers Fusion Applications in many other options, such as SaaS and OnDemand. As part of the OnDemand offering, the applications can be hosted at Oracle, the customer site, or the hosting vendor's sites.

Written firmly from the perspective of enhancing the manageability of Enterprise Applications, and based on years of working with Oracle's application customers, Richard brings a unique and insightful perspective to the subject. So while this book includes a valuable introduction to Fusion Applications, as well as an overview of effective application system management, the synergy of these two subjects together multiplies the value of each and provides essential information, guidance, and advice that all interested parties should know and use.

Paul Brook
Vice President
Applications Support
Oracle Corporation

# Acknowledgments

I would like to thank everyone who helped turn this from a nice idea into a real book. Special mention goes to Lisa McClain and Wendy Rinaldi for believing in and supporting the project and to Stephanie Evans for guiding me and answering all of my questions. Also special thanks to Arushi Chawla and Vasundhara Sawhney (Glyph International) and Lisa Theobald, who together improved almost every sentence I wrote. I would also like to thank my managers at Oracle, Ashish Kalra and Kuldeep Chaudhari, for fully supporting this extra-curricular project.

Special thanks goes to Kai Pigg, my technical editor for this book and actually most of my daily work! His dedication, expert advice, and guidance on every section of every chapter probably makes him closer to a co-author. Almost every day you have a lesson for me.

# Introduction

## Goals

This book seeks to provide four main benefits to the reader:

- **Information**   It provides background information about Fusion Applications, which is useful whether you are creating an implementation plan, looking at future uptake, or simply improving your knowledge.

- **Strategy**   It helps you understand the need for and content of a high quality Fusion Applications management strategy and plan.

- **Reference**   It forms a practical reference guide for those running Fusion Applications.

- **Support**   It complements the existing documentation and training material, all in the context of application management.

In addition to these core benefits, the information in this book can be useful for many other purposes (such as for internal training).

## Approach

I have spent more than a decade in-the-trenches of Oracle's Applications Technical Support teams, and I am now helping develop the service delivery model for Fusion Applications. This helps me bring not only technical and product knowledge, but also the experience of real situations and problems, to offer insights into best practice solutions as well as the unique capabilities of Fusion Applications.

The subjects covered in this book assume you have some basic familiarity with enterprise applications; however, because Fusion Applications is completely new, all concepts are explained fully as we go. The topics covered range from some detailed explanations of technology-based areas (such as diagnostic logging), to some more general principles of system management (such as application lifecycle models).

The focus remains fully on managing the Fusion Applications instance; and although other subjects such as implementation and customization are mentioned in this context, you should consult separate resources for more detail. The appendix of this book provides further reading resources to help with that.

The structure of this book is intended to help you first build a basic understanding of Fusion Applications, then do the same for Enterprise Application Management. Finally, the two are brought together into a complete integrated picture. The discussion then focuses on how the tools, services, and processes of the Fusion Applications environment can be leveraged to deliver successful system management.

# Intended Audience

With such varied content, this book has a wide range of potential readers. The most obvious of which is the IT staff, particularly system and database administrators, who can use it to learn about Fusion Applications, how it can be managed, and the available tools it includes.

Senior management, from both IT and the business, can also benefit from the material in this book. These decision-makers can read the first few chapters to familiarize themselves with what Fusion Applications is and then read on to get an understanding of what it takes to own and run it successfully.

The roles that exist between IT and business, such as system analysts and business superusers, will also find the content helpful. The innovative software solutions that these roles focus on usually require a good understanding of the architecture of any related enterprise applications, something this book provides.

The final audience for this book is the system implementer, from specialist consulting firms, to internal project teams. Because Fusion Applications will be implemented by those running existing Oracle

Applications (E-Business Suite, PeopleSoft, Siebel, JDE Edwards, and so on), plus companies replacing their non-Oracle legacy business applications, this book will inform implementers in both scenarios, without much need for any prerequisite knowledge of Oracle-specific technologies or solutions.

# A Brief History

Oracle Fusion Applications may be brand new, but its roots go all the way back to 1987. After ten years of successfully selling the database and development tools, and watching almost every customer use these in slow and expensive business application development, Oracle decided it could help (and profit) by writing the most common business applications and distributing those to its clients.

Oracle Applications began with Release 1 (1987), which centered around general ledger and purchasing applications. Payables was then added, and just two years later (1989) Oracle Applications Release 4 included receivables, fixed assets, and revenue accounting. By the end of 1989, more features were added, with Release 6 including the first Human Resource Management System (HRMS) application. With Release 7 in 1990, basic manufacturing products were released as well, including inventory and order entry.

Three years later, Release 10 was available. This became the well-known *character version* (10C), which saw project accounting added, and the *Smart Client* (10SC) version followed a year later (1996). By 1998, and Release 10.7, we saw significant expansion of the financials, HRMS and manufacturing products, as well as the addition of Business Intelligence capabilities. By release 11*i* in 2000, Oracle had renamed the applications to the E-Business Suite, and added several customer relationship management (CRM) applications.

Although more products and features were added in 11i.x and Release 12, the next five years were dominated by the acquisition of other enterprise resource planning (ERP) product vendors, most notably these: 2004 added PeopleSoft (with J.D Edwards), 2005 added Retek and G-Log, and 2006 added Siebel. With all these products and suites added, 2007 saw the initial formation of a Fusion Applications Strategy, with the aim of designing and building a new suite of applications using the best parts of each Oracle-owned product suite, and based on the latest technologies available (many also through acquisition).

# Evolution

As the Oracle Applications product offerings continued to increase in depth and breadth of features, the evolutionary growth of several other areas have influenced what we now have in Oracle Fusion Applications.

## Business Applications Evolution

Since 1951, when British food manufacturer and tea-room owner J. Lyons and Company first used its LEO1 computer to calculate overnight production schedules, businesses have unequivocally understood the benefits that computation can bring: to get more done, faster. In these early days, basic hardware was capable of only short processing routines and therefore it was up to each organization to develop its own way of using it. As hardware adoption grew with more standardization, the emerging software industry allowed the purchase of prewritten applications for groups of common tasks, such as account functions and payroll, reducing the need for programming.

As hardware capabilities grew, software vendors built out their offerings to include more and more features to support more business operations. These aggregated applications became behemoths that supported all manners of tasks, particularly those involving financial and manufacturing, and were labeled by Gartner in 1990 as Enterprise Resource Planning (ERP) applications.

This is where Oracle Applications fitted initially, and it quickly expanded its scope. The focus was both to match the features of niche applications and offer it as part of a preintegrated set of supporting applications. This was a successful strategy, and it matched perfectly to the needs of large corporations, which wanted wide-ranging features while avoiding costly integration. It also followed the evolution of its technology underpinning, moving from dumb terminals server-side apps, to client-server forms-based apps, to HTML-based web applications.

It's interesting to observe how the use of technology in business has evolved, too, and how it is increasingly seen for what it really is—an enabler—as opposed to having any intrinsic value in itself. With the dot-com bubble burst, the days of "tech for tech's sake" are gone, and it's plain to see from current use of both business (such as Oracle) and consumer (such as Apple) technology that "it's all about the applications."

Another good example (although currently without much business relevance) is the excitement around augmented reality—where a cell phone's built-in camera is linked to real-time location services and the resulting mash-up application shows a graphical overlay of data and annotation that enhances the view of the real world. Just imagine for a minute how this could be applied to business. It could form a business intelligence tool, where the day-to-day operations are running, and as you view a graphical model or position a linked camera at each area (a machine, a department, a location), the software application generates an overlay view of data, trends, and forecasts for rich analysis and decision-making. It's certainly different from the traditional reams of printed reports, that's for sure!

# Purpose Evolution

Precisely how applications are used in business has evolved as well, and it continues to do so with Fusion Applications. Software applications started as simple number-crunchers, doing the repetitive, number-based work quickly and accurately. This reflected the core capabilities of the early software. These applications reduced the number of processing clerks needed, which directly affected the bottom-line and in turn began to offset the high cost of the computer system.

As the automation of administration work continued, applications began to add management reporting functions, so that the data being compiled could provide a deeper operational understanding and support data-based decision-making.

As applications matured, businesses trusted them to perform more core tasks safely with minimal supervision. This shifted the focus away from reacting to past operating problems to performing proactive analysis to look for improvements. A new generation of business application features evolved to fit this need, most commonly known under the umbrella term of *Business Intelligence*. These sat alongside the core applications and provided a variety of standard analysis reports, and when further insight was needed it was relatively easy to add customization or to create new ones. Oracle Applications had (among other things) the Discoverer product that forms a popular method of performing operational analysis.

Built on top of process automation, standard reporting, and data analysis now comes a new stage in the evolution of purpose. Business applications now collect operational data in incredible detail, store vast amounts in readily accessible format, and use it within algorithm-based engines that take detailed analysis to the next level, offering predictive modeling capabilities and even recommended actions to take. In a way, the software has gone from slave, to co-worker, to master. The recommendations are often based on sets of prewritten rules, though self-learning concepts along the lines of artificial intelligence are starting to appear more and more.

## Evolution of Access

As with the evolutionary stages mentioned above, the profile of who uses the enterprise applications has changed too. To start with it was usually only the programmers who submitted the processing instructions, however this quickly switched to data entry clerks as basic inputs were required before the number-crunching could take place.

As input mechanisms improved through embedded technology and networking, more data was captured at the point of origin, such as the shop floor or the point of sale. At the same time, more application features where added, meaning that almost all job roles across the organization involved either inputting data or running reports.

With the evolution of using the Internet for business, new application access methods have become feasible and delivery mechanisms such as Software-as-a-Service (SaaS) and cloud-based deployment are hot topics today. These models outsource the complexity of managing the application to a specialist hosting company, leaving businesses to focus on their core competencies. Cloud-type deployments are particularly interesting because they include the ability for resources to scale up and down across the shared data center dynamically (that is, between customers) and automatically, based on real-time request volumes. This has been measured as increasing average server utilization from 5 to 60 percent, representing a huge potential cost savings that still doesn't overload the hardware.

This is especially relevant as, thanks to Internet technologies, enterprise applications are more accessible than ever, with each instance available to employees across to the business, from a Chinese manufacturing team ordering raw materials, to the CEO in Switzerland approving bonuses. This open access also extends between businesses, where external parties such as suppliers and customers can log into each other's application systems and automatically exchange large volumes of transactions, documents, and messages. And all of this is expected to be available and fast, 24 hours a day, seven days a week.

# User Experience Evolution

Each release of Oracle Applications has encompassed the latest developments in user-interface design; however, as the breadth of the product grew, having to reengineer every last page, form, and report to change the look and feel of the user interface became somewhat impractical. This extra work would have probably resulted in a smaller number of new features in each new release. Instead, Oracle used the new user interface designs intelligently, by first redesigning those features that would most benefit the user.

The original look and feel of Oracle Applications was based on the early Oracle Forms product, initially providing a terminal-based text view into the application. This endured up to Release 10, when Oracle released its Smart Client version. This installed an Oracle Forms client on each PC to help serve up a more graphical user interface (GUI). In 1998 and the 10.7 release, Oracle's Network Computing Architecture (NCA) changed the Oracle Forms client to run as a smaller Java applet on each PC. Release 11 quickly followed and its Java Forms client became much richer. This release also saw use of the GUI spread from only a few area to adoption across the entire application suite.

The evolution continued by moving further away from original client-server requirement for a set of forms on each PC, instead downloading forms from the server on demand via the Java applet. This greatly reduced the application footprint and its ongoing maintenance requirements. By 2000 and E-Business Suite release 11i, the Internet-based browser user interface was being widely adopted, especially for intranets, and Oracle began delivering a few specific products in HTML-based pages, facilitating the access to some common features such as raising requisitions and completing expense reports. With each of the 11i.x releases, more and more products adopted the HTML-based user interface, and by 11.5.10 (2004) these pages were based on a standard browser-focused user interface design pattern, known as Oracle Applications Framework (OAF). This continues into Release12.x, where the latest OAF developments include rich browser-based features such as partial page rendering, personalization by user by page, and a declarative extensibility implementation.

Now with Fusion Applications, Oracle has taken the OAF development principles to the next level. Based on the same Model-View-Controller (MVC) design pattern that existed in OAF, Oracle has written Fusion Applications using its own new user interface development environment called Application Development Framework (ADF), part of the JDeveloper Integrated Development Environment (IDE). This offers developers all the power and flexibility of enterprise application development, yet delivers it in an easy-to-use, often declarative way. Each resulting page is based on the open-standard Java Server Faces and acts as a container for other useful objects, from other page fragments and tabbed-regions, to a large number of individual widgets such as data tables, drop-down lists, charts, graphics, maps, and buttons. This approach takes all the advantages of an easy to use 4GL-like development environment such as Oracle Forms, and creates lightweight but powerful Web 2.0–style browser pages.

This helps Fusion Applications immediately meet the expectations of tomorrow's workforce, the so called Generation-Y. This audience uses Adobe Flash, HTML 5.0 and AJAX-based user interfaces, and although these originated from consumer applications such as those found in Apple's iStore or Google's Gmail, it now forms the basic expectation of any software application.

Large implementations often fail because of misunderstood requirements and end user resistance, but with Fusion Applications and its focus around high quality user experience, the risk of failure is significantly reduced.

# Better Systems Management

The inherent power and flexibility of the new generation of Enterprise Business Applications presents a range of challenges for traditional systems management. This book explains how to use Oracle's Fusion Applications not only to meet these challenges but to turn them into new and exciting improvement opportunities. Here are three simple examples:

- **Complex architectures and distributed management tools** Fusion Applications comes with many features for managing its complex architecture, and this book helps you locate them, understand them, and bring them all together for practical use.

- **New technologies**   Fusion Applications leverages the latest developments in software, having many more constituent components than its legacy cousins. Although all components are important, this book focuses on the most significant knowledge and management challenges, and it covers them using simple terms and with practical examples.

- **Business goals**   System management should be closely aligned with business operations to ensure that appropriate tools are used to run the business successfully. This is often overlooked in preference of technology-only discussion, but it remains a core theme in this book.

# CHAPTER
## 1

# A Fusion Applications
# Product Overview

I t's probable that no one person can completely understand the whole of Fusion Applications—not because of its complexity or a lack of information, but simply because of its size and scope. The broad range of easy-to-use functional features support all core business operations, while behind the scenes it runs a complex platform of technical components, each with intricate setup, function, and execution. Fusion Applications contains hundreds of functional features within each product area, and the first release of Fusion Applications comes with more than 80 product areas.

*(Hundreds of features × 80 products) × (Platform complexity) = You get the picture!*

Although this overview covers all the key areas that are essential for an appreciation of Fusion Applications, there remains a strong emphasis on leveraging additional chapters and reference material for specific detail. To cover even the foundation-level information, without running into thousands of pages, this high-level discussion is divided into four sections and two chapters.

This chapter is focused on the finished product itself—what kinds of things it can do from a business and end user perspective—and is divided into two main sections:

- **Business architecture**   The business operations supported by Fusion Applications.

- **Functional architecture**   How the application hangs together.

Chapter 2 takes the discussion a step deeper, providing an overview of the technology components that run underneath the Fusion Application product features, since this is essentially the responsibility of the Application Manager. This chapter included the following two sections:

- **Technical architecture**   The technologies at work and the complete technology stack.

- **Fusion Applications ecosystem**   Additional supporting frameworks and components.

To explain the purpose of each component, this discussion starts with the business-user details and drills down through the supporting technologies underneath.

# Business Architecture

A recent cultural shift is at the heart of Fusion Applications: the emphasis on technology as a real business enabler. As organizations continue to tighten their IT spending, all investments must provide significant (and immediate) benefits to the bottom line. Return on investment (ROI) really matters now; where once technology was viewed as having the potential for improvement and competitive advantage, this must now be clear, and, most importantly, it must be proven.

So how has this shaped Fusion Applications? The first step was to review the best-in-class features of each of the existing Oracle Application products, those that many businesses were already using to ensure their own success. Next was extensive requirements gathering, based on the needs and desires collected from literally hundreds of organizations. Subsequently, everything was rigorously designed with a core focus on enhancing simplicity, completeness, and flexibility. These factors ensure that Fusion Applications is more focused on supporting real work processes than any of its predecessors.

## The Business Process Model

One simple goal runs through the whole of Fusion Applications: to support a comprehensive list of best practice business operations. This list was built from several sources, including industry experts, Oracle's own Application product features, as well as detailed consultation with some of the world's most successful organizations. This analysis captured the precise way in which many organizations actually work, from boardroom to shop floor. Two simple examples of business process flows (actually known as *composite* flows) are the processes and actions involved between the purchasing of raw materials to analyzing subsequent supplier payments—the procure-to-pay flow—and the process that starts with a customer sale and ends with being paid for the goods—the order-to-cash flow. Clearly, the closer the application features are aligned to what business users actually do, the more successful its adoption will be. This set of best practices upon which Fusion Applications features are based is known as the *Business Process Model (BPM)*.

The BPM is leveraged in several ways in Fusion Applications. This includes tying code components to functional activities (via *Logical Business Objects*), organizing the user interface flow (via *taskflows* and *activity guides*), and ensuring that all the supporting documentation and online help is provided in the right place and at the right time.

The BPM structure is based on a hierarchy of nodes that starts by identifying the industry context and then decomposes it into four child flows, as shown in Figure 1-1.

Starting with Level 0, Industry, each level provides a finer level of detail than its predecessor, with Level 4, Task, being the precise actions a business user would perform in his or her job. The BPM content remains "application agnostic" at Levels 0 to 3, with only Level 4 providing details that are specific to Fusion Applications. An example of this hierarchy is the Level 1 Business Area of *Procurement* that has 12 child Level 2, Business Processes, one being *Manage Requisitions*. Manage Requisitions itself has four child Level 3 Activities, such as *Approve Requisition*, which in turn has seven Level 4 Tasks, including, for example, *Reject Requisition Request*. The BPM architecture

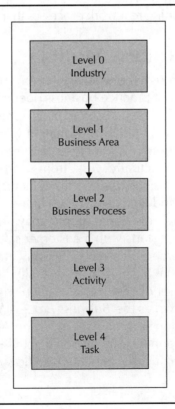

**FIGURE 1-1.** *The BPM hierarchy*

forms an outline for all Fusion Application functional features, and with around 11,000 tasks, it covers all core business operations and many additional operations.

**NOTE**
*Version 1.0 of Fusion Applications focuses on common core flows that apply across many different industries. Therefore, the Level 0 contains essentially just one cross-industry root node. Further, more 0 levels are planned for forthcoming releases.*

As well as being a design architecture, the BPM (unsurprisingly) has its origins firmly in Business Process Engineering. This allows organizations to map the capabilities of Fusion Applications to their own internal business processes and procedures as part of requirements analysis. Taking this a step further, using the standards-based tools available (such as Oracle's Business Process Management Suite) and the modular nature of the Fusion Applications business processes, you'll find it easier than ever before to perform setup, configuration, and even extension to meet those needs. (The book's appendix contains further reading on BPM and Business Process Engineering.)

# Fusion Applications 1.0 Features

Even in the first release, Fusion Applications includes a broad set of features that support the majority of day-to-day business operations. As discussed, product features are arranged primarily by BPM; however, for simplicity and clarity, all features are also categorized into a high-level product grouping, known as a *product family*. Each product family may contain part or all of a business process—for example the Procure-to-Pay business process is mostly part of the Procurement product family, but the final stages of the flow around invoice reconciliation and payment fall into the Financials product family. An overview of features in each of the six product families in Fusion Applications 1.0 is discussed next. You'll find more information in the Appendix.

## Financial Management

This product family represents a full suite of accounting and financial management tools that will satisfy most private sector business needs (with public sector and budgetary control features anticipated later). It includes General Ledger, Accounts Payable, Accounts Receivable, Asset Management, Payments and Collections, Cash and Expense Management, and a range of supporting common modules and reporting capabilities. It also natively supports many key legislative requirements of the major geographical territories (such as USA, Western Europe, Asia, and Latin America), although full localization support will be developed in later releases. In addition, Fusion Financial Management is immediately ready for integration with Oracle's Hyperion product range, offering exceptionally powerful financial performance analysis.

## Project Portfolio Management (PPM)

This product family includes full support for the following: Project Costing, Project Billing, Project Control, Project Performance Reporting, Project Integration Gateway, and a range of integrated analysis reports. This family focuses on private sector businesses and does not include the budgetary control pieces in version 1.0. One key benefit of Fusion PPM is that it has native integration with Oracle Primavera, offering powerful features to support projects in many vertical industries such as engineering and construction, utilities, and high-tech.

## Human Capital Management (HCM)

The HCM offering covers all the core features required by modern enterprises, including Human Resources, Global Payroll, Workforce Service Delivery, Total Compensation, Workforce Management, and Talent Management. Each of these comes with embedded performance indicators and powerful reporting capabilities. As with the other features, this is primarily focused around private sector use in version 1.0.

## Supply Chain Management (SCM)

This product family offers the following product features: Product Information Management, Asset Management, Global Order Promising, Cost Management, Distributed Order Orchestration, and Logistics (that includes Shipping, Receiving, and Inventory). Fusion Applications version 1.0 does not yet include full manufacturing support, such as Materials Requirements Planning (MRP), Quality, or Work-in-Progress. Arguably, the most exciting offering for SCM is in its Distributed Order Orchestration (DOO) product that provides a new central solution for the management and fulfillment of sales orders. Leveraging the latest technologies, DOO offers unprecedented levels of flexibility that should meet the needs of almost any organization.

### Procurement

The Fusion Procurement product family offers a wide range of features that help make the corporate buying process much more efficient and effective. This includes features for Purchasing, Self Service Procurement, Sourcing, Procurement Contracts, Supplier Portal, and Supplier Model. It also includes comprehensive performance management and spend analysis reporting.

### Customer Relationship Management (CRM)

The CRM product family offers a broad range of features, specifically based around Sales and Marketing activities for version 1.0. This includes Customer Master, Sales, Marketing, Mobile, Outlook Integration, and the same detailed reporting capabilities. In addition, the CRM product family hosts the complimentary Incentive Compensation product and features.

### Governance, Risk, and Compliance (GRC)

To satisfy the need for business operation control and recent regulatory requirements, this product family offers the following features that are fully integrated with the other product families: Financial Compliance, IT Risk and Compliance, Issue Manager, Risk Manager, Access Controls, Transaction Controls, and Configuration Controls.

# Functional Architecture

Many concepts and features are included in this section—they all simply provide the flexibility to implement Fusion Applications in a way that best suits an organization. These common datasets and internal business structures form the foundation upon which transactions are processed, features operate, and performance is monitored.

# Functional Architecture Objects

All Enterprise Applications contain objects that are defined once and then reused in many places. Common examples are employee data such as e-mail addresses and job levels, and organizational structures such as departments, divisions, and addresses. The following six concepts will provide a basic understanding of the core functional structures within Fusion Applications. As we'll discuss later on, truly effective Application Management requires a strong appreciation of all the underpinnings of the application, both technical and functional.

## Trading Community Architecture

Transaction-related data is usually denormalized in enterprise applications, so storage is optimized and any changes are made only once. Examples include the definitions for suppliers, customers, people, locations, and contact details. So that every Fusion Applications feature can access these definitions in a uniform and consistent manner, a central data model is used to help optimize designs, features, and even system performance. This model, the Trading Community Architecture (TCA), is an evolution of the same model that existed in E-Business Suite. As demonstrated in Figure 1-2, the TCA model represents physical objects such as people and companies as *parties*, and allows each independent party to have one or more *relationships* among themselves and

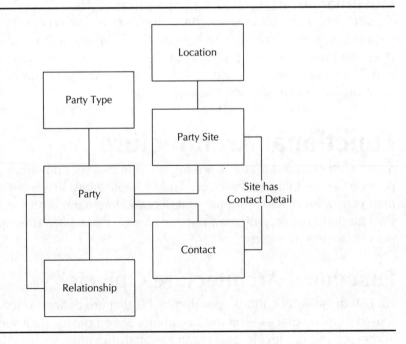

**FIGURE 1-2.** *A section of the Trading Community Architecture*

other parties. An example is the employee relationship between a person party and a company party. A party can also have one or more locations (addresses and some contact details) recorded as *party sites.*

This standardized data model is leveraged right across Fusion Applications and forms a vital ingredient to ensure the integrity of the basic functional data. Although all of this will remain essentially invisible to the business user, the Applications Administrator will occasionally benefit from a basic understanding of the model. Potential uses include analyzing issues around functional setup, assessing extended reporting needs, and managing database performance.

## Enterprise Structures

All businesses have internal subdivisions, which may be geographical, such as international or regional departments, or delineations related to work specializations, such as purchasing, production, and sales. All Enterprise Applications need to mirror these internal structures to ensure that they accurately represent and support each part of the organization. Fusion Applications has taken the best such capabilities from the existing Application products, added some new pieces, and delivered its own method for setting up what are known as *Enterprise Structures.*

To emulate the organizational structure inside the application, *business units* are used to represent logical or physical divisions. Business units roll-up into parent *Enterprise* business groups. Business units have two main purposes: they are used for the grouping of data, functions, and transactions for better management and reporting, and they are a method by which common reference data can be shared.

Here's a simple example: The California Business Unit provides centralized procurement business functions (that is, a purchasing department) and associated item data for five other West Coast business units, with the Florida Business Unit providing the same for five East Coast business units. In addition, the Colorado Business Unit may provide all invoice payment and accounting functions for the whole organization. In this example, orders can be reported based on each of the ten separate business units that raise them, the two business units that provide the centralized purchasing function, or even just the Colorado Business Unit that manages the centralized finance. This all helps improve administrative processing (especially for shared service centers), and it supports all performance analysis and legislative reporting needs.

In addition to Business Units, Fusion Applications contains a method for creating *legal entities.* This allows separate legal reporting (such as accounting, fiscal, and tax) for each discrete finance and employment structure that exists, and it is most commonly used between different countries.

## Effective Dates

Fusion Applications is designed to flex with an organization, and as organizational changes occur, the application can be adjusted accordingly. Adjustments are commonly required to the active reference data within the application—for example, from active order attributes to employee's job codes.

Date Effectivity is the mechanism by which any reference data can be quickly made inactive or active. In addition to making immediate changes, data can also be scheduled for use on future dates as well. Retroactively, the Date Effectivity feature ensures that all historic transactions retain their original reference data, improving performance reporting and audit capabilities, as well as helping to eliminate potential mistakes.

## SetID

Although the Date Effectivity feature allow organizations to version-control their reference data, SetID simply acts as the container in which reference data can be created. Each separate set of reference data is associated with one or more specific Enterprise Structures (also illustrating how these functional architecture pieces work together). Since this data needs to be defined only once, no duplication or associated maintenance overhead occurs. Using our earlier example, the California and Florida business units that perform buying functions might be assigned one SetID for Project Expenditure Types, allowing them to assign customer orders to the appropriate internal projects. A different Project Expenditure SetID might then be used for other business units that specialize in the fulfillment of internal orders only.

## Tree Management

Fusion Applications users can not only set up reference data, but they can also organize it into custom structures that represent its internal relationships. Tree Management allows you to create tree-like hierarchies, first by registering a *Tree Structure* and then associating data values to it. A simple example would be the job roles and teams within an organization.

Tree Management offers several key benefits, many of which are also applicable to other Functional Architecture components. Although trees are exceptionally flexible, they remain independent of any specific implementation, allowing the same tree to be reused in many different places. This reduces the maintenance overhead resulting from data changes. Another key benefit of having data structures represented and stored in a consistent way is that they're readily available to the advanced analysis and reporting capabilities prevalent in Fusion Applications. Although there are some other advantages, one final simple point is that trees represent a very powerful visual metaphor. This is demonstrated in Figure 1-3, where the page allows the business user to understand immediately the relationships involved, while ensuring accuracy and security at all times.

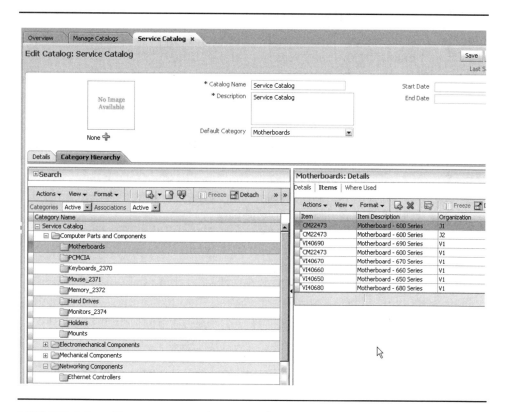

**FIGURE 1-3.**   *Tree structure shown in the Item category*

## Approval Management

Business transaction approval is a compulsory feature for Enterprise Applications, and Oracle Applications successfully used a workflow-based system for many years. Both E-Business Suite release 12 and PeopleSoft version 8 also include advancements that provide the implementation-independent setup and execution of a rule-based approval system.

Fusion Applications has taken this concept even further by leveraging the Approval Management Service (AMX) that exists as part of the Human Workflow Business Process Execution Language (BPEL) capability inside Oracle Fusion Middleware. This again abstracts many pieces of the approval process and dedicates best-of-breed tools to complete specific tasks, such as building the approvers list, sending alert notifications, and processing responses.

# Functional Setup Manager

Although this book does not delve into the world of application installation and implementation (for many reasons), and although detailed resources are included in the Appendix, one setup-related piece is definitely worth discussing here. With its origins and intentions similar to that of E-Business Suite's iSetup product, Functional Setup Manager is a self-contained feature that provides a platform upon which the implementation can occur. Centralizing the functional setup in a single integrated tool helps eliminate substantial project complexity and allows actions to be planned, executed, and reported, all within the context of the Fusion Application instance itself. That's not to say it totally replaces full-scale Enterprise Application project planning; however, within its own limited scope it is simple, flexible, and comprehensive.

Functional Setup Manager has two main capabilities. The first is the mechanism to define an *Implementation Project* and then choose the desired products and features that will be implemented (known as *offerings, features,* and *options*). As shown in Figure 1-4, this project will then automatically contain a sequenced list of all the actions required to complete the related setup (in a *task list*), automatically factoring in any dependencies that may exist.

Each task can have additional information and documents associated with it, which, together with completion tracking and team collaboration features, provides powerful management capabilities. Projects can also be extended to include any additional organization-specific tasks required, such as extra integration work. For applications administrators, it's immediately obvious how this will prove to be invaluable, representing a useful tool for the management and control of functional setup data.

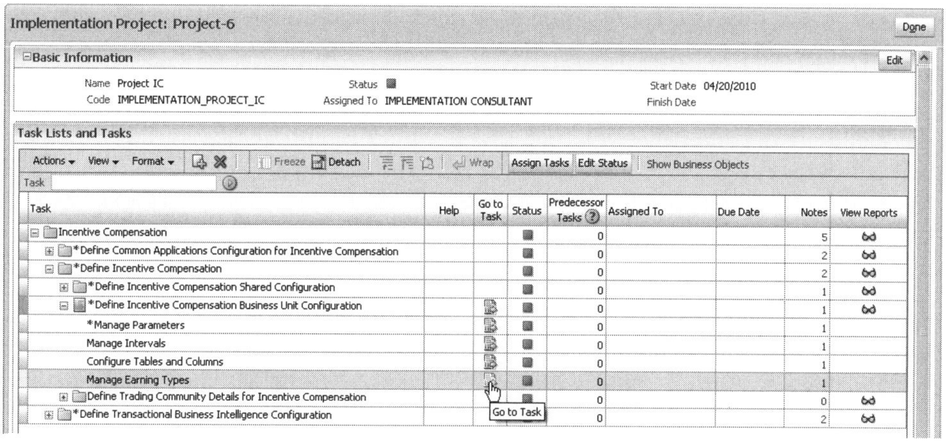

**FIGURE 1-4.**   *Functional Setup Manager showing tasks within a project*

The second main feature of Functional Setup Manager is its ability to import and export functional setup data. Export and import files are based on a set of standardized templates, which themselves can be part of a *Configuration Package* to allow further extension and customization. While hugely beneficial for implementation, this feature is also useful for application administrators who are responsible for many separate instances; at the press of a button, some specific setup values (or everything) can be made available and quickly imported into another instance ready for immediate use. This marks a significant improvement on traditional methods such as unwieldy database dumps and complex custom extract scripts.

Finally, Functional Setup Manager has an associated tool that provides some technical implementation services. The *Topology Manager* acts as an internal store for data that links the logical separation of implementation and setup (pillars, offerings, options, features, and so on) with the physical deployment details, such as business objects and end points for services and applications. This represents more of a back-end repository, and although it's helpful to be aware of its existence and function, it's not really a systems management tool, despite its name.

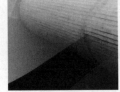

# CHAPTER
## 2

# A Fusion Applications
# Technical Overview

his chapter explains the general principles, technologies, and architectures upon which the Fusion Application features run. With literally thousands of Oracle products at its disposal, Fusion Applications leverages the latest technical advancements, product releases, expert functions, and comprehensive capabilities. Although most technology solutions are based on the latest releases of native product sets, Fusion Applications has also served as a catalyst for further extension and advancement. To cover the wide-ranging technical landscape, even at a high-level, this discussion is divided into five main areas:

- **Technical Architecture Fundamentals**   Explains the basic technologies and principles used across the applications.

- **The Technology Stack**   Looks at which Oracle components are used to deliver the structures explained in the preceding section.

- **A Processing Walkthrough**   A simplified example of how users' common actions can trigger each part of the technology stack and how the components work together at runtime.

- **Coexistence Overview**   How Oracle Fusion Applications can work with other enterprise applications right out of the box, using Oracle's prepackaged integrations.

- **The Extension Architecture**   How configuration, personalization, and extension are all possible within Fusion Applications.

Fusion Applications uses a huge range of technologies, and, as such, it's impractical to think that you can achieve a deep level of understanding of every last piece straight away. This section provides just enough detail to help you form a suitable basis upon which a sensible and practical approach to applications management can begin. The concepts discussed here are further discussed in additional chapters and supplemented by the references in the Appendix.

# Technical Architecture Fundamentals

This section provides an outline of the key concepts used throughout Fusion Applications, starting with the business users' view and drilling into each platform component from there. Although you may already understand some of these basic concepts, it's still worth your time to review them all to understand the Fusion Applications context.

# The User Interface

As explained in Chapter 1, Fusion Applications emphasizes the evolution of the way in which traditional enterprise applications interact with their users. With its user interface flow engineered around Business Process Model (BPM) Level 4 tasks, it more closely mirrors the daily work involved in common job roles. This creates a user experience (UX) that is intuitive and visually attractive, and most importantly enhances productivity. It has been estimated that Fusion Applications has cut the number of clicks, fields, and forms that are normally required to complete a task by about 70 percent, quickly delivering significant efficiencies. The Fusion Applications UX architecture contains a few basic elements that are helpful to understand.

## Dashboards

As with all modern enterprise applications, Fusion Applications is not focused solely on the speed of data input and transaction administration. Much of this has already been automated, and the focus is now firmly on providing business users with answers to two key questions to help users perform their jobs more efficiently:

- What do I need to know?

- What do I need to do?

Fusion Applications uses dashboard pages to provide each specific user, based on his or her functional role, with a variety of views (portlets) into the application. First, a general welcome dashboard includes information from all across the application. In addition, each specific functional area or business process (such as Finance Manager or Procurement Buyer) will have its own dashboard (Figure 2-1) for reviewing a more focused set of information, where it's possible to take direct action.

Top-level welcome dashboards commonly contain two specific components, along with tables of summary data and charts. The first component is a *Worklist* and provides a summary of all pending notifications, approvals, and to-do action items in one central place, all based on the

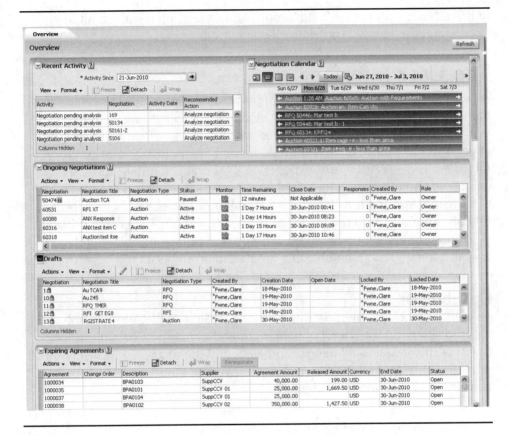

**FIGURE 2-1.** *An overview dashboard page for supplier negotiations*

users' job role. Items in the Worklist can be selected and right-clicked to see a list of common actions to take. The second common component in welcome dashboards is the watchlist. This region contains one or more functional objects (transactions, people, accounts, etc) that have been flagged as being of particular interest and are therefore eligible for close monitoring. Any specific attribute can be included in the watchlist, such as statuses, values, and quantities.

## Layout
The pages that make up the Fusion Applications user interface are constructed around a standardized set of *design patterns* that ensure consistent layout, content types, and styles throughout. At the highest level,

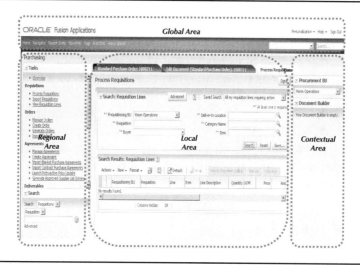

**FIGURE 2-2.**   *The Fusion Applications page layout*

each page is composed of four main parts, as illustrated in Figure 2-2. The top *global area* holds all the menus and links that apply to every page, maintaining a parent context within which the product features run. This offers navigation, collaboration, and help functions. The *regional area* offers users some helpful features that support the overall business process in which they are currently operating. The central *local area* is the heart of the page's focus, where users can interact with the data related to the task being performed. The final *contextual area* is, as its name suggests, a place for additional information that supports the current task, specifically that of the local area.

## Web 2.0 and Social Networking

Fusion Applications is designed to support the next generation of information workers (often known as *generation-Y*), whose expectations of application usability far surpasses that offered by traditional enterprise applications. The term *Web 2.0* is commonly used to encompass these expectations. Some examples of such features include pages that are composed of dynamically refreshing real-time data (such as Flash and Asynchronous JavaScript and XML [AJAX] data); that contain rich graphical components such as maps, charts, and fit-for-purpose diagrams; and that have embedded collaborative techniques such as wikis, network diagrams, and instant messaging. Fusion Applications is up to this challenge and provides a host of components that exist either as discrete services from the underlying technology platform (such as WebCenter) or as powerful widgets embedded directly into the user interface pages.

Fusion Application is not littered with these components just for the sake of looking good or following the latest trend. Each Web 2.0–style component has been selected for inclusion because it offers significant improvements and efficiencies over using an alternative, and it helps maintain a professional and easy to use approach to the overall design.

## Embedded Analytics

The graphical components of the user interface substantially support the presentation of complex data in an easy-to-consume way, and Fusion Applications leverages a standard set of tools to embed them in the most appropriate places. This is accomplished primarily by another standard design pattern and a set of specific components that work seamlessly with the Oracle Business Intelligence Enterprise Edition (OBIEE) server to keep the information up to date and accurate. More detail on how this works is provided later in the section "Business Intelligence."

# The Model-View-Controller Architecture

So how do these front-end principles link to the back-end processing? The whole of the Fusion Applications interface was written using Oracle JDeveloper 11g and its embedded Application Development Framework (ADF). Native to this is the Model-View-Controller (MVC) architecture, a standards-based development paradigm that is available for many different programming languages. It uses many of the same principles found in E-Business Suite's Oracle Application Framework (OAF).

In its most basic interpretation, the *Model* is a software layer that handles all the interaction with the database (or any data source) and controls the execution of the business logic code. The *View* is, as the name suggests, responsible for the display of the application user interface, and the *Controller* is essentially the wiring between the two that handles page flows and events as they occur. Abstracting the code objects into these layers has two main benefits: First, it facilitates a modular approach by using sets of self-contained objects, and, second, it greatly reduces internal dependencies, reducing maintenance and promoting code reuse.

Oracle ADF itself actually abstracts the Model layer further, specifically breaking out pieces around data persistence, object-relational mapping, transaction management, and business logic execution into a *Business Services layer*, implemented in Fusion Applications within ADF Business Components (ADFbc). This leaves the remaining Model layer in control of connecting these business services with view/controller pieces via its data binding and data control components.

# Business Logic Execution Architecture

Fusion Applications actually represents a complete set of Java enterprise applications, deployed in the Oracle WebLogic Server (WLS) Java 2 Platform Enterprise Edition (J2EE) runtime environment. In addition, a small percentage of business logic runs outside of the Java runtime environment, namely some Procedural Language/Structured Query Language (PL/SQL) code for a few data-intensive activities, and some C code for a few well-defined, mature processes that need that lower level of control.

Further details on code standards for Fusion Applications can be found in the developer guides listed in the Appendix.

# Orchestration

It will come as no surprise that Fusion Applications has been totally built around the Service-Oriented Architecture (SOA), having more than 1000 web services covering all its major functional objects and their associated tasks. This runs on the native Oracle SOA Suite technology, taking specific advantage of the Business Process Execution Language (BPEL) and workflow features therein. All of the artifacts and metadata that make up these features are open standards–based.

# The Security Architecture

Security has always been imperative for Enterprise Applications, especially with internal security breaches forming a significant problem. All modern enterprise applications contain a wide range of features and integration points that could potentially expose any unsecured entry routes. Examples might be misconfigured independent servers and unsecured application programming interfaces (APIs) that can be invoked to produce undesirable results. Another concern is how interfaces into Enterprise Applications are evolving, with more devices being used for business tasks, such as mobile and handheld applications, all working in real time with both internal departments and external partner organizations.

Fusion Applications addresses these concerns with a range of security solutions; however, underpinning each of these is a security architecture known as *role-based access control* (RBAC). Fusion Applications is based on the *segregation of duties* principle, meaning that access is broken down into specific tasks that are closest to what people actually do in their daily jobs. These tasks are grouped into roles that are then applied using the RBAC approach.

The purpose of RBAC is often summarized in this way: *Who* can do *what* on *which* set of data. This is implemented in Fusion Applications in the following way: The *who* is represented by a *Job Role*, itself composed of one or more *Duty Roles*. This Job Role gets either explicitly or automatically *provisioned* (assigned) to new users. The *what* identifies a particular level of *Function Security*, meaning it *defines* the privileges contained inside Duty Roles that control the range of associated work tasks. Finally, the *which* represents *Data Security*, defining specific datasets upon which a user can apply actions (via function security). An example would be that for one user with a Job Role of FL-Buyer, purchase orders associated with the California Business Unit can only be viewed, whereas orders from the Miami Business Unit can be both viewed and edited.

Another security measure that is increasingly important is the control of personally identifiable information (PII). Fusion Applications defines three levels in which all data is categorized, with specific controls on PII data. The first category is *Public* and has no extra control. Examples might be simply company names and addresses that are used everywhere, including on external documents. The second category is *Internal-Public* and provides an extra layer of control for more sensitive data using Data Security. An example here might be a person's work contact details. The final category is *Confidential*, and this data is secured at all levels, including storage in the database, communication through the network, and of course in the user interface. Examples of confidential data are bank account numbers and user's passwords.

With security a key part of the applications administrator's role, extensive details on the technologies and their related management tools are presented in later chapters.

# Data Storage and Retrieval

The database traditionally forms a stable foundation for data-centric enterprise applications, onto which everything else is built. You've seen how Fusion Applications leverages various advanced features for capture, manipulation, and presentation of data, but the basic architecture for storage and retrieval remains fairly constant. That said, two particularly innovative features come with Fusion Applications.

First, Fusion Applications has a unique deployment framework known as the *Pillar Replication Framework*, which, although not part of the initial release, will allow for separately distributed databases to contain different functional parts of the application. Internally, Fusion Applications splits the application features into groups of product families, each one known as a pillar. Consider, for example, three pillars. The first pillar may contain Financials and Supply Chain Management (including Project Portfolio Management [PPM] and Procurement), the second pillar is Human Capital Management, and the third is Customer Relationship Management. Each of these three pillars will run in its own, separate database instance. To keep all the dependent data (such as product items, employees, and enterprise structures) synchronized among the pillars, Fusion Applications will use a technology platform component, Oracle Data Integrator (ODI), an evolution of the acquired Sunopsis product. This will perform the Extract, Transform, Load (ETL) and Master Data Management (MDM) type functions. More details on ODI are provided in the next section.

In addition to the planned Pillar Replication Framework, Fusion Applications will natively leverage Real Application Clusters (RAC) for performance and scalability. RAC is Oracle's virtualization technology that provides Enterprise Grid Computing support for the Oracle Database. In a nutshell, this allows organizations to run each single database instance across several different physical servers. This, together with the Pillar Replication Framework (and similar flexible middleware deployment options), provides a wide range of capabilities that should satisfy almost any complex topology and capacity requirement.

# The Technology Stack

This section represents a particularly significant section of this book, because it covers the complete spectrum of components in the Fusion Application Technology stack. Although specific reference material (listed in the Appendix)

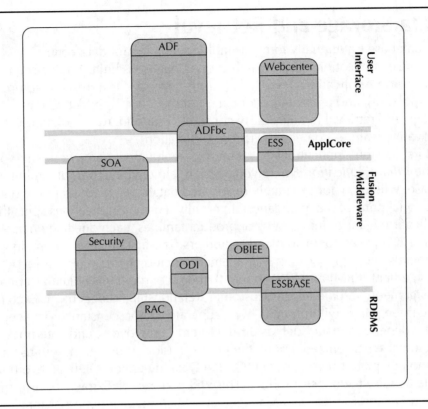

**FIGURE 2-3.** *Fusion Applications technology stack summary*

will cover each component in much more depth, Fusion Applications administrators first need to identify and appreciate the anatomy of the system. Then they can begin to understand how these components work together. Again, the focus of the discussion is on understanding the application technology to support the requirements of the business; we won't discuss technologies for their own sake.

Figure 2-3 provides an overview of some of the key components of the Fusion Applications technology stack, and we'll look at each piece in turn. Chapters 5 to 10 provide more detail on how an applications administrator would manage each discrete component, or at least those in a specific class.

# The Front End

As with most effective and seemingly simple solutions, behind the rich and intuitive Fusion Applications user interface sits a considerable amount of complexity and technology.

## Application Development Framework

As mentioned earlier, Oracle's Application Development Framework (ADF) provides most of what the business users see. The View layer, built as part of the MVC architecture, provides the user interface pages, forms, and components, with the Controller layer handling the user interaction such as button clicks (known as *events*). ADF is based on, and fully compliant with, the open standard specification for Java Server Faces (JSR 127) for the development of a rich user interface. Oracle's implementation, ADF-Faces, remains compliant with the standards but offers an extended range of more than 100 AJAX-like client components that provide powerful yet standardized ways in which business users can interact with the application. Examples include maps, graphs, and pivot-tables.

The Fusion Applications ADF layer also merges the View and Controller artifacts to ensure that pages look and work in an integrated and consistent manner. In addition to components and pages, ADF contains a *taskflow* mechanism that controls precisely how processes navigate from one object to another, such as page navigation and code calls. Taskflows are discrete components, being reused whenever a specific sequence of steps is required.

Although this section doesn't go into pages of developer-level detail, clearly it's important that the applications administrator understand the technology behind the user interface, as maintaining its availability and performance represents an obvious priority. To assist with this, later chapters offer more detail, together with some utilities and diagnostics for monitoring and troubleshooting. In addition, for those organizations creating and running customizations and extensions using their own ADF objects and code, full supporting details can be found in the developer guides listed in the Appendix.

## Simple Validation

Sitting behind the user interface is a layer of embedded logic that performs basic validation on both the data entered and the events fired. This logic operates by two main techniques: *Expression Language* (EL) and *Groovy Scripting*. Expression Language provides an easy-to-use syntax for handling the data held within the application session, reducing the need for full Java code execution to handling common or simple actions. Groovy Scripting provides a Java-like language that is used a little closer to the business logic, commonly within the MVC Model layer. Similarly to EL, Groovy offers a lightweight way in which to execute simple logic such as attribute value calculation and explicit validation routines.

# ApplCore

As mentioned, Enterprise Applications try to use common components everywhere possible. Although we touched on these earlier, some other common technical components also provide services to the application. A small subset of these are uniquely provided to satisfy enterprise application requirements, and are extensions to the standard technology products. This forms a thin component layer that exists near the top of the technology stack. In Fusion Applications, this layer is known as ApplCore (Applications Core technologies).

In Fusion Applications, ApplCore is a much thinner layer than the equivalent inside the other Oracle Applications products, mainly because it directly leverages the advanced capabilities from the latest versions of the technology products (Database, Fusion Middleware, and so on). Minimizing the footprint of this layer by using native technologies greatly reduces internal dependencies, processing complexity, and the overall maintenance needs. The following provides an overview of the main ApplCore services.

## Attachments

For many transaction documents and business objects, the addition of unstructured organization-specific material can be very important, but an application form or field to hold it may not be always available. A simple example could be the technical specification of complex items on a purchase order—probably not something that's needed on every order and hard to imagine how suitable fields might be arranged on a page. The solution in most enterprise applications is for business users to upload supplemental documents and attach these to specific parts of a transaction document, such as an order line. Enterprise applications often limit the uploaded documents in terms of size, but not on file types or formats.

Oracle Fusion Applications provides this same attachment capability in all suitable places, leveraging Oracle's Universal Content Management (UCM) product range, and specifically the Document Management Repository features (formerly Stellent). This permits attachments of various types, including URL, text values, and any types of file. All attachments are put into an internal category foldering system, shown as a graphical file/folder hierarchy (similar to Windows Explorer), which together with an attribute keyword search and version control, makes them easy to find and reuse. All attached files can also be automatically virus-scanned and are secured by the standard application role-based security, controlling all basic actions, such as view, add, rename, and delete.

## Flexfields

The concept of flexfields originated from E-Business Suite, where it proved a powerful and popular feature. Very simply put, flexfields provide a customizable, yet supported, way of defining implementation-specific data entry fields for use across the application features.

Traditionally, flexfields come in two types. Key flexfields are multi-part identifiers used to represent a specific value that's built up from one or more other values (known as *segments*). A simplified example of a Key flexfield might be the four segment value for an account code (such as 0129-210-1200-99), where the first segment (0129) is the account number, the next is the department, the next the division, and finally the cost center.

The second type of flexfield is the *Descriptive flexfield*. This provides additional database and user interface fields (known as *attributes*) that can be used however and whenever an organization requires them. This is a quick and easy way to include additional information associated with transactions (such as an order).

In addition, Fusion Applications introduces a third kind of flexfield, the *Extensible flexfield*. This is somewhat similar in purpose to the Descriptive flexfield, but it allows for the creation of entirely new objects and the definition of custom relationships between objects and attributes. This offers organizations many more options for use.

Flexfields are exceptionally important in implementation phases, and although they introduce some complexity, their maturity and well-defined structure should make them a simple piece to administer.

## Profile Options

All software applications require setup and configuration to control precisely how they work. The functional features and processes inside enterprise applications are exceptionally flexible, something that is essential for use across different organizations and between different industries. The ApplCore layer offers a standard way to perform application setups and configurations, known as *profile options*. A profile option is a name-value pair that is set within a common user interface, stored in the database, and pulled into the user context at runtime as needed. A simple example (that you'll see again later on) is the profile option *FND: Log Enabled* that controls whether application diagnostic logging is turned on or off, and therefore has two possible values: Y or N.

Profile options are set within the context of a *level*, adding the extent to which the configuration applies. In our logging example, this profile option can be set at *site* level, meaning it applies to the whole application and all users thereof, or at *user* level, applying to just one specific chosen user. Again, you'll see examples of this later on.

Similar to flexfields, profile options have been part of E-Business Suite for many years, and although some minor evolution has occurred in Fusion Applications, much of the structure remains mature.

## Audit

Fusion Applications implements the Fusion Middleware Audit Framework to provide full access to audit capabilities on the components operating in the technology stack, from security processes to specific product applications. ApplCore provides a standard audit policy as a baseline of audit constituents, which should be reviewed and extended upon implementation, using the extensive tools available. The framework also provides standard reporting capabilities, as well as integration to Business Intelligence (BI) components for setting up notification and alerting rules.

## Internationalization

Fusion Applications is available in eight languages in version 1.0, with more to be added in additional releases. National Language Support (NLS) preferences are stored for each use and also include time zone, date and number formats, and calendar style. These preferences are managed by the technology stack, allowing Fusion Applications to load the appropriate runtime context quickly at login, and then adjust all the pages and components using its embedded metadata framework on top (described later).

In relation to internationalization, it's helpful to have a basic understanding of exactly how Fusion Applications manages the user interface text. Two techniques are at work inside the application. The first, *resource bundles*, handles all the ADF-Faces user interface component labels (known as *strings*) from the text on buttons and tabs, or simply from the entry-field labels. These are deployed as files (.xliff), imported at runtime, and linked to ADF component attributes and their underlying code objects.

The second technique handles all the *messages* that are shown to the end users when they take an action on the system. Examples might be a confirmation message that a change was saved and a warning that a process cannot be completed. The text for these messages is simply queried directly from the database based on the current session language. These messages also commonly contain tokens for inserting dynamic values such as the current transaction number. As you'll see, more serious error messages are even used to trigger system management functions automatically, such as extra logging and the creation of an *implicit incident*.

## Taxonomy

Underpinning Fusion Applications is a structure that ties all application technical components together into a logical hierarchy. With such a huge system of thousands of individual artifacts (e.g., code and definition files) this structure, known as the Fusion Applications Taxonomy, is essential to promote accurate object reuse and modularity, and to provide detailed dependency information.

The taxonomy is a simple hierarchy with four basic levels, starting with Product Line (Fusion Applications), then Product Family (e.g., Financials), then Product (e.g., General Ledger), and finally a value known as the Logical Business Area (LBA), which represents a leaf grouping of components based on their use, for example, GL Calendars. The LBAs can be nested also, creating further levels where required. All components are then assigned an appropriated taxonomy value.

The taxonomy is used in several places in Fusion Applications, albeit under the skin of the visible activities. Provisioning and Patching are the main consumers of taxonomy information; however, there are other features that use the structure to interrogate and display information related to Fusion Applications, such as the Enterprise Manager Topology diagram displayed in Figure 7-1 later.

# Fusion Middleware Extensions for Fusion Applications

The next level down in the technology stack is Oracle Fusion Middleware (FMw); although another small subset of components exist in the standard Fusion Middleware products, they have been especially enhanced for use with Fusion Applications. These components are similar to the ApplCore layer, but strictly speaking, they're technology components implemented for applications, as opposed to pure application pieces. The two most significant parts of this layer are the Enterprise Scheduling Service and Approvals Management.

Again, most other Enterprise Applications contain many more similar such components, specifically developed to meet application-specific requirements. Although these might have been fit-for-purpose at one point in time, parts can quickly become outdated if they are not constantly refreshed, representing a significant dependency and maintenance overhead. Upon closer inspection, you'll find that it's clear that many of the services provided are not really unique to any one application, and the latest releases of Oracle's Fusion Middleware provides most of these services to support all enterprise application development and execution.

## Enterprise Scheduling Service (ESS)

This feature provides a method of executing units of work at specific times and in specific sequences, similar to the batch processing of older enterprise resource planning (ERP) applications. This requirement may seem rather old-fashioned in today's always-on, super-powerful systems. Most applications administrators know that enterprise applications often contain terabytes of live data, and performing large updates can seriously impact resources and performance; those non-urgent requests are better scheduled for quieter times.

ESS represents a mechanism whereby its internal *scheduler* accepts specific units of work, known as *jobs*, to be started at certain dates and times within specific resource constraints (time, Java threads, and so on). The jobs themselves are registered by the *client* business application (such as General Ledger, Payroll) and are not actually run by ESS itself, but when the specific time is reached, ESS performs a callback to the client that kicks off the work.

ESS has features such as its own log records; detail on-job request dependencies (shown as a tree hierarchy); and the simple ability to review (and purge) past, current, and planned load. All ESS jobs are secured via the same RBAC policies and roles that exist within the client application itself.

## Approval Management Service

The Approval Management Service (AMX) abstracts the transaction document approval processing from any specific implementation and then provides a range of management services to use as required. The technology to do this is based around the FMw Human Workflow product. This includes prebuilt integration to the notification capabilities and the especially designed Fusion Application Worklist user interface component.

AMX supports all manner of approval processes including the following:

■ Both static and dynamic approver list generation

■ Serial and parallel approval paths

■ Graphical presentations of approval hierarchies

■ A wide range of business rules, identity, and decision services

■ Context sensitivity to derive runtime attribute values

■ User interfaces for easy configuration and predeployment testing

The creation of approval rules tends to occur mostly during implementation; however, applications administrators should again be aware of the component parts and the processing mechanisms involved.

## Oracle Enterprise Crawl and Search Framework

Fusion Applications leverages Oracle's Secure Enterprise Search (SES) technology to provide keyword and category-based search results across a number of data sources (database and non-database), all while making sure the right information is shown to the right person. The internal crawler process first gathers information based on its own security implementations, and the resulting index is stored in an especially hardened database. Finally, all search results are carefully secured using a range of options including access control lists, query time authorization, and combinations of the two.

On top of this base functionality, the Enterprise Crawl and Search Framework was created especially for Fusion Applications. It provides a set of standard APIs into the SES platform, it integrates with the applications-based RBAC security model, and it has a range of standard user interface display options. This helps ensure a complete and consistent search experience across all of Fusion Applications.

As with managing any data repository, there are some significant considerations for applications administrators here, especially regarding managing data sources and their security, scheduling internal processes, and optimizing performance. Further details and activities are explained in Chapter 5.

# Core Fusion Middleware

Oracle has continued to evolve its Application Server, Middleware, and Development Tools, through acquisition and new product creation. They are currently represented by a cohesive and integrated platform for developing and running applications, namely Fusion Middleware. This layer is application agnostic, meaning that many of its open standards–based components can be used with any compliant enterprise application. Although the references in the Appendix provide more detailed content on Oracle Fusion Middleware itself, following are a few key pieces to give you a quick summary of their use in Fusion Applications.

## WebLogic Server

Although it leverages specific components for specific tasks, Fusion Applications is primarily a set of Java EE Applications, deployed within the WebLogic application server Java runtime environment. Since such a large number of these deployments exist across Fusion Applications, the scalability features inside WebLogic provides a solid platform while retaining flexible implementation options. For those unfamiliar with WebLogic Server, the following simplistic summary of the Fusion Applications architecture should prove helpful.

WebLogic includes three main groupings:

■ **The managed server** This is essentially the Java Runtime Environment (JRE) within which application Java code executes in one or more Java virtual machines (JVM).

■ **The cluster** This is a group of one or more managed servers that may be running across one or more machines. Capacity adjustments can be made quickly and easily by adding managed servers or physical machines to a cluster. Clusters are also used to ensure availability, as one managed server can take over should another fail.

■ **The domain**   This is a container in which all the managed servers and clusters are grouped. The domain allows servers with similar requirements to be managed together. This management is accomplished by a dedicated managed server instance that must exist in each domain, known as the *administration server*. Additional Fusion Middleware components are also commonly configured at the domain level.

As explained at the start of this chapter, Fusion Applications is divided into product families based on the particular business features they implement. Each product family has all its Java EE applications deployed to one WebLogic domain. This domain contains several clusters within which applications are deployed (roughly one per managed server), plus the administration server that handles all internal management functions (including running Fusion Applications Control). The detailed configuration needs and dependencies of each product family domain are handled as part of the Fusion Applications installation and provisioning process.

In addition to having clusters for each Fusion Java EE application, two more are required within each product family domain. The first is used to host the SOA Server infrastructure (SOA-INFRA) and its related composite applications. The second additional cluster is for an instance of the ESS, itself running as a Java EE application (known as *ESSAPP*).

The only additional WLS logical container to mention is the *farm*. A farm is the top-most grouping, within which domains, clusters, and all administration and managed servers are held. It is specifically implemented for use by Fusion Applications Control to allow application administrators to manage the system as a whole.

Clearly, the management of the WebLogic environment represents a sizable portion of the applications administrator's role, and later chapters provide plenty of background information and descriptions of the standard tools available. The discussion also adds some insight into how to use some helpful extra features and introduces some recommended management practices.

# ADFbc

As mentioned, working away behind Oracle's ADF is ADF Business Components (ADFbc). It continues the support for the MVC architecture by providing a range of back-end services. Specifically, it provides the data binding capability for use in the Model layer, and it supports the creation of the components for the Business Services layer.

ADFbc's data binding occurs in complete accordance with the open-standard JSR-227 recommendation. This states how declarative data access should be defined between user interface components and the underlying functions of the Business Services layer, running in a J2EE environment. In ADFbc, this occurs via the data control and its list of data-aware user interface components.

As its second core capability, ADFbc allows for the creation and execution of business services, and it does this by implementing a specific set of code objects. Fusion Applications fully adheres to this, and the two most fundamental objects in this layer are the *entity object* (EO) and the *view object* (VO). Simply put, an entity object provides an abstraction of the physical data model in the database, built to represent a logical business object and its properties (such as persistence). For example, each line on a Requisition can be represented by a *RequisitionLineEO* object. The code logic performs actions on the EO object itself, and the changes are automatically propagated to the underlying database by the ADFbc platform. Relationships between EOs are defined by another object, known as an *association*.

View objects are simply containers for queries that pull data from the database (SQL), with any relationships between them defined as *view links*. An example from Fusion Applications is *RequisitionLineVO* that simply queries item lines for a given requisition ID. View objects are also rolled-up into parent containers known as *application modules* (AM), and these load related VOs at runtime, plus contain additional properties such as transaction control definitions.

As mentioned, this is all abstracted and deployed as open-standard XML metadata files because it removes any hard coding of implementation detail, meaning that ADF-based applications can be implemented in a range of different J2EE environments. For Fusion Applications, this standard-based, best practice development architecture represents the most efficient and effective way to develop and deploy enterprise applications.

So how do we go one step deeper, into the real application processing logic and the technology stack involved there? In simple terms, once the entity object defined in ADFbc is updated it will raise a new *business event* through the use of something known as the *Event Delivery Network* (EDN). Other code objects will *subscribe* to that event and be listening for it. Once triggered, the event will pass along any associated data and begin the next phase of processing. A simple example might be when an order is updated the EO raises an associated event, which in turn fires a human workflow process to notify the buyer to approve the change. Later sections continue drilling into this execution process thread, but we need to pause at this point to look at another important technology stack component.

## Business Process Execution Language (BPEL)

In simple terms, although SOA-based web services (and other components) form a modular architecture, they still need gluing together to deliver an execution flow that closely matches to what the business user is trying to achieve (the BPM flows). Rather than the traditional method of hard-coding this wiring in the code, BPEL steps in. Using standards-based XML formats (such as BPELWS), it allows for the declarative definition of business process execution flows. This is partnered with a language upon which the middleware platform can execute to chain together discrete services and programs, forming what is known as *composite* applications.

In Fusion Applications, all processes are built using JDeveloper's BPEL Designer, and the BPEL Process Manager forms the execution engine that runs within the WebLogic SOA-INFRA cluster. As mentioned, BPEL processes may be kicked off by an event, such as a button click on the user interface, and the subsequent processing runs in its own context and according to the predefined logic.

Clearly, it is important for the Fusion Applications administrator to be able to monitor, manage, and troubleshoot all the executing process flows in the system, and later you will see how to use tools like the BPEL Console to review the process execution.

It's easy to make comparisons between BPEL and the Oracle Workflow component that's used in the Applications Unlimited products. This is a somewhat fair comparison, although BPEL is a more complete architecture for embedding business processes, plus it has much broader support for different service providers. Oracle's BPEL Process Manager runs a separate subcomponent called *Human Workflow* that, similarly to Oracle Workflow, provides dedicated features to handle interaction with business users within a process flow. Human Workflow provides many features to support the assignment of *tasks* to specific individuals or groups of *participants*, including the management of priority and deadlines for completion, the sending of notifications and reminders via various communication channels (not just e-mail), as well as standard methods for processing responses and passing the results back into the BPEL process flow. Figure 2-4 shows a simplified BPEL process that involves Human Workflow (the NotificationTask node) to notify a user of a pending task and to process the response.

As you may have worked out, the AMX and the Worklist component are both part of BPEL Human Workflow. They leverage several of its advanced task administration features, such as parallel approvals, escalation, and delegation.

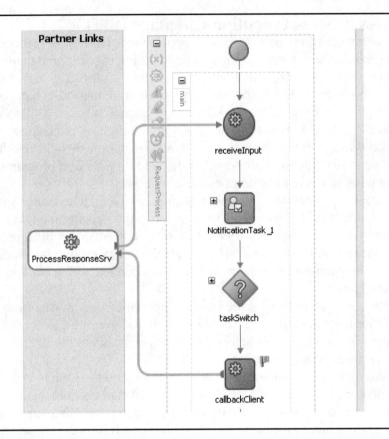

**FIGURE 2-4.** *A simple BPEL process with Human Workflow*

One other BPEL component used in Fusion Application is the *Activity Guide*. This is similar in concept to regular BPEL process flows, except instead of chaining together programmatic services or human workflows, it is primarily focused on high-level functional features and user interface components only. A simple example is the linking together of the steps involved in on-boarding a new employee into a company. The Activity Guide for this would include setting up ADF taskflow elements such as the payroll and benefits information, and performing legal and contract administration. Activities Guides can also be used to support disconnected tasks that are external to the Enterprise Application, such as creating an e-mail account or even issuing a security badge.

Fusion Applications includes full support for activity guides and presents them intuitively within its dashboard pages, so all related actions can be carefully monitored and tracked. Using the employee on-boarding example, the dashboard includes a simple progress bar with an associated tasklist, showing each item's status with drill-down links for more detail.

One final BPEL component of which applications administrators should be aware (but by no means is it everything) is *Oracle Business Rules* (OBR). This forms a method in which to apply complex policies, regulations, or computations, based on the well-known Rete algorithm. Like the Human Workflow components, this is represented as a specific node type within a BPEL process and governs how the execution process will flow. Each Business Rule node has its inputs and outputs linked to a reusable rule definition—a *ruleset*—created declaratively in the Rules Designer and stored in a rules library. OBR provides many advanced features for the implementation of organization-specific logic, although its use does require a certain level of expertise. The Application Administrator should be aware of this moving piece, understand what it does, and know how to manage it.

One additional comment regarding Fusion Applications specifically is that although the BPM levels (particular Level 4 tasks) may represent logical containers for BPEL processes, there is no consistent physical link between BPM and BPEL in version 1.0. This may expand in future releases, where the whole business process, including the execution logic, is held and managed in one all-encompassing business process repository.

## Oracle Mediator

As discussed, BPEL primarily represents a way in which to organize the discrete components of a composite application into one or more flows that mirror the business process activities the organization needs to complete (such as procure-to-pay). Although BPEL Process Manager forms the engine for process execution, it does not handle the invocation, management, and monitoring of the services it calls. This is done by Oracle Mediator. It works inside the SOA infrastructure, performing several of these orchestration-type functions. At the most basic level, Mediator forms the XML message handling mechanism through which almost all activities occur.

Following are a few basic examples:

- **Service invocation**   The messages passed between the components within a web service execution are all handled by the Mediator, supporting both synchronous and asynchronous invocation.

- **Business events and the Event Delivery Network**   Where events are raised upon specific action, the associated messages are handled by the Mediator.

■ **Message transformation**   Since many components have different interfaces, Mediator performs the transformations required to get them working together.

■ **Routing rules**   Mediator can also validate and perform message routing based on the content of the messages, as part of specific rule definitions.

For applications administrators, Mediator also handles any internal exceptions (such as network interruptions), as well as those returned by the web services it calls. It provides a detailed error handling and reporting process together with its own logging mechanism.

## WebCenter

Moving aside from business logic processing and back into user interface technologies, Oracle WebCenter sits in the Fusion Middleware stack and provides several services that integrate with and complement those already discussed.

Oracle WebCenter complies with the JSF standards of the ADF component, further enriching the end user experience and enhancing productivity. It focuses specifically on bringing Web 2.0–type features into Enterprise Applications, producing what some call *Enterprise2.0*. Fusion Applications, to leverage many parts of WebCenter. Following are some examples:

■ WebCenter spaces and portals for management dashboards

■ WebCenter Composer to perform runtime user personalization and more extensive customizations, based on a declarative and metadata driven architecture

■ WebCenter Services provides various social media services, including the following:

   ■ Wiki and blog for the publication of user content

   ■ People Connection for graphically showing relationships

   ■ Tags for adding keywords to objects and data to help with searching

   ■ Instant Messaging and Presence (IMP) to promote collaborative working

With so many flexible and powerful features readily available via WebCenter, applications administrators may need to consider specific implementations carefully and monitor usage for such things as resource capacity control and even potential misuse.

## Business Intelligence

As mentioned in the introduction, one of the key drivers of Fusion Applications is the move beyond processing transactions toward providing organizations with the tools needed for informed decision-making, whether it be optimizing order fulfillment schedules or making accurate sales forecasts. The implementation of these analytical type features has traditionally been a separate, dislocated effort, with the resulting tools found in another system, often away from the live transactional data. Fusion Applications integrates its intelligence capabilities into the work area interface, allowing patterns to be spotted and actions to be executed all in one place, greatly improving accuracy and efficiency.

Fusion Applications leverages several key technologies to manipulate raw data into a solution that is responsive, secure and accurate, while retaining comprehensive coverage.

- **Oracle Business Intelligence Enterprise Edition (OBIEE)**   The OBIEE server provides extended analytical capabilities and access to various data sources beyond only the transactional data, most significantly Hyperion Essbase, an Online Analytical Processing (OLAP) server that provides scalable and responsive multidimensional data warehousing. Together, these form the foundation of the BI technology used across the whole of Fusion Applications, from the components embedded in ADF pages to more detailed analysis workbenches, scorecards, and reports.

- **BI Publisher**   Previously called XML Publisher, this component takes customizable report templates and uses the XML transformation of real-time data to produce extremely high-quality reports. It's easy to use and supports even Microsoft Word–based declarative templates, and can be used to create multiple page reports that can contain a range of embedded analytical functions.

- **Oracle Business Intelligence Applications (OBIA)** As with the existing Applications products, Fusion Applications leverages a set of prebuilt intelligence reports, dashboards, scorecards, and other solutions for use within specific application products, such as Human Resources, Financial Accounting, and Supply Chain. These components have evolved from detailed analysis of best practice for BI, making sure that the right people in the organizations have access to the right information upon which to base effective decision-making.

- **Oracle Transactional Business Intelligence (OTBI)** Specifically developed for Fusion Applications this provides real-time reporting on live business data while leveraging the advanced display capabilities of the OBIEE server. This is most often used in the embedded analytics mentioned earlier.

- **Enterprise Performance Management (EPM)** Specifically designed for upper management, Oracle provides advanced solutions that leverage the entire set of application data and, based on an organization's own guidelines, thresholds, and targets, perform complex computations to provide business performance information in a notify-by-exception, actionable, and easy-to-monitor format. Traditionally, this has been through things such as KPIs and scorecards; however, Fusion Applications also includes a range of innovative methods and in-situ user interface components. EPM includes strategic and forecasting analysis tools based on operations such as supply chain optimization, financial budgeting and planning, asset and workforce management, and sales and marketing effectiveness. Several technical components are at work here, including Crystal Ball, the Hyperion EPM solutions for departmental and industry verticals, as well the Essbase modeling capabilities. The applications administrator needs to understand the moving pieces and ensure supporting management plans are appropriately created, undertaken, and maintained.

## Oracle Data Integrator

As mentioned, ODI's role in the Fusion Applications technology stack is primarily based around data synchronization. ODI extends the standard ETL process of data migration into a process that first extracts and then, as one more flexible step, performs both the load and transform activities together (E-LT). ODI is also based on the SOA runtime architecture, meaning that service interactions are accomplished in the same way as the other Fusion Middleware components; for example, ODI can be called from a BPEL process.

ODI capabilities are leveraged in several places in Fusion Applications, and the following list touches on a few:

- To populate data in the BI data warehouse

- To migrate data from legacy systems being replaced by Fusion Applications

- To synchronize common data across the Pillar Replication Framework

- As part of integration to an external system (such as within a coexistence strategy)

- In MDM to synchronize the single source of truth

All these are touch-points for application administrators, and therefore we will go into more detail on the basic ODI processes and ODI's management in Fusion Applications, and mention some useful extended capabilities to meet organization-specific needs. Further specialist reading is provided in the Appendix.

# Identity Management and Security

Security is at the heart of Fusion Applications, leveraging Oracle's already world-class solutions across each and every part of the application, from user login, to logic processing, and down into data storage.

## User Authentication

Login authentication controls access to function and data security, as explained earlier in the chapter. Fusion Applications uses the Fusion Middleware authentication processes, via Java Authentication and Authorization Service (JAAS), to perform all its user authentication.

This includes several different technical components. It starts with basic user credentials being stored in one or more Lightweight Directory Access Protocol (LDAP) servers, such as Oracle Internet Directory (OID). For centralizing security, these LDAP servers may be distributed across different physical servers using something like Oracle Virtual Directory (OVD). The user credentials are then mapped to predefined security *roles*, managed by Oracle Identity Management (OIM). Where any changes are needed, the Authorization Policy Manager (APM) tool allows full role customization. In addition, where Single Sign-on (SSO) is required, Fusion Applications readily integrates with Oracle Access Manager (OAM).

At the application front-end, for most users the provisioning process is done by roles being granted to employees based on their work assignments, although in some cases (such as external supplier users), manual creation via OIM may still be required. Fusion Applications also supports importing users and roles from legacy systems via OIM and the HCM applications' Import Workers feature. Fusion Applications initially installs a few base users, although it does include a complete set of policies and roles to support each and every business process. Again, customization can be done using the graphical tools available inside OIM and the more general tool, Oracle Platform Security Services (OPSS).

As mentioned earlier in this chapter, Fusion Applications includes extensive features to ensure proper adherence to regulatory standards and controls, especially as part of its GRC product family. Obviously, this has interfaces into security and indeed contains some specific tools for that purpose. One example is the Application Access Controls Governor (AACG) that helps with segregation of duties inside GRC.

## Middleware Security

With so many components in the Fusion Middleware technology stack, a full discussion of security would warrant a book of its own (see the Appendix for a bit more information). Suffice to say, Fusion Applications uses all the best pieces. The following list provides a brief summary of some of the main security technologies it employs:

- All web services are secured using a standards-based WS-Security–compliant architecture. This is fully accessible through Oracle Web Services Manager (OWSM).

- In addition to the services it calls, BPEL processes have several other moving parts and therefore include a number of security components, from Secure Socket Layer (SSL) for communication, to the application of user security context for function and data security in process execution. The BPEL Process Manager is the primary tool for monitoring and administering business process security.

- ESS secures jobs by revalidating the security access levels from the requesting users' security context. It validates both their function and data security privileges (roles, policies, and grants) against the requirements of the objects being accessed in the job (such as Java, PL/SQL, and C programs).

- The User Interface and Business Logic components, such as ADF, ADFbc, and the BI components, are all secured by the user authentication (JAAS) mechanism. This common security implementation helps all these components perform their integrated tasks seamlessly and efficiently.

As mentioned, security is an exceptionally important part of the applications administrator's role, and with the middleware forming such a large part of Fusion Applications, plenty of further discussion is warranted.

## Database
The security technologies at work in Oracle Database 11*g* are well publicized, and Fusion Applications makes use of the best of these in a fairly standard way. So what is specifically notable for Fusion Applications? As mentioned, PII represents data that needs securing to protect individuals from being identified, contacted, or located by anyone unauthorized to do so. Fusion Applications contains about 50 fields that are categorized as *Internal-Public* and about 30 categorized as *Confidential.* To enforce strong security, it leverages the Oracle Database Vault capabilities when storing and communicating PII data.

# A Processing Walkthrough
This section provides a simplified illustration of how a user action will trigger the parts of the technology stack, demonstrating how the parts work together at runtime. As a suite of composite applications, Fusion Applications does not actually have the linear execution paths that are more characteristic in traditional enterprise applications (user interface to database and back again). The different components running inside Fusion Applications often work at the same time, frequently as part of the same user interface page and triggered from the same event. Figure 2-5 shows an extension of the technology stack overview provided, adjusted to show a high-level view of the relationships between some of the parts discussed so far.

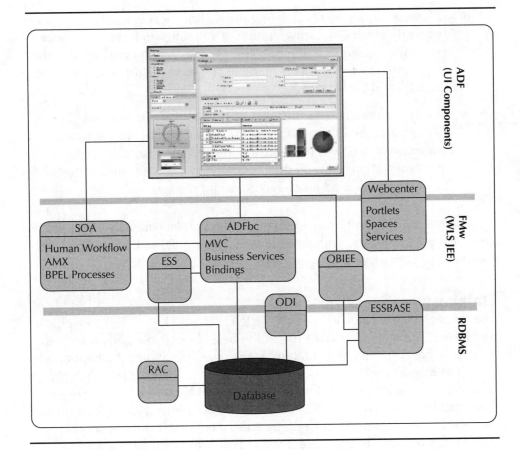

**FIGURE 2-5.** *How the technology stack works together*

To provide at least a rough outline of a common execution path, the following is a broad sequence of activities that could occur through the technology stack. It is broadly based on submitting a page of data by the business user, such as creating a new purchase order.

1. The user visits the application URL and basic session information is established (cookies, and so on).

2. The user logs in, invoking the full suite of identity management capabilities from OID and into OIM for the association of function and data roles (and their policies) to their session. The associated dashboard, with only authorized regions, data, and capabilities, is provided to the user.

3. The user completes the form and clicks the submit button. The request invokes any embedded ADF validations (Groovy, and so on) and fires the controller code. The controller methods commit some data (via entity objects) at this point.

4. The controller and the page then raise an associated business event within the ADFbc layer and any associated subscriptions are triggered (via EDN). Where the next step represents a large piece of work, the processing may split so that the user session is released to continue forward and the back-end processing runs behind the scenes.

5. Event subscriptions invoke the Mediator to handle subsequent messaging to and from an associated BPEL process flow.

6. The BPEL Process Manager starts the flow and executes the associated steps based on the data it has received. As it runs, it retains context data and runs associated web service calls in and out of the BPEL process, also orchestrated by the BPEL Process Manager and the Mediator. Many different actions and processes may be spawned, including Human Workflows, ESS jobs, and child BPEL processes.

As various threads of processing run, the associated data is updated through the system, so as soon as an activity occurs, the new data will be reflected in the application pages.

# Coexistence Overview

Not all organizations will want to replace their entire enterprise applications in one go. It's a hugely expensive task, and unless benefits and return on investment (ROI) can be proven, it's likely to be out of the scope of near-term strategy plans. That said, many organizations will want to adopt the advanced features and more productive working environment offered by Fusion Applications, especially in business areas where significant improvements could be made. This is possible right away with version 1.0, using prepackaged coexistence integrations. These represent several functional features that have been specially designed to run in the Fusion Applications instance while readily integrating to complimentary existing Applications products. By leveraging the SOA, as well as technologies such as ODI, Fusion Applications is natively structured for this kind of process integration.

The first release includes planning for ten of these coexistence integration scenarios, and they focus on some of the best Fusion Applications features, without the need for a full-scale implementation or migration. It's seen as a relatively simple first step to adopt one or more of these integrations, which can bring immediate benefits to business users. Coexistence also represents the start of a flexible piece-by-piece implementation program that can be progressed at times most suitable for each organization.

The following list provides the coexistence scenarios that are planned for Fusion Applications in version 1.0:

- Supply chain management

  - Fusion distributed order orchestration, to non-Fusion order entry/fulfillment

- Procurement

  - Fusion shared spending, sourcing, and contracts, to non-Fusion requisitioning

  - Fusion Procure-to-Pay, to non-Fusion general ledger

- Project portfolio management

  - Fusion PPM, to non-Fusion PPM

- Human capital management

  - Fusion Talent Management On Demand, to non-Fusion HR

  - Fusion Workforce Directory Management, to non-Fusion HR

  - Fusion Incentive Compensation, to non-Fusion CRM

  - Fusion Workforce Lifecycle Management, to non-Fusion Financials and CRM

- Customer relationship management

  - Fusion Territory Management, to non-Fusion customer relationship management

- Financial Management

  - Fusion Accounting Hub, to non-Fusion financials

Clearly, coexistence is a great starting point for implementing Fusion Applications; however, this inevitably represents additional work for the applications administrator. Although managing both legacy and Fusion Applications systems in addition to a major integration piece is not for the faint of heart, in the real world, this is not so unusual. For example, during any upgrade or migration, there is normally a project phase when two systems run side-by-side for a period of time before the full switch-over is done and the old system is decommissioned.

# The Extension Architecture

Fusion Applications, and indeed all modern enterprise applications, come with a set of features and techniques to change and extended the way in which the standard software works. This is required, because although all the application features are reasonably flexible, they will never be able to satisfy the needs of every organization. Although many business analysts and consultants would push organizations toward standardization and less customization, sometimes an organization's unique attributes control profit margins and set them apart from others in the marketplace.

Traditionally, changes to the standard application increase the total cost of ownership, since applications are costly and complex to build, brittle to change, and complex to support. Ownership costs have been estimated as being around 70 percent higher for customized applications. Fusion Applications offers several solutions that allow organizations to make the most of their unique differences while mitigating most of the normally associated risks.

## Configuration

Fusion Applications comes with a wide range of options for setting up both the technology stack and the application features to work in a way that best fits a specific implementation. These configurations are fully compliant with the standard product and are therefore fully supported by the system operation. Some examples of this might include the configuration parameters provided as part of the installation process (inside something called *Flow Designer*), the business setup data used as part of Functional Setup Manager, or simply the profile options that are set within the system.

Application configuration setup usually occurs during implementation, although occasionally adjustments may be made for such reasons as organizational changes or as part of optimization efforts. The applications administrator will play a large role in configuration management.

# Personalization

Personalization represents the first level of system penetration in terms of making changes to satisfy nonstandard requirements. Truly effective enterprise applications should be sensitive to the context of each and every user, providing exactly what each needs to do the required job. Fusion Applications focuses on this from security roles and privileges, to the rich user interface design. Taking this one step further, through personalization it's possible for each user to configure the system him or herself so it looks, feels, and works to match users' individual expectations and preferences. This ranges from the size, shape, and content of the components displayed on each page, to configuring specific sets of query results that users commonly find useful.

Traditionally, many of these preference changes were lost upon user logout, but in Fusion Applications, everything is retained indefinitely. That said, no actual changes are made to the original page definitions; instead, each set of changes is stored separately and is quickly applied each time the user accesses the page. This is done using the Oracle WebCenter component known as Composer. For more extensive personalizations, beyond the scope of the Composer features, Fusion Applications leverages the Metadata Repository (MDS). Similarly to WebCenter, MDS stores all personalizations and reapplies only the changes using a layering approach. It supports multiple layers of personalization, applying one after the other, on top of the original base definition. This has many benefits, but most significantly it means the original base definition can be changed by a patch or upgrade without affecting the personalizations, as they're simply reapplied over the new version. Should a patch or upgrade significantly change the base definition, any personalizations that are no longer applicable (removed regions) are simply ignored. Personalizations are secured, and applications administrators can enable or disable the range of options available to end users.

# Extensibility

When the changes needed are actually in the processing logic itself, WebCenter and MDS personalizations are simply not up to the job. Extensibility takes over and comes with two main methods for making these more invasive system changes.

The first one is using the flexfield architecture mentioned earlier in this chapter. Fusion Applications supports user defined unique identifiers (key flexfields) and additional data fields, used either in a single usage context (dynamic flexfields) or in multiple different contexts (extensible flexfields). When appropriate, this is certainly the recommended path to take, since no changes to existing code or data objects are required to get started.

The second method is much less declarative and requires the use of Oracle JDeveloper to begin manipulating code objects to make the changes required. As a general rule, most standard objects, such as EOs, VOs, Java classes, and BPEL processes, can be *extended* by new objects. These new objects should implement all the same interfaces plus add any of their own. Objects that cause restrictions in interfaces or changes to processing logic, security, or adjusted database objects are not part of extensibility, and these come under the customization category, discussed next.

The results of extensibility projects, when done correctly, are again applied through MDS repository layers, ensuring that future-proofing and simplicity are retained throughout.

Where the applications administrator is required to manage extended objects, he or she needs a good understanding of the technologies, tools, and techniques involved. Although the administrator might not be doing the actual development work, a detailed understanding can prove helpful when he or she investigates application problems and analyzes the potential impact of system changes.

# Customization

Although most of the preceding three methods for adjusting Fusion Applications should suffice for the majority of organizations, inevitably some organizations' requirements can be satisfied only by serious changes to the base software itself. Usually this is a mixture of methods. Organization-wide personalizations are used to adjust the user interface, some extensions to standard objects (such as BPEL flows) get the system processes to match the business operations, and a few customizations are used to change the behavior beyond that of the standard feature configurations.

With Fusion Applications natively running on Fusion Middleware, leveraging a range of standards-based architectures, and integrating directly with the 11g JDeveloper integrated development environment (IDE) (via its own Fusion Applications customization role), any customization work required is now much simpler, more logical, and more manageable than it has ever been before.

# The Fusion Applications Ecosystem

You are probably beginning to appreciate how each functional application (General Ledger, Purchasing, and so on) is part of a broad landscape of supporting components, each with its own specific purpose. So far, we have discussed the pieces that run underneath the applications, providing the execution platform for their various capabilities. In addition to this is a second set of components that sit alongside and complement the applications, forming a kind of *ecosystem* to support users from both the business and IT operations.

## User Assistance

All Enterprise Applications are complex, and as such they include things like online help and documentation to assist new or inexperienced users. Fusion Applications, although designed to be easy to use, also has extensive information to help the successful completion of every task. Several new approaches within this content make it far removed from the traditional experience of wading through reams of static documents to find what you need to know.

### Content Structure

A strong focus is placed on providing users with just enough information to complete their tasks—not too much and not too little. Each concise unit of knowledge is discrete and independent, providing a modular structure that promotes the reuse of information in different contexts. As these all work together, they roll-up to form a comprehensive overall coverage. Each unit can take one of seven forms:

- Frequently Asked Questions
- Key Concepts

- Examples of Use

- Task Sequences and Relationships

- Demonstration

- Further Reference Information

- Glossary

The knowledge is available in a range of consumption formats including simple text, diagrams, screenshots, and interactive video segments.

All help content is structured based on the BPM model, so it's easy to move from a top-level business process to each individual activity and find information for all the tasks therein. Obviously, this navigational layout for the content very closely corresponds both to how the application works (such as task flows) and how organizations work, making the content easy to find and always relevant.

## Content Style

The user assistance (yes, it's seen as more than just online help now) in Fusion Applications has a few extra capabilities that take it beyond what is possible with traditional static content. First, as part of the advanced user experience (UX), several Web 2.0 (or Enterprise 2.0) features are available, based on integration with the WebCenter component. One of these is the ability to custom tag each item of content, so that keyword searches are more intuitive and the results are more accurate. Another neat feature is that each piece of content can be voted on by users, thereby placing popular and generally useful articles first in result lists.

Another exceptionally important capability is that all of the content can be edited or added to by anyone authorized to do so. The content is just as extensible as that in business process logic or the user interface components. No extra tools or particular skills are required to adjust help content, since the system itself provides easy-to-use features to make changes. This improves the traditional process considerably, since commonly business users would request changes and wait for suitable resource from the IT department, whereas now the administrator need only grant a business user the appropriate security role and the changes can happen as needed.

These changes, like other MDS-based extensibility, are future-proof, meaning that the original base content can be upgraded or patched, and any changes are just reapplied on top.

## Content Access

The user assistance content is available in essentially three ways. First is through *embedded help*. One example is the bubble-help available for most fields on each page, which provides a few explanatory words. In addition, some fields and buttons also offer pop-up help icons that provide a little more detail. A final example of embedded help is the format examples and alerts that appear for fields that accept only specific data types, such as dates and numbers. Embedded help provides almost everything required to understand and use the components on each page.

The second type of content is more wide-ranging, focusing on completion of work rather than usage of pages. This covers everything from understanding business process flows, to how to set up and complete detailed tasks. This content is known as *non-embedded help* and is held within the *help portal*. It comprises the seven different forms of content listed earlier (FAQ, Key Concepts, and so on) and is somewhat equivalent to the online help of traditional enterprise applications. When accessing this content, Fusion Applications shares the context of the active page with the help portal, ensuring that everything displayed is relevant. In the help portal, the extensibility, tagging, and other features come into their own, allowing all content to be tailored as required.

The third type of content is somewhat traditional, but nevertheless exceptionally valuable. Some content, such as installation instructions and system administration information, doesn't neatly fit into a functional Business Process Model, and it doesn't really work in the context of the application features. This type of content, mainly related to back-end system management, is provided as static PDF documents. That's not to say that some of it is not accessible from the help portal, as some functional setup documents are, but for the most part it forms a comprehensive offline library.

# The Supportability Architecture

Most enterprise application architectures are based around execution and capabilities, helping them deliver a long list of feature functions. Although this still remains true for Fusion Applications, an additional underlying architecture runs through the whole system, known as *supportability*. Supportability can be defined as the ease with which problems can be diagnosed and resolved, or more simply put, how supportable the software is. Fusion Applications has a baked-in range of support-related technologies, utilities, design patterns, and best practices, so that when something fails, the relevant details are captured and provided for further analysis. In the future it's likely that this will form the basis for automated system diagnosis and may be self-healing, the panacea for delivering lower total cost of ownership (TCO). For now, a few specific pieces make the applications administrator's job substantially easier.

## Diagnostic Logging and Tracing

Fusion Applications comprises several business logic execution environments, such as Java, PL/SQL, and BPEL, which all work together to provide the application features and functions. Should the code in any one of these environments fail to perform as expected (exceptions, poor performance, or simply illogical results), running inside such a complex technology stack it would be difficult to identify precisely what and where the failure occurred. Fortunately, Fusion Applications contains a unified logging mechanism, so that all code writes its debug output (including exceptions, data, and processing statuses) in a consistent manner, in standard format, and to a uniform location.

Later chapters provide full explanations of how these logging mechanisms work in each execution environment. We'll look at how they can be configured, monitored, and their content used for successful applications administration.

## Application Diagnostic Tests

With thousands of business features that can be used in hundreds of different configurations, it's not just the software code that needs support, but also the setup and use of these features themselves. By starting the problem analysis at the highest level—looking at what the business user is trying to do—many issues around misconfiguration and misuse can be avoided. The validation of business features is supported in Fusion Applications by the Diagnostic Test Framework (DTF).

Similar utilities exist in other Applications products, such as E-Business Suite's own Diagnostic Tests, however, for Fusion Applications, this platform provides a very flexible and powerful method for business users to begin troubleshooting from within the product itself.

In summary, this framework offers the following key features to help detect and diagnose problems in application functions and features:

- Each diagnostic test provides a detailed report output. Tests can also be chained together so that one report can contain a full suite of related diagnostics.

- A separate dashboard is provided for managing all diagnostic tests and their execution, accessible from anywhere within Fusion Applications. Test runs can also be prescheduled and batched using the dashboard.

- Each diagnostic test is fully secured based on the standard application Data and Function Security access privileges.

- Tests can accept one or more input parameters, allowing them to be executed for specific sets of data. For example, tests can be run for individual transactions or within a particular context, such as for a particular user or business unit.

- The use of diagnostic tests remains flexible to suit specific purposes and needs. They can perform such functions as validating technical and functional configurations, qualifying the setup of business objects (such as enterprise structures), verifying transaction and data integrity, and checking the results of process execution. Tests can also directly call application logic to validate parts of a process.

- Although commonly used when reacting to a problem, these diagnostic tests can also be used in a proactive manner to check for potential problems that, if not resolved, might have severe downstream effects. For example, prior to running the processes for the close of a financial period, diagnostic tests can be run to validate the health of the functional setup and the transactional data, and any corrections can be made before processing begins.

- Each diagnostic test is associated to a business process, making it immediately accessible to business users, directly within the context of a problem. In addition, like the help content, diagnostic tests can be custom tagged for such purposes as linking a specific test to one specific event.

### Diagnostic Framework

With the 11*g* release of Fusion Middleware and the Database Server, Oracle has introduced an underlying platform for the capture of system information upon any serious failure. This is known as the Diagnostic Framework (DFw), and its adoption extends to Fusion Applications as well.

In summary, this framework provides a detection mechanism so that whenever a problem with a predefined set of symptoms (or signature) occurs, a dedicated process is launched and collects all associated system information, such as logs, traces, dumps, and diagnostics. Fusion Applications leverages this framework so that when the product logic handles a particularly serious error, it will automatically raise an associated alert (known as an *incident*) and ensure all related information is captured.

Interestingly enough, in Fusion Applications this framework actually leverages the two previously discussed supportability features, whereby Fusion Applications incidents will include application diagnostic logs and traces, plus they will execute any diagnostic tests that are associated with the problem signature.

# Next-Generation Manageability

Although Fusion Applications is more complex than its other Oracle Applications cousins, more tools and utilities are available to manage that complexity. This book is intended to provide information in a meaningful and applicable way. As such, we will look in detail at the various dashboards, consoles, and systems management programs that exist, both in the technology stack as well as those extended to be part of Fusion Applications.

Although the discussion will focus specifically around Oracle Enterprise Manager as the central systems management tool, to encompass the complete Applications Management remit (as discussed in the next chapter), the focus is somewhat broadened. We'll look at various other utilities and techniques that, when combined, offer a deeper overall awareness, covering all aspects, including the health of the business processes and the application processing, performance of all the supporting technology stack components, and monitoring such things as the database, the operating system, and even the network and hardware.

# CHAPTER
## 3

# Successful Enterprise
## Application
## Management

**B**efore joining Oracle, I worked as a programmer, a data analyst, and, especially relevant to this discussion, a system administrator. I worked with a range of enterprise applications, both home-grown and off-the-shelf. Most of these were based around typical back-office processes such as inventory management, order fulfillment, production processing, and sales and marketing. My experience also includes consulting on implementations for multinational organizations, and even project managing one particular enterprise application implementation, integrating with more than a dozen separate systems. This experience taught me many things, and with nearly a dozen subsequent years helping Oracle support some of the largest organizations on the planet, I think I am in a reasonable position to impart a few pearls of wisdom. This makes it sound like the following discussion is going to be a long list of hints and tips, and although I do offer some, the most valuable contribution I think I can make at this early stage is to keep things simple, understandable, and most of all complete. From this you can take what you need and transfer it into meaningful actions in your organization.

It seems pretty unlikely that you would be reading this book without some experience of Enterprise Application management, and in fact you could well be far more experienced than I. But, clearly, Fusion Applications isn't something you would decide to take on for just a bit of extra fun, and therefore this discussion is once again written from the bare-bones up. I guess the one phrase that clearly sums up why this is a sensible approach is "assumption is the mother of all ****-ups"—a phrase I first heard from an engineer while looking for natural resources aboard a semisubmersible oil rig floating around the Atlantic Ocean! Another job role from my somewhat varied past.

# What Is Enterprise Application Management?

As is somewhat traditional when discussing IT systems, we'll start with an analogy. Most machinery comprises a closed-loop system when it comes to management: it simply runs. Although, eventually, one of the perishable parts will fail, it's a relatively simple process to find the problem and install a replacement part. Many pieces of modern software are not too different from this ideal picture, especially small, self-contained programs that perform a specific set of operations with fixed inputs and outputs.

Unfortunately, despite our technical discoveries and inventions, this machinery analogy cannot be realistically applied to enterprise applications. The wide range of moving parts, input and output possibilities, setups, configurations, and customizations make this kind of closed-loop model impossible, certainly for the foreseeable future. With all these variables, together with things such as sudden environment alterations and workload fluctuations, the enterprise application is likely to react even to the smallest incremental change and is generally much more sensitive than any simple machine. So perhaps more like a house (or even a spouse), the enterprise application needs regular care to ensure its health and happiness.

# Definition and Goals

It makes sense to define the enterprise application management role and what it constitutes, since this will significantly help explain and structure what follows in this book. Quite simply it is the role that accepts the responsibility for the enterprise application, making sure it's adequately accessible to users. Enterprise applications are at the heart of most daily business operations, and they can significantly influence a business's effectiveness. Whether you're a CEO or an order processing clerk, if the enterprise application doesn't perform well, you probably won't have a very productive day.

Let's start with five basic tenets of enterprise application management:

- **Reliability**  Ensure that the features consistently operate as intended.

- **Availability**  Ensure that all features are available whenever and wherever expected.

- **Performance**  Ensure that all work can be completed within an acceptable timescale.

- **Optimization**  Ensure that the software helps meet the organizational objectives.

- **Governance**  Ensure that features and data are available only to authorized users.

You'll notice the inclusion of unbounded statements here, through words such as *intended, expected,* and *acceptable.* This is deliberate, and it indicates that each implementation should establish its own detailed definition for practical use. For example, an organization might specify that in the production instance, the actual availability should be no less than 95 percent of the scheduled up-time, or perhaps that the performance threshold for the rendering of the Payables dashboard should be between 0 and 5 seconds. Obviously, this kind of detailed breakdown can quickly get unwieldy to manage; however, we'll look later at some tools in Fusion Applications that are specifically designed for this purpose.

# Role Introduction

Now that you have a basic idea of what you can achieve with enterprise application management, let's look at what kind of individual might manage enterprise applications.

Traditionally, large organizations have many different applications (sometimes hundreds) in their overall operation, and with finite resources, it's often the existing roles that are forced to take on those applications that fit closest with their job profile or skill set. Even Oracle's existing Applications products (E-Business Suite, PeopleSoft, and so on) may not have dedicated individuals or roles assigned to their management, instead being grouped together and managed with other applications based on similar technologies or purpose. Although this is understandable, Fusion Applications' broad range of features and its deep technology stack mean that dedicated efforts are needed to ensure that effective management goals are delivered.

Let's look at some of the traditionally related roles, and see how a new hybrid role is indeed required.

## The Systems Administrator

This role is the staple of the IT department, and provides general installation, configuration, and troubleshooting for any and all technologies in use. This ranges from operating systems and execution environments, to more specific specializations such as networking and hardware.

Although Fusion Applications requires its own dedicated technology stack, this still sits over the standard technology platform and therefore the system administrator function remains vital. In fact, with more software components, complex topology and integrations, and deployment options, the system administrator skills and tools are as important as ever.

## The Database Administrator (DBA)

It's often the DBA who gets loaded with supporting enterprise applications. The applications' data-centric nature means that traditionally the DBA is often closest to the applications, and their skills are regularly required. This does change somewhat with Fusion Applications, since the database forms one of many separate technical components. Obviously, the same data-centric nature remains, but the modular system architecture allows for role specialization and should release the DBA to refocus his or her time on more productive tasks.

## The Applications Super User

The consumers of the enterprise applications are the business users, and a senior role is used to ensure that the available features appropriately meet the users' needs. This role performs all basic functional setups, manages all processes, and generally performs small tweaks to improve feature use. Also termed power-users, they are granted extra privileges so that they may access more advanced functions that can help optimize their teams' working environment. Examples in Fusion Applications might be access to the Page Composer tools for making site-level page changes, or even perhaps access to the flexfield configuration pages.

Interestingly, Oracle makes a recommendation that an administrator be defined for each application type, providing specialist management of the processes and features therein. This role is mainly technical and becomes particularly pertinent when the Pillar Replication Framework is available. Until then, it could be good practice to adopt the same effort based on each product family (which are not dissimilar to pillars), as it will help promote a good understanding of the functional processes and setups.

## The Security Manager

For large organizations with many distributed systems and disconnected applications, managing IT security can be a full-time job. Even in today's world of centralized security solutions and unified login processes, there are always additional security tasks to manage. As connectivity continues to proliferate in business, protecting valuable intellectual property and corporate data from competition-driven prying eyes is a high priority to the IT department, the boardroom, and increasingly to the public relations team.

As the business backbone, the enterprise application should provide a suite of security management services that, as well as basic tools, should provide support for embedding safeguards, good practices, and comprehensive enforcement and monitoring procedures.

## The Systems Analyst

Sitting halfway between IT and business operations, the traditional systems analyst role is tasked with designing software solutions that help solve business problems. This is often achieved with the help of outside consultants who also bring their own expertise and recommendations. It's interesting to consider how large organizations traditionally used this role to help design bespoke proprietary software applications, but with the evolution of both new technologies (such as SOA) and enterprise applications, there is greater flexibility and ready-made options available to meet most business requirements. And although this has somewhat reduced the need for very large-scale implementation development projects, a role that is able to leverage the features of the enterprise application to meet the real business objectives remains exceptionally important.

## The Helpdesk

Despite (and perhaps because of) the evolution of software applications, organizations need user helpdesks. Although the majority of helpdesk work involves desktop support, in larger organizations the helpdesk team also accepts enterprise applications issues. Helpdesk agents are rarely skilled in the enterprise application features or in complex troubleshooting, however.

The helpdesk often acts as a first-line interface, performing basic triaging of issues, and then routing complex problems to the most suitable roles, such as system administrators and DBAs. Although this model might work for smaller or more simplistic applications, enterprise applications have become so powerful, pervasive, and essential to everyday tasks, that they now require their own dedicated support resources. The related support processes and procedures need to be very well defined and clearly structured, and this will heavily involve the enterprise application manager.

## The Hybrid Role

Although the enterprise applications manager has to be a kind of superstar, possessing a broad range of skills, the depth in which they need to specialize in any one of these skills is not so great. Basic knowledge of various areas should suffice for the most part, where particular specialists can be called in when more expertise is required.

This is especially true for Fusion Applications, since most of the technology administration is accomplished using Oracle's standard platform tools, such as Oracle Access Manager and Oracle Identity Manager for handling user security. The enterprise application manager should be able to perform basic activities in all of these tools, but as in our example, additional expertise might be required from the security expert for advanced tasks.

One additional background point to make quickly is that we're discussing roles within an organization, not specifically individual job titles. This distinction is important, since one job title may include several different roles. It's often not necessary (or economical) for too many people to be looking after the organization's systems, and indeed by using some of the tools we'll see later, the time and effort involved in performing management duties can be significantly lowered.

# The Principles of Enterprise Application Management

So far in this chapter, the five goals of enterprise application management have been defined, and we've looked briefly at the kind of roles and abilities involved. Now let's bring together these concepts by looking in a bit more detail at what the enterprise application management role actually involves.

## Reliability

As mentioned, the enterprise application needs to exude the same strength and quality that serves as the foundation for the rest of the organization. An unreliable enterprise application will have numerous negative impacts, with some of the obvious ones being the following:

- **Frustrated and annoyed end users**   Taken to the extreme, good workers will consider leaving an organization when they cannot complete their jobs to their own satisfaction.

- **Slowing and even preventing the completion of core business tasks**   This can impact all areas, from production and sales, to wage payments, and even cash-flow.

■ **Impacting external partners** For example, if you are trying to process invoices to pay suppliers but the system keeps failing, it will not be long before suppliers' impression of the organization will become negative.

So what must the enterprise application manager do to avoid reliability problems (beyond selecting a good quality enterprise application in the first place)? This can be best illustrated by looking at some of the fundamental activities that are part of the role.

## Resource Monitoring and Management

With so many moving parts in the technology stack, it's vital that the manager keep a close watch on the availability of key resources. This includes the usual set of common resources, such as physical resources like memory, disk space, CPU, and network connections, and also configuration-based constraints, such as those for the Java virtual machine (JVM) and the database tablespaces.

With so many discrete components running inside modern enterprise applications, occasionally problems with one resource will not be immediately obvious, since it will be related only to one or two specific activities. For example, one component's logging may not be appropriately configured, and as it tries to write more lines to an already huge file, it may experience problems that only affect a few specific processes. Understanding and monitoring all the core resources being used is vital.

In Fusion Applications, many of the technology stack components run as Java EE applications themselves, making the resourcing and monitoring of this infrastructure layer especially important. This forms a key part of the availability utilities discussed in Chapter 7.

## Preventative Support

A good enterprise application management plan includes many proactive elements. These are vital to mitigate the downstream affects that software problems can cause to the business operation. As an example, all enterprise application vendors will issue regular software updates that include fixes for known issues. Until full system management automation is mature enough to be totally trusted, it's up to the enterprise application manager to review these updates and to ensure that those that contain pertinent fixes are implemented, ideally before those issues are encountered.

This can also be taken beyond simply checking for known issues. At regular intervals, the enterprise application should be fully reviewed to validate the finer details of the system health. On a day-to-day basis, the key resources and performance indicators will be monitored and fine-tuned; however, dedicated time must be set aside for more in-depth analysis to help pick up on any early warning signals and spot optimization opportunities.

It's important that all proactive work be explicitly scheduled, since it often gets pushed aside as seemingly more urgent things come up. It's vital to keep on the right side of the curve, making improvements and avoiding potential issues, and not to fall into the hamster-wheel of working on one problem after another.

## Reactive Issue Resolution

When serious problems occur, they will inevitably require the involvement of the enterprise application manager. As the subject matter expert and general owner of the system, the manager is ultimately responsible for researching and applying solutions. Problems almost always come in different shapes and sizes, although it is possible to define a few high-level types.

- **Questions** Users often require more detailed information or assistance to understand how to complete a particular activity. The enterprise applications manager will therefore require expertise and experience to answer these questions, although this should be supported by availability of additional reference resources such as documentation, knowledgebase articles, and other specific experts.

- **Problems** Users occasionally experience failures or unexpected results when trying to complete a task. Failure-type problems are defined by a set of symptoms that make up a *problem signature*, and each occurrence of a problem is known as an *incident*. Problems may also include behind-the-scenes technical issues that might not yet impact end users, but will still require resolution. The skills required here tend to be focused around troubleshooting, execution analysis, and general technical expertise.

■ **Improvements** The performance goals set for (or by) the enterprise application manager will often require immediate attention and action. This kind of reactive optimization effort again requires troubleshooting and analysis skills, along with a clear understanding about the intention of the targets that may require some business operational knowledge.

As part of the reactive issue resolution process, the enterprise application manager should be integral to the internal support procedures—for example, by helping to ensure that the right kinds of issues are routed to the right teams and individuals. They should also be instrumental in the design, delivery, and monitoring of sufficient training for all those involved. All too often, knowledge becomes siloed, and unless detailed information (including reference material) is shared, the enterprise application manager will be quickly overrun with requests for assistance.

In addition to the internal resolution process, the enterprise application manager will be responsible for occasionally working with external software vendors and partners for issues that cannot be resolved in-house. This will require expertise in using the vendor's own support tools, utilities, and processes. We'll revisit the issue resolution process, together with some Oracle specific tools, in more detail in Chapter 11.

# Availability

For enterprise applications, downtime is not really an option. When key parts (or all) of the system are unavailable, business operations quickly grind to a halt, and it's rare that organizations properly provision for manual backup operations (except perhaps in some military or medical type industries). As such, the enterprise application manager should be well prepared to ensure that the application is (or at least seems) continuously available.

## Continuity

Sometimes unexpected situations occur (notwithstanding acts of god), and the enterprise application manager should maintain a full *disaster recovery* architecture that helps provide a relatively uninterrupted service, certainly for the key features of the application. Clearly, the closer the application features are to the completion of the core business tasks, the more costly outages are. Although the detailed process for defining an adequate continuity plan (such as detailed *redundancy* measures) is beyond the scope of this short discussion, it remains a vital part of the enterprise application manager's role. Fortunately, the Oracle technology stack has various *high availability* tools, and most of these are available for use by Fusion Applications. We'll look at various fail-over options as well as backup and recovery strategies in Chapter 7.

## Instance Provision

In addition to the live *production* instance of the enterprise application, it's recommended that you have multiple additional installations to meet the needs of the organization. At a minimum, the following are recommended, and of course there may be one or more instances of each type:

- **Preproduction instance**   This instance is used as a copy of the production instance and is intended to replicate the same setup and data. It can have various purposes, but most commonly it's used for training new users and testing new features. It is usually carefully controlled and the setup and data is refreshed regularly. Some organizations do not use a formal Preproduction instance; however, for the extra confidence and production-like testing gained, it can be used to great effect.

- **Test instance**   This is a sandbox-type instance, used for pretty much any activity. Its data will be periodically refreshed from the other instances, and therefore there may be a few guidelines on its use. Uses include somewhere to first try new ideas and adjusted setups, as well as a test-bed for some more invasive customizations, upgrades, and patches.

- **Development instance**   These instances tend to be provisioned for the software development teams that enhance the system with customizations, advanced configurations, as well as new integration solutions. Again they're periodically refreshed with new data and are carefully controlled so that complex and expensive development work is properly managed.

## Systems Integration Availability

Although Fusion Applications is a complete suite of products and features that handles almost all business operations, it's quite likely that some organization-specific applications will exist, and that some level of integration between the two will occur.

All integrations require expert management to reduce their complexity that can lead to frequent failures and subsequent complex diagnosis. Every external or internal piece that even lightly touches the enterprise application must be well designed, well written, well understood, and well documented so that it can be properly managed and supported. In Chapter 6, we'll look in more detail at integrations, and together with customizations we'll consider a few good management techniques. Let's take a brief look at a few basic integration requirements.

**Internal Systems Integration**    These include off-the-shelf specialist applications, programs developed in-house to support a specific need, or even huge systems that have evolved to form an important part of the operation. Examples might be proprietary manufacturing software, service administration tools (such as insurance policy handling), or perhaps simply point-of-sale solutions. The integration pieces between these systems have a habit of being quite large and rather complex. It is therefore critical that the enterprise application manager be involved in their design, development, and testing. Going forward, to support these pieces, it is vital that the enterprise application manager ensures that each integration piece is accompanied by detailed reference material and clear ownership is maintained should any changes be needed.

In addition to large-scale integrations, some unified custom utilities will be linked to offer additional services to help end users. Examples are portal access systems, administration and productivity tools, and expert knowledge systems. Although these pieces may seem smaller, the same standardized approach should be taken in ensuring proper support for every piece.

In discussing integrations, we should consider the Fusion Applications Coexistence solutions. These prepackaged integration solutions allow organizations to run parts of Fusion Applications with their existing Oracle Applications product set, and form a simple first step toward full adoption. It is therefore likely that the enterprise application manager will spend considerable time and effort in understanding, administering, and optimizing these coexistence integration solutions.

Another integration scenario that is popular is to have parts (or all) of the enterprise application hosted by a third party, eliminating much of the overall maintenance overhead. Where this is used extensively, the enterprise application management role becomes mainly concerned with handling integrations to and from the hosted systems. Most organizations currently adopt hybrid approaches to this On-Demand, Cloud-based, or Software-as-a-Service (SaaS) model, meaning some core parts of the application are kept in-house and then integrated with specific parts that fit especially well with the hosted deployment model. Managing this mix is something we'll revisit in Chapter 11.

**External Systems Integration**    Enterprise applications are intended to form the heart of the business operation, and as with any part of the organization, they cannot be successfully run in total isolation. Close relationships with suppliers, customers, and partners will ultimately lead to lower costs, more efficient processes, and better profit margins. So although the center of the enterprise application works alone, its reach must extend beyond the organizational boundaries, accepting inputs and providing outputs with key external systems.

A simple example flow is how supplier systems can be automatically sent purchase orders upon their approval, acknowledgment and shipment notices are received back from suppliers when those orders are processed, and upon item receipt suppliers automatically send in invoices requesting payment. All of these messages need accepting and processing in an efficient and fault-tolerant way to avoid slow manual intervention that can put a high-volume organization at a virtual standstill.

Another slight twist to external integration scenarios is that sometimes intermediary brokers form a hub of connections between trading partners and provide transaction message routing services between enterprise application systems. From the retail sector, web sites such as eBay and Amazon Marketplace offer elements of these services, and most enterprise application vendors offer (or partner to offer) more broad-scale services. Oracle offers its own Supplier Network (osn.oracle com) for precisely that purpose. In addition, integration partners may provide a wide range of services, both for transaction processing and additional capabilities such as banking services, third-party tax calculation services, and all manner of other value-added offerings that require direct links to the source system, sending data to and fro.

Specifically for Fusion Applications, the architecture also lends itself to integration with advanced Web 2.0 features, such as communication tools (like VOIP), internal wikis or web applications, and existing portal solutions. Although these are specific to technology integration, they still represent an overhead for the application manager.

# Performance

Reports regularly state that for web-based applications, the primary reason for user drop-off is poor performance. Usability surveys show that after just a few seconds, users start repressing buttons, reclicking links, and generally becoming impatient. We know it's true, because we do it ourselves—despite the fact that most enterprise application managers are actually a lot more tolerant of usability issues, since they understand the complexity operating behind the scenes. Truth is, although there may be technical or indeed logical reasons that something is slow (it represents a lot of processing work), business users don't care and quickly begrudge having to use a system that doesn't respond quickly.

I know some web-based applications that actually make a point of responding to users quickly. These applications forgo showing the user the traditional confirmation message when something has completed ("Your entry was saved") but instead run all the processing in the background and allow the user to continue using the system immediately. Of course this has to be carefully coded to control execution context flow, as well as to avoid any potential dependency and integrity conflicts.

Although users might accept the fact that their skill level may occasionally slow them down, it's generally seen as unacceptable to have to wait for the system to respond. This seems harsh, but it's actually not a bad thing. It makes software developers work smarter, encourages technology advancements, and generally keeps everyone trying his or her best to meet the increasing demands from the business, ultimately delivering more value.

Enterprise application performance can be broken down into a few specific areas, and later we'll look at some specific monitoring and troubleshooting tools.

## Monitoring Performance

Clearly, the enterprise application manager is not going to be sitting around watching performance statistics scrolling down the screen all day. It's boring, a poor use of their time, and usually completely unnecessary. So the work here is based on establishing the processes that need monitoring, implementing and managing the metrics that can be used to quantify that performance, and creating alerting and resolution mechanisms that handle violations of a set of acceptable thresholds. This sounds much better than screen-watching.

Three classes of performance data should be considered:

- **Failures**   Connections and processes run so long that either they never complete or they exceed an internal timeout and a low-level termination is performed. This kind of situation can have some painful consequences inside an application, affecting both the end user experience as well as the application data itself.

- **Peaks and troughs**   Performance thresholds should be set against anticipated load, with both upper and lower limits, and when these are violated, some investigation should occur to determine why. When lower limits are broken due to poor performance, it usually represents a capacity or processing problem, but it's worth mentioning that on the flip-side, improvement opportunities may exist where upper limit data can potentially signify underutilized resources.

- **Bottlenecks**   As well as monitoring continuous data, the enterprise application manager will engage statistical analysis methods to compare and contrast performance metrics between systems, configurations, time, and numerous other environment variables. Analysis should be based on a representation of the end-to-end execution flow of business logic, such as the process of the creation of an order. The performance data can then quickly be used to monitor which parts of a process are the slowest, and based on the profile of the processing load, any bottlenecks can be identified. Based on this, optimization projects can be built that should deliver significant extra value for business users.

Let's also look quickly at the kind of performance data the enterprise application administrator is particularly concerned with, and since the complementary roles discussed before (system administrator, DBA, and so on) also do performance monitoring, it's helpful to have some demarcation to prevent a duplication of effort.

**Business Process Performance**   This highest level category sits closest to the business users and is usually where the most value can be added, since it's concerned with validating the performance of work task completion. Obvious examples are transaction creation, transaction processing, and approval processing, in addition to somewhat smaller things such as the notification backlog.

Although they are the most logical to track, these are often the most complex issues, since the multitude of moving parts and variations between transaction types and parameters means it takes considerable expertise to monitor the full detail accurately. That said, it's important to invest heavily in this area, and it's a core task for the enterprise application manager. Fortunately, Fusion Applications offers some excellent tools in this area, courtesy of its integration with Enterprise Manager and Business Activity Monitoring.

**Applications Technology Performance**   This category handles the next level down in the technology stack, the core services that the application uses to execute its own logic. Examples include the response times for the application UI pages, SOA messaging, Java EE server performance, database connections and query performance, and batch transactional throughput. Some of these areas may require collaboration with domain experts such as the DBA, however, the enterprise application manager should be able to identify areas of concern and perform basic troubleshooting steps. Again Fusion Applications is well equipped with various tools.

**Pure Technology Performance**   In working closely with specialists such as system administrators, the technologies upon which the application is founded should also be monitored for performance. Most large organizations will have a standard set of tools for monitoring known components, such as operating systems and server hardware.

With enterprise applications potentially distributed over many separate machines on the network, keeping track of this low-level data remains vital to get a full picture of the service that is eventually delivered to business users. As a simple example, problems with one machine's CPU can readily affect a specific subset of application components on that server, resulting in problems only in one specific piece of the enterprise application. As an example, in Fusion Applications, the Enterprise Scheduling Service (ESS)–hosting server (or its surrounding network) may experience problems and the consequences felt only in those tasks (jobs) that are passed to it, leaving the remainder of the application unaffected. Without some visibility to this low-level performance data, it can take a long time to identify the cause of such an issue.

As usual, the most basic elements to monitor include the CPU cycles, memory and disk I/O, and the traffic between the key nodes in the network. As mentioned, this is really the domain of the other specialists, and a wide range of performance monitoring and analysis tools are available. The enterprise application manager should ensure that these tools are accessible, that they fully understand the core information therein, and that they have acceptable processes to involve other experts when required. Oracle's Enterprise Manager includes low-level monitoring to offer what is known as an *applications-to-disk* view through all the technology stack pieces.

## The Capacity for Performance

The enterprise application should be suitably resourced based on the vendor's recommended requirements list (or similar benchmarks), which usually provides a minimum outline for basic items such as memory, disk space, and CPUs. Using this as a baseline a *capacity plan* would have been put together during the implementation project, usually based on projected loads calculated from existing system usage profiles. Going forward, the enterprise application manager will need to update and maintain this plan frequently to ensure that all parts of the system are adequately resourced based on immediate, near-term, and long-term load projections. This is especially true in our modern world of rapid organizational change, where speedy mergers and acquisitions are now commonplace.

Although all this isn't new, all too frequently a lack of capacity is first highlighted by an application error whose cause is simply related to the depletion of available resources. The professional enterprise application manager must build in the capacity planning with his or her monitoring profiles, so that when load is consistently reaching defined thresholds, and optimization solutions are either exhausted or simply unsuitable, it will trigger a review of the capacity plan and all the appropriate actions (such as placing orders).

**Resource Scalability**    In enterprise applications, scalability can be described as how well the allocated resources are used based on changes in load (often also known as *utilization*), and how efficiently additional resources can be added to manage those potential changes. In the modern IT landscape, innovations such as virtualization and cloud-based deployment provide new options for organizations to better manage their infrastructure and resources.

Most enterprise applications are built to leverage scalable architectures and components inherently, and as discussed in Chapter 2, the native Fusion Middleware and Database components used in Fusion Applications are exceptionally strong in this area.

**Capacity Lifecycle**   As discussed in Chapter 4, it's a well-accepted method to view all IT operations (including enterprise applications) in terms of a lifecycle, where each area is managed according to its maturity level. These lifecycles start with conceptualizing requirements and solutions, flow into design work, continue through implementation and utilization, and finally head toward retirement.

Clearly, nothing within or underneath the enterprise application stays constant forever, and although the application itself requires updates and upgrades, clearly the same applies to the entire technology stack, the network, and the hardware it sits upon. The average lifespan of hardware servers is estimated at between three and five years, and together with all the other hardware components (storage drives, routers, switches, and so on) and software installed (operating systems, database, middleware, applications), the mean time to failure (MTTF) calculation is an interesting consideration.

The applications administrator needs to work together with the other roles in the IT department to ensure that the lifecycle of components is considered and monitored, ideally so that pieces are updated or swapped-out before they fail. This may seem like potential overkill, but it can save significant pain and can also reduce the cost of having fully redundant resources sitting idle while waiting for what might be a somewhat predictable failure.

# Optimization

As mentioned, the core goal of the enterprise application is to help the business be successful in any way it can, be that through better productivity, more efficient operations, or new business intelligence insights. In addition to ensuring that the enterprise application is in suitable health to achieve those goals, a range of additional improvement activities can be included in this role.

## Improvement Projects

The enterprise application will be monitored based on the expectations of the IT and business users; however, these expectations should not be permanently fixed and there should be a strong desire to constantly improve the service levels offered. The enterprise application manager should be looking to spot opportunities for improvement, either based on performance data analysis or simply by keeping up to date with new options and features and taking the time to consider their potential impact on the organization (both positive gain and negative disruption).

While keeping within the scope of certification and licensing, improvements should be considered for all the layers in the enterprise application, from new business features, improvements and new capabilities in the technology and communication components (such as uptake of the Web 2.0 features in WebCenter), and even optimization of the base hardware and networking.

## Planning for the Future

Like it or not, the enterprise application will change over time, mainly through updates, upgrades, and the odd configuration adjustment. Although some of this may be a necessity (for example, to remain supported and certified), progressing and evolving the enterprise application should also be seen as an opportunity. It's certainly important to couple its future planning with that for the overall organization, so that new application features are leveraged at the right time and in the right way. It sounds obvious, but so often different departments (including IT) follow their own agendas and development paths, with only cursory relationships to each other. In fact, decoupling departmental entities regularly leads to frustrated business users who see their tools change in a conflicting or delayed manner when compared with their business objectives.

## Configuration, Extensibility, and Customization Management

Enterprise applications are exceptionally flexible, a characteristic that allows them to be used in a wide range of industry types and organizations. This, as explained in Chapter 1, especially applies to Fusion Applications. Significant control is required to keep the system in a *known state*, and the application manager is ultimately responsible for ensuring that all significant configurations, extensions, and customizations are properly supportable.

The following list highlights some example considerations that the enterprise application manager must act upon to ensure control with regard to changes to their application:

- Planning and impact analysis of each customization should involve the application manager; results should be clearly communicated to all stakeholders so that the resulting overhead and risks are known, approved, and suitably mitigated.

- All significant application alterations should be documented in a consistent and complete manner, with all material kept in a single standard repository. The content must be immediately updated when any changes occur.

- All customization coding occurs using a consistent set of practices, design patterns, methodologies, and tools. These should all be well documented and should be understood and available to the enterprise application manager.

- Customization coding should include full and proper exception handling and debug logging. Both should be implemented using established and standardized mechanisms. It should also be possible to remove or disable custom code should problems be found, allowing the original standard processes to continue until a resolution is determined.

- Customization coding that interacts with standard application objects should do so in the intended and supported manner. All testing of this should be completed and the results available for reference.

- All configurations are kept within their intended value range and type.

- Configurations are thoroughly tested, based on both common and occasional use-case scenarios. Failure testing should also be completed to enhance durability. In addition, all related configuration changes should be tested together to ensure that no conflicts occur.

■  Extensions are accomplished based on the standard mechanisms provided and supported by the software vendor(s). Deviations or alternative interpretations should be outlawed, or if absolutely necessary, they must be accepted and handled as customizations.

■  Ideally, at least one relatively up-to-date instance should not contain any significant alterations, especially extensions and customizations. This is exceptionally helpful for troubleshooting problems because the instance can be used to identify the influence of the alterations on the standard product.

We will revisit the management of configuration, extension, and customization again in Chapters 6 and 11. You'll learn about tools, techniques, and recommendations for use with Fusion Applications to address many of the points mentioned here.

## System Design Consultation

As the expert on what usually represents the largest and most significant software application used by an organization, the enterprise application manager should be aware of all new developments in related systems infrastructure. This might range from network adjustments to the implementation (and creation) of complementary programs and applications.

Although standard testing may unearth any problems or conflicts, by that time only reactive and often costly solutions are possible. Instead, it's better if the original design considers any specific enterprise application factors that might cause issues.

## Cost Reduction

Enterprise applications are never cheap, although when used properly, they can and should show a good ROI. As well as ensuring that features are maximized and end user complexity is kept to a minimum, enterprise application managers can keep costs down in a number of other ways.

The two most expensive parts of the enterprise application in terms of ongoing overhead are the electricity consumption of its servers (and their environment) and the payroll for those supporting it. Although some of this is fixed, the enterprise application manager can take some simple measures to make improvements. For example, many utilities are available for tracking server utilization and power management, and these often come with hardware and operating systems without much additional cost. In terms of efficiencies to lower headcount, by monitoring utilization and processing the enterprise application manager should be able to make some recommendations on potential areas for business process re-engineering or even the potential outsourcing of some higher-cost pieces.

Experience tells us that the clearer the planning at the start, the more likely efficiencies will be realized. And although cost control might seem obvious, just assuming it will be properly addressed is a frequent mistake.

## Increasing Supplier Efficiency

Working in isolation gets you only so far, and the enterprise application manager will have to engage with a number of external suppliers to get things done. This may include outsourcing and implementation partners, specialist consultants, hardware and networking vendors, and of course the enterprise application vendor (including technical support). Generally speaking, the better those relationships, the more likely the enterprise application will truly oil the wheels of the organization. Organizations that properly leverage the appropriate services available to them encounter fewer unexpected problems, and indeed any they do find tend to have a lower business impact and a better resolution time. The same is also true when the enterprise application manager takes the same open, collaborative approach when dealing with internal teams, whether these are their helpdesks, business users, specialist experts, or project teams.

# Governance

The enterprise application manager is the custodian and guardian of the system, and in this connected world, needs to approach all aspects of this responsibility in a complete yet pragmatic manner. This work comprises four main divisions, and the real key to success is to ensure that the plans build in a strong sense of commitment to enforce meticulous and rigorous adherence to a high-quality set of targets made up of both metrics and expectations. Further reading on aspects of governance is provided in the Appendix in this book.

## Security

Security is probably the most important part of the enterprise application manager's role. It's even more important than availability, since once the system comes up it must be secure, or else it will have to be shut down again. Each interface that the enterprise application has with the outside world must be secured, and with increases in the flexibility that comes with such things as SOA and J2EE-based applications in general, there are more interfaces to secure, including the following:

- **End user security** The careful monitoring of data and function roles, their administration, and the provisioning to end users.

- **External intrusion** The headline-grabbing attacks performed by potentially malicious individuals. With more remote access points and mechanisms than ever before, this is a significant priority.

- **Internal violations** Often cited as actually more common than external intrusions, and although they are mostly covered by end user security, the enterprise application manager needs to watch for employees trying to access restricted areas of the system.

- **Networking** This involves the interception of data during its transportation, often via open Internet communication. Although not uncommon, it is relatively easy to avoid. This may also include aggressive network-based attacks intended to disable the system, such as Denial of Service (DoS) attacks.

- **Exporting** The loss of data that has been extracted from the enterprise application. Although often simply resolved by properly securing the export features, other solutions are available, such as encrypting all data as it leaves the system.

- **Integration** It's crucial to ensuring that all touch-points into the application involve the same level of authentication that is applied to end users.

- **Physical security** Access to the hardware used to run the enterprise business application must also be secured. This also includes any hardware running integrated or complementary components that may themselves contain access routes in.

■ **Information and communication security** Standard corporate guidelines should be followed in terms of distributing sensitive application information via email, instant messaging, and other Web 2.0 tools such as blogs and wikis. Similar to exporting, although information is outside the system's influence, all reports should be secured and all sensitive fields masked as appropriate.

■ **Offline storage** Ensure that the archived system information is fully secured. This may be dedicated system backups or simply old transaction audit data. Again, a similar approach should be taken to the exporting element.

## Data Cleansing

In addition to securing the access to data, the enterprise application manager is responsible for ensuring data health. This means looking out for potential duplication, redundancy, and corruption, as well as trying to understand and optimize its usage profiles.

**Duplication** All modern enterprise applications contain tools that address some of the most common data problems, such as stale and duplicated business data. A simple example might be where the same supplier record exists once in the payment systems, again in the order capture and processing system, and for a third time in external marketing tools. If it remains unsynchronized, this data acquires different properties and often key information is unavailable to those who need it.

The tools within Master Data Management (MDM) provide methods to consolidate and cleanse old data, and create a single-source-of-truth record. They then synchronize that record (and future updates) across all of the application features.

**Data Quality** Unhealthy data leads to all kinds of downstream problems that can directly affect business users. This ranges from failures running financial reconciliation processes, sales people unable to follow-up on valuable leads, or CEOs unable to see trends to support strategic planning decisions. Clearly, a system with poor data quality will be of little use to anyone.

Although the enterprise application manager doesn't create, update, or own the business data per se, he or she has a duty to try to ensure that it remains as useful as possible. Examples of poor quality include missing data, duplicate data, outdated data, or simply incorrect and corrupt data. Although the data itself might be outside the enterprise application manager's ownership, the actions taken upon it (inserts, updates, deletes, synchronization, and so on) are done by the system that they manage, and therefore they have an important role to play.

A huge range of potential causes can be blamed for poor data quality, and the enterprise application manager should be on the lookout for unusual data patterns, processing problems, and abnormal usage profiles that may provide early warning signs that something is awry. Some common causes of data problems include the following:

- System failures midprocessing, leaving trailing and orphaned data records.

- Poorly written data manipulation scripts that are out of sync with sensitive data models.

- Manual imports and updates that originate from unvalidated (poor quality) data sources.

- Integrations with external systems whose data may be of poor quality, or where there is an incomplete match between the source and the target records.

- Abandoned and incomplete functional setup, leaving behind malformed reference data.

**System Purges**    Enterprise applications, a lot like lofts, continuously tend to collect items that are not really of use anymore, but do not get automatically tidied up after their relevance has past. The most obvious example is the processing log (and data) that gets created during the execution of large and significant programs. Left unchecked, data can build and build until it actually starts to occupy so many resources that it influences the real-time system activity, usually observed as a performance issue.

All enterprise applications provide utilities for managing this background data, but it's down to the enterprise application manager to set up, implement, execute, and monitor a method for running these at suitable intervals. Often the programs themselves will include built-in utilities for cleaning up the mess they create, a simple example being that most software servers (database, web server, application server) will include configuration for cycling their own log files. Again, these do not automatically know when and where to archive logs, so various parameters have to be set first.

It's essentially down the enterprise application manager to review all the data that the system is accumulating and verify if and when suitable archive or removal (purge) should be performed. Obviously, each type of data will have its own rules, and it may require detailed consultation with all the particular affected parties.

## Information Gatekeeper

With much of the business operations flowing through the enterprise application, all manner of records and reports will be needed. As with data quality, the enterprise application manager may not be the owner of the data, but he or she is instrumental in ensuring that the right person has suitable access to the information they need.

The following list provides some simple examples of the kinds of information and reports that will be commonly required:

- **Business operations management**   Business performance intelligence

- **Technical system management**   User and processing performance

- **Regulatory auditing**   Compliance against official and internal standards

- **Data management**   Includes transactions, security, data quality, and archiving

In addition to this standard reporting, most organizations have their own unique information requirements and use additional bolt-on reporting tools to achieve analysis capabilities. Enterprise application managers will be involved with the implementation and management of these (often third-party) specialist solutions to define additional standard reports plus create on-the-fly custom data displays. This ad hoc analysis and reporting capability helps business and IT staff build deeper insights into the overall performance and provides a more holistic view of information spread among different logical and physical areas.

## Managing Change

In making efforts to optimize the enterprise application, or even just keep it up to date, change is inevitable. But without proper change management, the enterprise application can get quickly out of control and into a situation in which it contains unsupported configurations and where additional changes can cause multiple subsequent problems.

Change management is a major focus in IT, and most enterprise software vendors provide tools and methodologies to help. The planning, tracking, and audit of change is key for the enterprise application manager, who should be well equipped with appropriate skills, experience, and resources. It is interesting to note that change management is often focused around technology-based changes and less frequently includes the functional setups that are part of an enterprise application. Let's therefore look at these two types of change separately.

**Technology Changes**    The technology stack upon which the enterprise application runs must be tightly managed. The two components, technology and functionality, work as a partnership, and like all good partnerships, this one must be based on mutual understanding. Should changes cause the technical platform to stray beyond what the application functional expects (and is certified upon), it can have catastrophic effects. As such, careful control is required regarding such things as hardware, operating systems, and databases. This control also includes additions and changes to any associated integrations and nonstandard software, as again the operation of the enterprise application assumes a "clean" standard system environment.

**Business Changes**    Essentially, two levels of business changes actually closely mirror the upper logical layers in the enterprise application. The first level includes changes to the core application setups such as security role profiles, the available products and features, and what languages can be used. The enterprise application manager usually assumes most of the responsibilities here.

The next level up represents the configuration of how individual features operate, such as the numbering scheme used on business transactions, or the optional fields shown on specific pages. Here the enterprise application manager must work closely with representatives from the business to ensure that the features they require have been appropriately resourced.

In addition, the enterprise application manager may have occasional involvement in changes made to the business objects setup in the application, such as reference data and structures. When major business changes occur (such as merges and acquisitions), it will be important to ensure that the enterprise application is capable of properly supporting any new usage profiles that may result, such as an increase in user load. It's obviously good practice to estimate and validate this ahead of time, rather than omit this and run into problems later on.

One final, but significant, point to make is that the enterprise application manager is responsible for upgrades and updates to the products and components, and as such planning and managing this will demand significant amounts of time. As mentioned, other material attempts to cover this area in more detail, and together with implementation, is best focused on in dedicated, fit-for-purpose content. To make an incomplete attempt to cover this area would simply add confusion and be of little practical use.

# Defining Success

The degree to which the management of the enterprise application is seen as a success is difficult to define, and it's likely that one person's vision of success represents a problem to someone else. A good example is the decision of whether to keep an application on the latest release or not. Keeping it constantly patched and updated is seen as good IT practice, whereas this represents disruption and extra work for business users who have to run validation and acceptance tests. For them, a relatively static system is preferable.

As discussed, the modern enterprise application is no longer a collection of linear software programs overlain by a static set of front-end forms. The distributed and open nature of SOA, the orchestration by flexible Business Process Execution, and a Web 2.0–style user interface, means that the enterprise application manager needs to have a dynamic set of tools, services, and skills to keep up. As the pace of innovative application development continues to increase, it pulls with it even higher expectations from application users, making the enterprise application manager role ever more crucial.

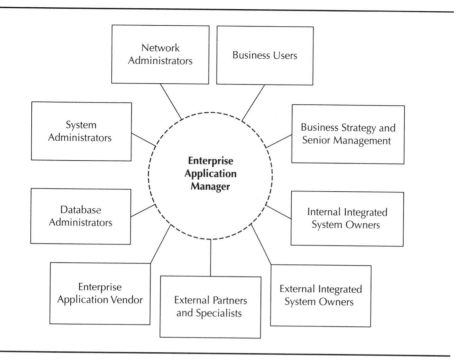

**FIGURE 3-1.** *The interactions of the enterprise application manager*

As illustrated in Figure 3-1, the enterprise application manager also represents a pivotal role in the organization. He or she must be more than just a technical expert, regularly acting somewhat like a broker who is able to understand the needs of the customer (the business) and then negotiate the best deal possible from suppliers (the IT department).

# The Benefits of Success

Although this is somewhat obvious, it's worth quickly summarizing some high-level goals for enterprise application management, since (as mentioned at the start of this chapter) assumptions are generally a bad idea. Each organization should create its own detailed definition for success (and failure), based on its own requirements and vision. From this, the enterprise application manager can fully define his role and build a framework of corresponding tools and methods.

Following are the key elements of successful enterprise application management:

- **Business enabler**   The focus is making the operation of the organization as effective as possible, from ordering paper clips, to hiring and developing staff, to managing payments. Although features support all the operational tasks, real value can be added by ensuring that its use is seamlessly embedded into those tasks, making them more productive and simultaneously capturing data for reporting and analysis. The competitive advantages that can be gained through operational efficiency should result from employing the enterprise application, and not in spite of it.

- **Preventative and proactive support**   Nothing works at 100 percent all of the time (especially people), and the traditional view of the enterprise application manager would be of someone who spends most of her time putting out fires, jumping from one urgent problem to another. This is unappealing to everyone, and taking early steps to ensure effective support systems are in place can reduce this kind of work substantially, leaving more time to focus on value-added optimization activities. With the proper approach, such as ensuring that workarounds exist should key processes fail, any issues that do occur will have a lower impact to the business.

- **Efficiency**   The enterprise application manager needs to ensure that the finite resources available to them are used intelligently. This ranges from IT resources such as hardware, memory, and network capacity, to resources that the business users waste in trying to use the enterprise application to meet their needs (time and effort). By paying close attention to the needs of both the system and the business, the enterprise application manager sets up the scales to balance out his resources, and at the same time keeps an eye out for new tools and techniques that will help him get more from the resources he has. An example might be performing analysis on extensibility and personalization projects, to ensure that the changes made to improve end user productivity do not impact other areas or system resources. Other examples might include leveraging SaaS deployments and better system integrations, both of which can help drive efficiency. Keeping tight control on resources and costs has rarely been so important, and the enterprise application manager must play his or her part.

■ **Strategic and future-ready**   The enterprise application manager must ensure that the system is robust enough to meet the immediate needs of business users, but also make sure it retains enough flexibility for tomorrow's requirements. As most of us aren't clairvoyant, this isn't easy; however, by working closely with vendors, partners, and business planning teams to understand all prospective directions, an amalgamated strategy can be built and managed.

# The Impacts of Failure

Not achieving the successes mentioned here can be seen as a failure, although these somewhat ethereal goals are not specific enough to be simple hits-or-misses. This means that a sliding measure of the extent to which they are met is the best way to look at them, with perhaps a chalk-line rough minimum target.

Apart from not hitting targets for success, true negative targets are (for some reason) somewhat easier to define. Let's quickly revisit the core definitions for enterprise application management; from these, it's easy to picture where real failures may lie:

■ **Reliability**   Ensure the features consistently operate as intended

■ **Availability**   Ensure all features are available whenever and wherever expected

■ **Performance**   Ensure all work can be completed within an acceptable timescale

■ **Optimization**   Ensure the software helps meet the organizational objectives

■ **Governance**   Ensure features and data are available only to those suitably authorized

These definitions can be used to form the goals for excellence, but they also represent a minimum set of requirements that, if unmet, cause issues for both the business operations and the IT department.

The ultimate problem occurs when business users cannot complete the tasks they are employed to do, halting either the money-making operation or causing cost escalation. Either way, negatively affecting the bottom line is never good. Where issues are perhaps not quite as bad, effects generally tend to include wasted time, reactive support (back to fire-fighting), user frustration, and a general loss of productivity. Also, any negative impressions of the enterprise application can seriously affect adoption, especially for infrequent users who often remain skeptical of its added value within their specific role.

One way organizations define a set of minimum performance standards is by the use of Service Level Agreements (SLAs). These are used explicitly to quantify the requirements of all stakeholders (mainly business users) and may be based on both internal metrics provided by monitoring tools, as well as acceptable deviations and threshold ranges. Some monitoring tools embed SLAs into their functionality, providing notification upon potential or actual violation. SLAs are a good solution where metrics can be used to measure service delivery; however, true measurements of success should also include softer targets, such as those within the optimization and governance parts of enterprise application management.

# CHAPTER
## 4

# The Fusion
# Applications
# Lifecycle

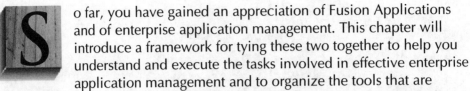

o far, you have gained an appreciation of Fusion Applications and of enterprise application management. This chapter will introduce a framework for tying these two together to help you understand and execute the tasks involved in effective enterprise application management and to organize the tools that are available for use. Almost all effective workers, from artists to builders, first carefully prepare their tools and raw materials before they embark on a significant piece of work, and we'll do the same using this framework.

When it comes to IT management, a number of recognized *lifecycle* frameworks are used by successful organizations to help them get the most from their technology investments. Probably the best known example is the Information Technology Infrastructure Library (ITIL). It would be remiss to ignore these well-respected practices, and therefore a few key examples are summarized here with regard to their use in enterprise application management.

This chapter will apply what you've learned so far and conceptualize a new lifecycle model. This model can be used throughout the remaining chapters, applied in the specific context of Fusion Applications.

# What Is a Lifecycle Model?

The most popular models for managing IT Infrastructure are based on a flow-type design, showing what activities are most applicable over a complete time span. Using an analogy, the human lifecycle helps us visualize how an infant changes into a child, grows to a teenager, and into an adult. By observing each of the phases in detail and noticing the changes between them, you can gain a clear understanding of the complete subject. The key to using lifecycle models is to absorb the underlying knowledge and then build on top your own specific set of requirements and goals that are accurate, measurable, and directly applicable.

As outlined in the generic IT solution lifecycle flow in Figure 4-1, these models help guide organizations to make the right decisions early, provide a path to follow as solutions are constructed and implemented, and even assist with decommissioning when components are no longer of use.

This type of model also allows individual systems to be easily recognized based on their *maturity* through the lifecycle and ensures that appropriate

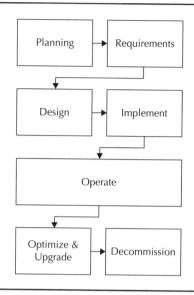

**FIGURE 4-1.** *A generic IT lifecycle type model*

considerations and actions are being taken at each point through their evolution. With IT a constantly changing field and software tools becoming more and more like replaceable commodities, this type of model provides a guided path and tracking mechanism that managers can use to ensure that their systems remain up to date and are the best they can be for the business.

IT management has traditionally been ad hoc, and based around internal processes and procedures that have evolved over time (often through bitter experience). With the advent of some publicly available open lifecycle models, any organization now has access to what is generally regarded as industry best practices, a fact that is regularly validated as successful organizations frequently admit to their use.

Generally speaking, lifecycle models are also surprisingly complete, representing the standard needs of most organizations, and can be applied by both the chief technical officer (CTO) and the engineer. For IT management in particular, the wealth of all-encompassing frameworks that are appearing proves they're certainly in vogue. These are early days for many of these models, however, and their evolution continues as they adapt to the technology and operating models they attempt to support.

# Example Lifecycle Models

Several popular lifecycle models are used by IT departments today in their quest to manage their infrastructure. In addition to providing general background material, the following sections will help you to understand the key parts that apply to enterprise applications and to learn how use them to build our own more precise model.

# Software Development Lifecycles

Let's visit some popular methodologies for software application creation. Since these models ensure that the application actually has the features that are needed by end users, it's a natural next step to use them to consider provision and ongoing management. Dozens of different application development models are in use today, and many are used within the same organization or even the same project. None has emerged as the ultimate "right way," and their suitability is often best determined by the properties of the task at hand. Since most development models are based loosely on the software development lifecycle (SDLC), let's look at a few popular examples.

## The Waterfall Model

As one of the most traditional methods, this model is based on a sequential set of predefined activities that logically feed off each other to achieve an end result. The process begins with the analysis and specification of the base requirements, upon which a full design is written. This is then implemented through coding and any integrations are built. The system is then tested and validated before live deployment to end users and the final maintenance stage is reached. A detailed review marks the end of each phase and is used to ensure that all work is complete and the next phase can begin. Although reasonably comprehensive and logical, the waterfall model is often criticized because of its structured and formal nature, which sometimes means that retrospective adjustments are difficult to implement because past phases cannot be easily revisited.

## Iterative Development

Replacing the sequential nature of the waterfall model are several development models that perform each task in the development process several times, refining and improving the final solution each time. Often basic outlines are created on the first pass, and initial testing provides clear feedback on any major changes and extensions that are needed. The repeated cycling through the requirements, design, testing, and evaluation phases uses small subsets of features, allowing each iteration to be relatively quick. The target here is to spend as little time as possible in coding unvalidated areas (reducing potential rework) and to help ensure the final product truly meets the requirements. Although traditionally limited in their project scope, iterative development projects are often continuously expanded, building on past successes and resulting in reasonably broad results.

As an extension to some of the iterative principles, Agile software development models include additional simple execution methods into the feedback mechanisms between iterations, further reducing the traditional structures that can obstruct important information from contributing to system improvements. An example of an Agile method is the Extreme Programming model, which starts by taking the understood requirement and building the basic tests to be used later. By outlining these validation routines early on, you can immediately focus the development effort, and after the routines are implemented (and tested), the other stages such as design are completed. This seems odd compared with the more logical sequential methods, but it is surprisingly effective and popular.

## Rapid Application Development (RAD)

Moving away from SDLC models, the RAD-type models provide a structure that includes more flexibility and more active engagement of those involved in using the end products. Prototyping and iterative testing cycles are used to ensure that what is being created meets the expectations and requirements originally laid out. These models are also well suited to frequent change, since products begin small and evolve over time. This means they can flex and change along with changing requirements, as opposed to all-encompassing monolithic systems that might meet every initial need but are quickly outdated as things change. Although originally popular in consumer commodity software such as small utility applications, this small but flexible mechanic remains popular as the proliferation of web-based commercial applications and services grows (including SOA-type integrations).

# Application Lifecycle Model (ALM)

From the name alone, this sounds the most applicable model; however, upon closer inspection, you can see that this is not entirely the case. ALMs are based on the same principles as this chapter, in that for an enterprise application to be properly managed, it must be based on a predefined set of rules, activities, and processes.

Unfortunately, there are no universal ALM models, and the majority of ALM content tends to focus on specific software vendor tools. What material there is has a strong bias toward internally developed applications, with most detail on the upstream development phases and substantially less in the post-deployment management activities.

The areas of focus for ALM include the following:

- Project management

- Requirements analysis

- Modeling and design

- Change and configuration management

- Build, test, deploy, and release management

- Issue management

Unsurprisingly, ALM outlines often resemble the basic Product Lifecycle Management (PLM) processes used in the creation of physical goods. The traditional steps, starting with idea conception, running into design and creation, and finally to service (including maintenance), do seem to have been translated across to the software development realm and ALM.

So although some basic outline principles are relevant, this currently lacks detail on precisely what kinds of actions and activities are included in managing a prepackaged enterprise application.

# Information Lifecycle Management (ILM)

ILM focuses on the classification of data based on its usage profile. Data falls into several basic groups, although precise agreement on these varies based on the unique requirements of every organization. Fundamentally,

ILM represents a rough lifecycle of data over time and according to use, with the following as commonly used divisions:

■ **Active use**   Online data that forms active documents and records—examples are orders, items, and people.

■ **Semiactive use**   Reference data that is associated with active documents and records. Examples might include trading partners, reference agreements, terms and conditions, and general enterprise structures.

■ **Historical data**   Documents, records, and reference data that must be kept for occasional use. This data is normally important in performance reporting that includes meeting regulatory requirements.

■ **Archived data**   Data that is no longer used for day-to-day work but must be kept for potential reference, often focused around regulatory and legal compliance.

■ **Expired data**   Data that has no feasible purpose and should be removed.

ILM represents a useful lifecycle model to help identify specific volumes of data and to map these to data storage tools and devices. With both structured and unstructured data volumes ever increasing, it's well known that high performance storage costs roughly ten times more than archive-type media. To help you properly distribute data on the most economic medium possible, modern access mechanisms can be used to make any performance concerns relatively immaterial.

Although architecting a mechanism for ILM may be an important tool for the enterprise application manager, its narrow, data-centric focus leaves many other areas untouched.

# IT Service Management (ITSM)

Most large organizations are looking at (or already using) IT Service Management for their technology infrastructure management. It uses a service-orientated approach (such as the SOA technology) to manage how the IT department provides business users with the tools and services they need to complete their tasks and meet their goals. The aim of ITSM is to quantify IT spending properly, in terms that relate to business operations, and to be able to measure the quality of the services therein. By trying to align IT better with business operations, potential high-impact areas for improvement can be much more easily identified.

Let's briefly consider whether IT elements really all fit as services. Certainly some sets of users require the delivery of certain core IT features so they can complete their daily tasks (such as create orders); however, many modern users get the most significant benefits from IT when it is provided as a tool to help them perform their own analysis and create business insights (for example, to determine supplier efficiency). Having or not having a tool may not be immediately obvious as being a service; however, since its availability and performance are usually provided by the IT team, it can be considered service consumption.

ITSM service quality is measured through the use of Service Level Agreements (SLAs) that define precisely what the service is and exactly what the minimum acceptable performance (quality) should be. SLAs are traditionally very detailed, and it often takes substantial negotiation involving all parties before an agreement is reached and is made effective. An SLA for ITSM services will commonly include the following:

- Overview and Scope (with both IT and business perspectives)

- Performance Expectations

- Tracking and Reporting on Service Delivery

- Problem Management and Resolution Process

- Violation Terms and Procedures

- Duties and Responsibilities (for both Producer and Consumer)

- Security and Legal Considerations

- SLA Review and Expiration Terms

Since IT services may also come from outside an organization (outsourcing/SaaS), the ITSM model can also be applied here, although this usually involves a much more detailed SLA.

ITSM forms a set of principles and can be implemented using a number of framework models. Let's take a look at some of the more common ones to see what we can learn for potential use in enterprise application management.

## Information Technology Infrastructure Library

Information Technology Infrastructure Library (ITIL) is a public framework for implementing ITSM in an organization. In its current version (v3) it is based on a set of five books that aim to cover a lifecycle of IT services, and as illustrated in Figure 4-2, it provides an outline to help organizations link their operational requirements to suitable approaches and solutions.

The first phase of this lifecycle (ITIL book) is Service Strategy and provides a central space in which organizations can continuously evaluate the kinds of services they might want to consume to achieve operational excellence. The second phase takes each of these services and defines the Service Design. This forms a translation of the business requirements into an IT solution, and as such is exceptionally important to get right.

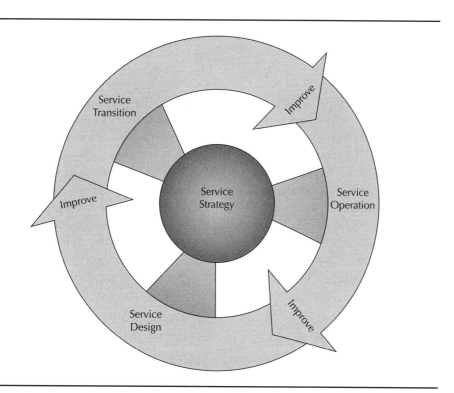

**FIGURE 4-2.** *An overview of the ITIL lifecycle*

The third phase, Service Transition, accepts the design as input and builds the corresponding solution. Although usually concerned with software development, it also includes hardware architectures, documentation, training, and all other parts of the complete service solution. The transition phase, as the name suggests, includes service deployment and full implementation with its consumers. With the solution built and implemented, the Service Operation phase proceeds, concerned with managing and maintaining delivery based on the parameters of the SLA. The final ITIL phase rolls into the mix the concept of Continual Service Improvement, so that the service provided today grows to meet the demands of tomorrow.

ITIL is exceptionally popular, especially in larger organizations, and although it is not a totally prescriptive guide to follow, it can certainly help organizations get a grip on sprawling IT infrastructures. Like all ITSM models, it allows for a clear rationalization of investments, both in terms of bottom-line financial costs and also vital resources such as time and effort. Sometimes this might represent a trimming exercise, but optimizing the IT service catalog to emphasize those with the most business impact should also help organizations increase the visibility of the contributions that IT makes, and prioritize the provision and expansion of key services for everyone's benefit.

## COBIT

Control Objectives for Information and related Technology (COBIT) is also ITSM compliant; however, it has a more prescriptive focus by providing a clear set of measurements for IT managers and auditors to be able to interrogate and monitor the performance and governance of IT resources.

Within its 210 specific measurements, spread across 34 IT processes, COBIT's coverage is similar to ITIL's, although it uses four core lifecycle-type domains, namely Planning and Organization, Acquisition and Implementation, Delivery and Support, and Monitoring and Evaluation. Indeed, some mapping between ITIL and COBIT has been done, highlighting the commonality here. COBIT is certainly more focused around governance than ITIL is, a fact emphasized by the official endorsement of its use in meeting the Sarbanes-Oxley (SOX) regulatory compliance.

# Applying the Generic Lifecycles

Although we didn't find an existing model that fully fits with enterprise application management, the few example lifecycles discussed so far do show some methods and activities that will inevitably apply. Let's look clearly at the benefits they offer, as well a few drawbacks.

# Benefits

It's interesting to look at a few points taken from software development, ALM, ILM, and ITSM models and see how these might be applied.

- Software Development lifecycles illustrate how understanding requirements is critical, followed by creating a properly detailed design. The iterative methods also illustrate how revisiting the design after testing allows for refinements to be made that can improve the overall solution.

- ALM offers an application-focused model and provides a high-level, end-to-end flow. Although many phases are not applicable for prebuilt enterprise applications, ALM may be useful when implementing extensive configurations or extensions that often represent a considerable project themselves.

- ILM offers a deep insight into application data and represents a helpful model that the enterprise application manager can use to architect this part of his or her work.

- ITSM models demonstrate how business user requirements should be very clearly understood, so that application functions and features are managed based on the well-understood and recorded expectations. They also introduce the importance of service control based on regulatory and internal governance guidelines.

# Limitations

Some key factors negate the full use of these models in enterprise application management:

- Software Development and ALM focus on upstream phases, and this is mostly irrelevant since enterprise applications are already designed and built.

- ITSM models apply across the whole of IT management and do not focus on enterprise application–specific factors or requirements.

- ILM covers only a small part of enterprise application management, plus it's possible other specialists (such as a DBA) might focus more on data storage.

- Like any model design to be applied in varied situations, there is inherent simplification and summarization in all of these models.

Generally speaking, these models touch on both enterprise applications and also IT Management best practices; however, rarely do they tie the two together or offer comprehensive detail. So let's design our own model.

# A Fusion Applications Management Lifecycle Model

The intention here is to take the enterprise application management principles we defined in the preceding sections and build a basic high-level but usable model. This is not intended to be all-encompassing or super-complex, but based on the lack of any reasonably useful equivalent, it should represent a good starting point. It should help get your organization thinking about the right topics in the right way.

Although the enterprise application forms a significant part of the IT infrastructure, it's by no means everything making many of the lifecycle models discussed too broad to be directly applicable (or too narrow in the case of ILM). We can, however, cherry-pick some key parts and put these into the actions, activities, and responsibilities that form part of enterprise application management.

It's worth noting that this new model could be considered a subset of ALM or ITIL, dropping in quite nicely as an optional extension where applicable. Indeed, ITIL does actually have a standard "Application Management" activity categorized as an *Associated Function*, but with no real detail provided.

The easiest way to begin to explain the new model we're proposing is to provide an overall diagrammatic representation (Figure 4-3), and then to discuss the key parts one by one.

The process of enterprise application management begins (#1 on the diagram) as an offshoot from the standard enterprise application implementation process, spawned around the same time as the overall design is created and well before the deployment phases.

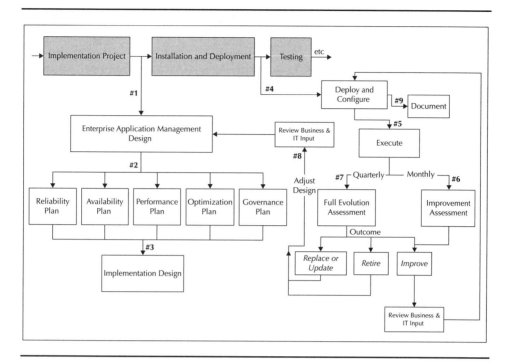

**FIGURE 4-3.**  *The enterprise application management lifecycle model*

The resulting Enterprise Application Management Design (#2) should be comprehensive and completed in a formal method to help ensure complete coverage of the five separate (although interconnected) plans. The design creation should include the use of structured methods to gather requirements and expectations from all the key stakeholders involved with the enterprise application. The results of this are then analyzed to ensure associated service delivery costs are acceptable, and once documented the final design (plans and associated services) is reviewed and signed-off by all parties.

The third phase of this model (#3) is a kind of subsection to the design and is focused on making sure suitable tools, processes, and procedures are implemented so that the content of the five plans can be properly resourced. When using the ITSM approach to IT management (including the enterprise application), this is also where the service definition would occur, so that each discrete part of the provision of the enterprise application to end users is encapsulated and can be properly designed, executed, monitored, and measured.

Obviously, each organization will want to develop its own unique implementation design that fits its own needs and structures. Care should of course be taken, since all too often, the system management plans and intentions are good but are not backed up by adequate resources (people and equipment), inevitably resulting in poor implementation and execution. Interestingly, the converse is also occasionally true, where fabulous tools are implemented but with little or no clear intention on their purpose or most effective use. Having a dedicated implementation phase based on a clear design helps make sure the right balance is met.

The fourth phase (#4) is spawned as part of the general enterprise application installation and deployment phase and represents getting the management tools, processes, and procedures set up and ready for use. Although this sounds somewhat trivial, this is often quite a complex task. In addition to establishing clear and efficient process and procedures (never easy), this step often requires considerable expertise in configuring complex software tools while maintaining security and not affecting the systems they monitor.

To emphasize the complexity involved in this phase, let's look at a few example activities:

- The installation and provisioning of additional software with suitable resources and security

- The configuration of the nodes, servers, applications, and processes that are to be monitored

- The insertion of minimum and maximum thresholds for alerting mechanisms

- Entry of personal contact details, including availability and contact procedures for use by the alerting mechanisms

- The setting up of emergency contingency plans and procedures

- The creation of regular maintenance policies and procedures (including patching)

- The setting up of all availability, reliability, and performance targets from the design

- The setting up of sample frequency, record taking, and data longevity

■  The adoption of security policies and procedures for system management, with many being mapped based on physical security rules

■  The allocation of suitable resources for proactive improvement and optimization-based projects

The fifth phase (#5) simply involves doing the management work, and it represents the normal operation after the design is implemented. Of course, it's possible that only core parts of a complete management design are implemented initially, and additional iterations are done for each subsequent management piece as additional tools and resources (including time) become available. It's also worth noting that at this stage, the full base specification for the system (configuration, architecture, and so on) should be carefully recorded (#9).

Once the enterprise application management design is in execution mode, the rest of the model (#6–9) is concerned with continuous improvement, ensuring that the process evolves with the changing expectations of business users, IT staff, and advancements within the enterprise application itself.

Our model also includes two feedback loops that iterate on different frequencies. The first (#6) represents a regular review phase that is performed to evaluate the output of the management process. This could be performed frequently, say monthly, with key stakeholders reviewing a set of performance reports to pinpoint problems in service quality (possibly against SLAs). The output of this should be either the reapproval of existing management activities or stakeholder-agreed adjustments to expectations, targets, or the enterprise application itself. Most changes are minor adjustments and fine-tuning and are fed back through the deploy and configure (#4) cycle, therefore including record-keeping (change management).

The second improvement loop (#7) is run less often, possibly quarterly or semiannually, and consists of a much more in-depth and formal look at the enterprise application management. It considers various influencing factors including these:

■  A 360-degree review of delivery against targets (that is, SLAs), including deep root cause analysis of unexpected results or incidents

■  Changes to the IT landscape, such as new services, tools, and systems whose intention is to run alongside (or integrate with) the enterprise application

■ Changes to enterprise application features being used by business users, such as new datasets and new business objects that may affect processing or storage

■ Forthcoming changes to the organizational structures that are mapped within the enterprise application, potentially affecting usage profiles

■ Creation of (or changes to) configurations, invasive personalizations, and customizations that have either occurred or are planned

■ Existing or forthcoming upgrades and updates to the enterprise application, its technology stack, and all related hardware and networking

All significant outcomes of this formal review exercise should feed back into the Application Management Design (#8), and all changes should filter through each of the subsequent steps in the proper manner. This then ensures the proper deployment and configuration of the changes (#4). Clearly this broader improvement loop is influenced more by the optimization and governance plans, whereas the more frequent review loop is more associated with the availability, performance, and reliability plans.

One final benefit of using such a model for enterprise application management is that it also helps enforce *Change Management*, something exceptionally important to troubleshooting problems as well as addressing general performance, security, and audit tasks. Step #9 on the diagram illustrates how this comes as an outcome of deployment, recording all actions applied to the system in a formal manner using an appropriate tool and method.

Now that we have defined a basic outline model, let's see what precise tools, services, and methods exist that can to turn it into a reality for managing Oracle Fusion applications.

# CHAPTER
## 5

# A Fusion Applications
# Management Toolbox

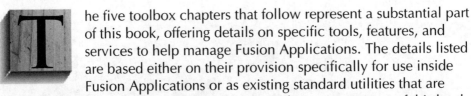

he five toolbox chapters that follow represent a substantial part of this book, offering details on specific tools, features, and services to help manage Fusion Applications. The details listed are based either on their provision specifically for use inside Fusion Applications or as existing standard utilities that are well suited for use with Fusion Applications. The main purpose of this book is to bring together the wide range of management capabilities available, in a directly applicable and practical format. To do that, we'll look at a multitude of things, with many items used for a range of tasks. However, the discussion retains a single purpose: managing Fusion Applications.

# Why a Toolbox?

Perhaps the question should be, why not? It's an analogy used time and again for a set of software utilities that can be used for a specific purpose. Programmers and system administrators have used similar collections of tools for many years and, although some may be embedded in the integrated development environment (IDE), they usually include a range of general purpose utilities such as debuggers, documentation tools, various templates, and version control tools. The enterprise application manager (just like the system administrator) needs this wide range of tools to implement his or her management plans.

The resources inside this toolbox are intended to fit the most common use cases and situations, including both proactive and reactive work. In some cases, more utilities will be needed, but almost all of the tools discussed here can be used in a flexible manner to provide information in almost any scenario. It's impossible to cover every potentially useful tool, of course, and therefore this discussion focuses on a core set of features, functions, capabilities, and services, and the detail in the appendix provides additional material.

The toolbox serves as a guide to *what to use and when*, so that when addressing a specific situation, you can recall the right information or quickly locate and review the specifics you need. It should therefore act as a reasonable reference as well as basic training material.

# Toolbox Scope

Let's define a few boundaries for our toolbox discussion, so that it's very clear what kinds of utilities are included and how the discussions are structured. As mentioned, we will simply discuss specific capabilities that exist within various tools, and their explicit use in Fusion Applications management. The documentation listed in the Appendix can be used to find details on all other aspects of the tools mentioned, including their installation and configuration. The intention is not to discuss one or two tools completely, but to highlight many different features that help satisfy the requirements of effective application management.

As you read this chapter, you'll notice that although some tools have specific use cases and therefore apply in only one area, other tools have a wider range of features and as such are mentioned several times, albeit discussing either a different specific feature or its use in a different context.

As with installation and configuration, the Fusion Applications documentation covers the basics of starting, monitoring, and stopping of Fusion Applications and all its components. Rather than repeat any of this, the intention here is to take a more holistic look at overall management and then drill down to provide examples of specific features that can be used to provide precisely what is needed.

Although the majority of the tools mentioned are additional software programs, the discussion does include other types of tools such as services, recommended practices, and procedures. Table 5-1 provides a broad summary of some of the tools we'll be looking at.

| | |
|---|---|
| Diagnostic Logging Frameworks | RDBMS Administration |
| Real User Experience Insight | SOA Management |
| Diagnostic Test Framework | Business Intelligence Management |
| Problem and Incident Management | Reactive and Proactive Support Services |
| Remote Diagnostic Agent | Security Management |
| Business Process Execution Management | Recovery, High Availability, and Fail-over |
| Oracle Enterprise Manager | Command Line Utilities |
| WebLogic Server Administration | Oracle Governance, Risk, and Compliance |

**TABLE 5-1.**  *A High-Level Toolbox Manifest*

# Toolbox Structure

The next five chapters retain the focus, purpose, and intent of the preceding toolbox discussion. We'll look at tools in the context of each of the five enterprise application management tenets from Chapters 3 and 4. Although this works in a hands-on approach as a reference, it also allows us to build out the design for Fusion Applications management by putting real detail into the model we defined. Simply stated, keeping this structure to the discussion helps ensure that the design plans actually match the execution. As a reminder, we'll use the following categories:

- **Reliability**   Tools that help manage features so they consistently operate as intended. This includes monitoring for (and ideally avoiding) general problems and errors.

- **Availability**   Tools that help maintain feature access. This is essentially ensuring that all services and components are up and running.

- **Performance**   Tools that help spot the early signs of poor performance and provide facilities to help resolve any mismatch against expectations.

- **Optimization**   Tools that help facilitate additional contributions to organizational objectives and improvements.

- **Governance**   Tools that help manage the security, integrity, audit, and general quality of application features and data.

In addition to these broad categorizations, a further subdivision is also made, corresponding broadly to the layers that exist within the application technology stack, discussed in Chapter 2. This is shown in Figure 5-1.

The first subsection of each category provides tools that are best applied within the management of the highest level application functions and features, essentially focused around Business Process task completion. Some of the corresponding tools may be accessible by business users so that they can be involved and ideally self-manage certain parts of the application.

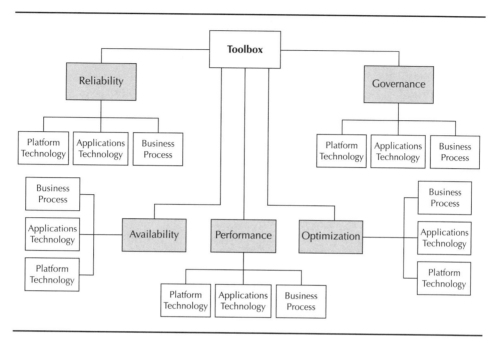

**FIGURE 5-1.** *The Fusion Applications Management Toolbox structure*

The next subdivision is the Application Technology layer, working under the features and functions. This is a useful category that often provides in-context information that helps capture important information. The final subdivision is the Platform layer, upon which all the components run. Core component, hardware, and operating system issues do sometimes arise; therefore, appropriate management tooling is most certainly required.

Using these three layers should help the applications manager traverse the technology stack when working on a specific problem or project, commonly important when looking for the type of information needed to move toward a truly effective solution.

# Toolbox Content

Several basic capabilities exist within the standard technology stack and related resources available for use with Fusion Applications. The list of potential tools, services, and features that *could* be of use is infinite, and it's neither practical nor sensible to attempt an exhaustive listing at this early stage of Fusion Applications evolution as a product. As such, we'll focus on core processes and the key moving parts, in the same way the application manager would initially prioritize his or her approach.

The tooling is not static, similar to the Enterprise Application Management Lifecycle model we built. You'll recall that we deliberately included two built-in continuous feedback loops into our model to ensure that all the tools and services are reviewed and made to evolve with requirements, expectations, and the application itself.

# Alternative Views

Although we're using our own lifecycle structure to lay out the toolbox, this information can be oriented in other ways according to specific use-case needs or individual preferences. One example might be to arrange and look at the tools with less emphasis on planning, and more emphasis on equipping adequately for reactive work. This is not to say it would include different content—it's just a different viewpoint. So the following categorization might be interesting to consider:

- **Monitoring**   How to identify problems across the whole system.

- **Analysis**   How to dig deeper when things go wrong or for proactive health checking.

- **Knowledge**   Tools and resources to promote ideas and good practices through better understanding.

- **Support Services**   Where to look to get additional help.

Another alternative and actually a more traditional view is to consider how to manage each technology stack a piece at a time. Using this approach and based on the outline in Chapter 2, the following might be used to organize the tooling required for success:

- Managing the application features

- Managing Fusion Middleware

- Managing the database

- Managing security

- Managing enterprise scheduling service

- Managing Business Intelligence

- Managing logging, tracing, and diagnostics information

- Managing high availability, backup, and recovery

Although useful, these additional views are commonly best used after an existing enterprise application has been implemented. In the next chapter, we'll go back to our original lifecycle model and look at some tools that can turn our great plans and intentions into a reality for Fusion Applications.

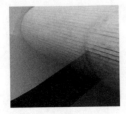

# CHAPTER
## 6

# A Reliability
# Management Toolbox

R eliability (as defined in this book) is about avoiding system problems, making core processes more fault-tolerant, or, when problems do occur, having capabilities in place so symptoms are spotted early and corrective actions are taken before downstream affects are too severe. The system's reliability is ultimately measured by the end user's experience, based on his or her exposure to unexpected interruptions, failures, and general instability. In extreme cases, reliability problems can lead to availability issues, as failures take down whole components—although we'll focus specifically on that later. So, in summary, some practical examples of reliability management tasks include the following:

- Proactive avoidance of known or potential problems.

- Reactive resolution of unexpected and new problems.

- Resource monitoring and management. This includes items such as hardware (CPU, memory, disk, network, and so on), as well as configuration-based constraints such as those inside the application, the Java runtime environment, and the database.

# Business Process Level

Ultimately, the business user needs reliable features for his or her day-to-day work, and although the technology underpinnings are vital, it's often the application configuration and use that leads to issues. As such, we'll first look at some tools to help investigate the health of the functional features used for completing normal business tasks such as creating orders, creating sales opportunities, or processing payments.

## The Diagnostic Test Framework (DTF)

Fusion Applications includes a purpose-built platform for running diagnostic tests. This platform runs alongside the application features and offers a set of executable tests. One or more of these tests can be run by any application user with the appropriate authorization. Each DTF test runs in the context of a single business process or feature, helping to interrogate the health of the application and its data, rather than focusing only on the underlying technology components. Tests commonly validate such things as user and feature setup, the configurations of related business objects, setup and use of any additional options and dependencies, transaction status and health, and general processing detail. Because tests are specific to one process or feature, content will vary from test to test; however, each test is supported by documentation that explains its use.

DTF tests commonly accept some input parameters such as a transaction number or a business object name, and they result in a detailed output report. Using the Diagnostics Testing Dashboard shown in Figure 6-1, tests can be run immediately as a single job, or they can be grouped and prescheduled as a collection of jobs.

DTF tests can also be triggered by *incident* creation, a feature that helps ensure failures include business process diagnostics along with technology stack information to provide a complete, end-to-end troubleshooting resource.

In terms of reliability, the Diagnostics Testing Dashboard can be used in two ways: First, it is an important reactive tool, helping you troubleshoot features and business processes when following up on user reported issues. Second, many reports can be run to validate the health of a process or feature before business users actually begin work. Although this is exceptionally useful during implementation and before major change activities, it is good practice to run these before any significant pieces of work are conducted.

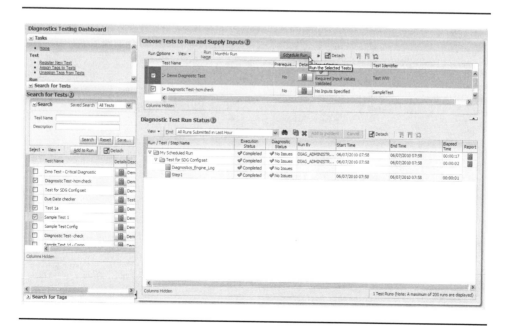

**FIGURE 6-1.**    *The DTF Diagnostics Testing Dashboard*

An obvious example might be validating related configuration and data reliability before running the period-close process within financials. This is also a case in which creating a group of proactive tests to run at regular intervals (such as monthly/quarterly improvement reviews) or in preparation for specific situations helps the business user and applications manager improve overall reliability.

As one of the more significant diagnostic tools in Fusion Applications, you'll see DTF used in more areas of applications management, and additional background information can be found in the Fusion Applications documentation, as listed in the Appendix.

## Functional Setup Manager

As discussed in Chapter 1, Functional Setup Manager provides a tool that captures a complete configuration snapshot of all application features and business processes. As shown in Figure 6-2, it offers easy-to-use navigation to the pages and forms where all setup is done, as well as export options in a variety of formats such as XML and PDF, intended for use as import in other instances.

As with the diagnosis of many types of end user reported problems, validating the related setups and configurations is a sensible first step before

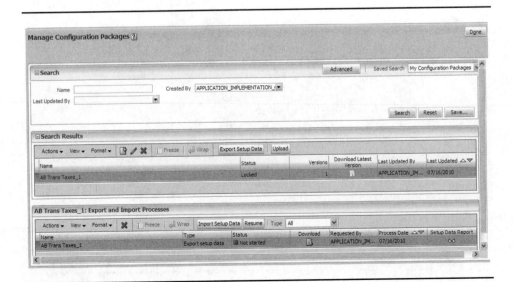

**FIGURE 6-2.** *Functional Setup Manager's review options*

spending time digging into complex technology stack analysis, such as reviewing log files. Functional Setup Manager can be used by both end users and application managers to validate setup information, particularly to look for gaps and anomalies related to one specific problem.

Despite not being originally intended for investigative purposes, the Functional Setup Manager features and capabilities can be tuned to fit a variety of the needs the application manager might have in checking reliability-related setups.

# Oracle Support

Although it might seem a little out of place to bring Oracle Support into this discussion so soon, as a resource to help improve the reliability of the application business processes and features, it would be a mistake to not mention it at all. As an advocate (and part) of the thousands of dedicated experts who help customers find solutions to their reliability problems every year, I can confirm that Oracle invests huge amounts of time and money in providing a range of services whose sole purpose is to help ensure customer success in using their software.

The service request resolution process forms the backbone of these services, but application managers should also use multiple proactive services to help monitor and manage their systems reliability. One specific example is Oracle Configuration Manager (OCM). OCM collects configuration data from installed systems and provides various tools for its analysis. In terms of use in investigating reliability issues, it's easy to spot any recent changes made to setup and configuration using OCM and to see the original values. In addition, as shown in Figure 6-3, Oracle Support provides a set of Health Recommendations that search the entire application system (including OCM data), looking for known problems or potential conflicts, and if any are found it provides clear advice on appropriate actions to take.

OCM and Health Recommendations are both embedded in the My Oracle Support web application and run alongside the following other useful capabilities and services:

- Powerful knowledge browsing tools that share the wisdom acquired from literally thousands of Enterprise Application and Technology implementations.

- Patch recommendations showing patches based on priority and those confirmed as missing from the host system (based on OCM collected data).

- Proactive alerts highlighting significant information, issues, and solutions.

- Community forums that include information, experience, and knowledge directly from other users of Oracle's products.

- Advanced Customer Support (ACS) services and tools that help you get even more value from the products installed.

These capabilities put access to existing solutions and useful recommendations in the hands of application managers and can help continuously ensure systems are as stable and reliable as possible. In Chapter 11, where we dig deeper into system health, we'll revisit a few

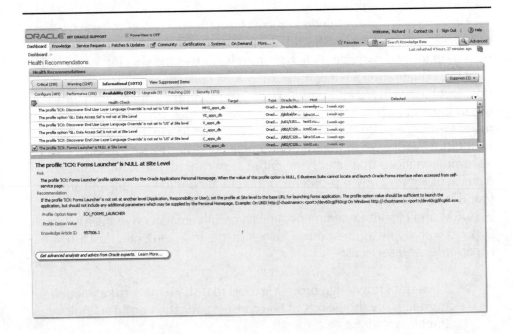

**FIGURE 6-3.** *My Oracle Support's Health Recommendations*

of these services and tools and show how adopting specific recommended practices can help transform the application management effort into a much richer partnership with Oracle Support.

# Applications Technology Level

The next level down in the technology stack covers the set of base components that directly support the application features and business processes. As mentioned in Chapters 1 and 2, this division is not always clear-cut, and here we group the management tools mainly based on their usage and relative proximity to the application features. Again, some of the larger tools will extend beyond our arbitrary subdivisions through their broad capabilities; however, for simplicity and clarity, we'll put each feature into our structure mainly based on the most common use cases.

## Incident Management

Those with an Information Technology Infrastructure Library (ITIL) and general IT Service Management (ITSM) background are likely to make an immediate assumption when the word *incident* is used, taking it to mean one specific instance of a definable problem. Although this definition holds true, for our discussion on managing Fusion Applications, it's extended by the implementation of the *Diagnostic Framework* (DFw), as discussed briefly in Chapter 1. Fusion Applications simply takes the basic ITIL definition and adds to it a set of diagnostic information for use in subsequent troubleshooting.

Indeed, in ITIL the term *incident management* is focused around restoring the offending operation or service to its previous good state, and *problem management* forms the guts of the determination of a cause and application of a solution. In Fusion Applications, these are combined so that the first incident of a problem has diagnostic information attached, initiating the resolution process immediately. Along with combining some actions, the tools discussed still support ITIL's *Service Operations* phase and are already used by many organizations implementing their associated helpdesk process and functions. Again, we'll revisit this whole area in Chapter 11.

Fusion Applications uses the DFw capabilities from Fusion Middleware specifically, and an incident can be created in two ways. The capabilities inherently form part of the investigation of reliability issues, and some evidence of the exact creation methods used can be found during diagnosis.

First, the application code can create *explicit* incidents by making a direct service call through the application's diagnostic logging framework to the incident JMX MBean API in Fusion Middleware. The alternative creation method, known as *implicit,* happens through the use of a specific predefined text string message that has been tagged so that its use spawns a process to create an incident (actually eventually using the same JMX call). For the end user, it's indiscernible how the incident was created, but as you debug and track logs, it is worth knowing that these methods exist and that they may be used interchangeably. In addition to the two creation methods from Fusion Applications, the DFw also runs in the Fusion Middleware and RDBMS layers, and they will create their own incidents upon any serious internal failures (such as ORA-0600).

Should the failure be not automatically captured by any of these three DFw implementations, the applications manager can trigger *manual* incidents at any time from just a few simple WLST commands (or from the Support Workbench, discussed a bit later).

Clearly, the display of all incidents created is useful from an alerting and tracking perspective; however, they also provide a rich diagnostic resource for investigating causes and solutions. The general intention of DFw incidents is to capture a complete picture of the system at the point of incident creation— in fact, they are often compared with an aircraft's black box flight recorder. Let's take a look at how incidents are created and then examine what they contain.

## Incident Creation

Incidents are created by the DFw when an error is caught by the product code. Then a process known as the *Diagnostic Data Extractor (DDE)* checks each error raised against a predefined list of errors that are eligible for incident creation. For the technology stack (FMw, RDBMS), this list is built into the framework and cannot be changed. For Fusion Applications, the creation is either hard-coded into the product or occurs implicitly based on data associated with user response messages stored in the database, which means that additional incidents could be created through a customization.

The DDE engine also knows what diagnostic data to collect based on the class of incident raised, which is essentially governed by the error message code (known as a *problem key*), such as FND-70 or ORA-01578. Next, the files are placed into the relevant directory on the file system (the *Automatic Diagnostic Repository*). It creates a new folder with the incident's unique identifier so that it can be easily found.

## Incident Contents

The contents of DFw incidents reveals what a valuable source of troubleshooting and diagnostic information they contain:

- **Diagnostic image** A dump of the WebLogic servers' own detailed diagnostic and status information.

- **ECIDCTX** The data associated with either the single Execution Context ID for which the failure was associated, or, when unclear, it captures all those available at that time.

- **DMS metrics** FMw uses the Dynamic Monitoring Service (DMS) for detailed diagnostic information for all of its components, and it represents a full dump of these at the time of incident creation.

- **JVM threads and class histogram** Detailed information on all running Java threads, as well as a class histogram.

- **ODL logs** The content of all diagnostic logs registered with the system, including those from Fusion Applications, based on the Execution Context ID (ECID) or 5 minutes before the incident creation time.

- **DTF test output** The DTF uses a method that allows specific tests to be executed upon incident creation, associating the resulting output with the incident. This occurs through the association of a message identifier (as used in implicit incident creation, which therefore becomes the *problem key*) and the registration tags used for one or more DTF tests. This is all pre-seeded in the application code, but could potentially be extended.

- **Database incidents** All the items mentioned here relate to FMw incidents as well as Fusion Applications incidents originating from Java. The database implementation of DFw also creates incidents and is used by Fusion Applications PL/SQL (Procedural Language/ Structured Query Language) code. These incidents contain relevant trace files, as well as a section of both the database alert log and, in the case of Fusion Applications, the applicable PL/SQL Oracle Diagnostic Log (ODL).

**Incident Storage**     Incident information is stored in the host file system in a repository structure known as the *Automatic Diagnostic Repository (ADR)*. This is a standardized directory structure for storing all diagnostic-related information. It replaces many common output directories—for example, in the database, a single directory (ADR_HOME/trace/) contains the trace files that were previously found in background_dump_dest and user_dump_dest. In standardizing directories, it facilitates the use of several management and analysis tools.

**Incident Management**     Three tools are available for looking at the incident content in Fusion Applications and its underlying technology stack. They all offer similar features, but two offer a command-line interface, while the other is part of the Enterprise Manager product.

The first is a set of WebLogic Scripting Tool (WLST) commands that can be used across the Fusion Middleware ADR directories for creating manual incidents, reviewing details of automatically created incidents, as well as retrieving file contents. A full list of all the commands is provided in the Fusion Middleware documentation.

The second solution, known as *ADRCI*, is the command-line interface for managing the ADR content. This tool offers various utility commands for viewing problems and their incidents. ADRCI is intended for the management of all of the ADR directory structure, and it therefore comes with various utility features that expand beyond DFw incidents. Similarly, since it's not only incident-focused, ADRCI does not allow the creation of manual incidents.

The final incident management tool is known as *Support Workbench* and is a feature of Enterprise Manager. As shown in Figure 6-12 later on, Support Workbench offers most of the same functions as WLST and ADRCI, but in a much richer graphical interface and with a few additional functions, such as the option to add system dumps manually into the content of an incident.

One additional feature of both ADRCI and Support Workbench is the option to *package* the incident contents held in ADR into a zip file, and to transmit that file straight to Oracle Support for use with a service request. The tool that does this is known as the *Incident Packaging System (IPS)*, which offers a few useful options, such as adding additional diagnostic outputs (such as the Remote Diagnostic Agent, or RDA) and allowing the administrator to add his or her own files.

Since all this detailed information is retained with every occurrence (incident) of a problem, if something should fail in a loop, it could quite quickly occupy valuable resources for many users. Fortunately, the DFw has a *Flood Control* feature, which means that a parameter can be set that limits the maximum number of incidents that will be created for the same problem.

Obviously, it's critical for reliability to monitor incident creation closely. Too many incidents could represent either an unreliable system or the capture of too many non-issues. Too few incidents, however, might mean many issues are going uncaptured. It's important that you verify that what is being observed on the back end correctly mirrors the real experience of the user base. It's also vital that for each unique problem, in addition to monitoring, the Fusion Applications manager initiates an effective resolution process where the incident data is properly involved. DFw Incident Management represents one of the key capabilities in supporting reliability problems in Fusion Applications, and much more detailed material can be found in the Appendix.

## Fusion Applications Diagnostic Logging

Most of the many moving parts in the software stack will be concurrently writing their own log output, with their own configurations and specific capabilities. The term *Fusion Applications Diagnostic Logging* refers to the log output that is created when a business end user invokes application code while using a feature and function to complete tasks that support the business operation—such as creating invoices, changing salaries, running payrolls, or creating orders. This type of log is clearly different from the logs that are written when an XML message is parsed, or a web server handles an HTTP request, though these are also intrinsically part of the overall processes.

Although Fusion Applications Diagnostic Logging is fully described in the official product documentation, the following overview focuses attention on features and practices that can help ensure reliability.

Diagnostic Logging can be enabled either through Enterprise Manager (Fusion Applications Control) for the whole system or by using Profile Options (see Chapter 1) to set it up at the individual user level. As with all systems, the day-to-day default values for logging should remain fairly low, meaning that the system is not constantly writing large amounts of output to the disk-based file system. Fusion Applications Diagnostic Logging provides a few methods to keep logging under control and avoiding overwhelming both the system and the reader of the output.

It's possible to specify precisely which part of the code for which you would like to write log output. Although this might seem to suggest that you require detailed knowledge of the source code, in reality, you can provide a reasonably broad configuration value that eliminates inapplicable areas. The profile option is *FND: Log Module Filter* and can be set in the system-wide Profile Options administration pages; Figure 6-4, however, shows an even easier option, in which each authorized user can set up logging himself using the Supportability page, invoked from the global Help menu anywhere in the application.

Notice the Logging Module field that contains the value of the module package name accepting, a user-defined value. This allows the clever applications manager to choose for what code he or she wants to see the log output, and it can be an effective way to find evidence of problems much faster than trawling through hundreds of lines of output. The field uses its own pattern matching, so precise module names and words are not critical, and, as shown, you can use wildcard characters as well. It also supports a comma-separated list, so that multiple outputs can be provided—useful for capturing the logs for the parallel execution flows inside Fusion Applications.

In addition to fields that specify what code will be writing log output, the Log Level field here (which corresponds to Profile option FND: Log Level)

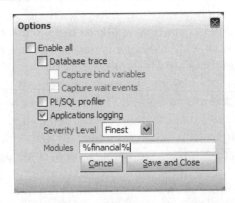

**FIGURE 6-4.** *Setting up Applications Diagnostic Logging through the Help-Troubleshooting menu*

controls the type of output that is written, commonly known as its *verbosity*. Following is a brief summary of the available options for this field:

- **Incident**  The highest level of logging provides log output for only the most serious issues. This generally applies to the platform (such as Fusion Middleware), where only critical issues require the capture of logs.

- **Severe**  This provides a little more output and is intended to help the applications manager review activity and take appropriate action. This is commonly the default setting value.

- **Warning**  This provides more output still and shows evidence of potential problems as well as plain errors.

- **Info**  This provides more output, and in addition to failures, it includes information on some basic system processing.

- **Config**  This includes all the preceding output, plus detail on the configurations used and normal system events.

- **Fine**  This is the first official debug level, and it provides all the preceding details plus basics on the code execution.

- **Finer**  A lower debug level that provides all preceding details plus more on code execution.

- **Finest**  The lowest, most verbose level of debugging possible. It provides full details on code execution along with configuration, data, and errors.

The Fusion Applications Diagnostic Logging also includes advanced configuration, as shown in Figure 6-5, from Enterprise Manager, with important options to specify Supplemental Attributes for additional output (XML or text) in the rich ODL content, as well as file location and, of course, rotation parameters.

Fusion Applications managers will adjust these logging controls so that they can get as much pertinent information as possible when investigating any reliability concerns using the Application Diagnostic Log in concert with logs from the other components in the technology stack. The nature of the ODL standard structure for logging content is such that each log

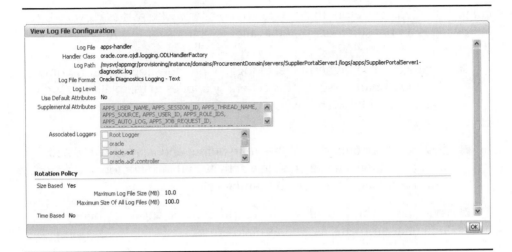

**FIGURE 6-5.** *Configuration of Applications Diagnostic Logging*

statement is associated with rich information, such as user, ECID, module, and timestamp. Although this makes the logs exceptionally useful, it also limits their use in their raw format, as eyeballing them can be almost impossible. We'll look at the replacement tooling in forthcoming sections.

Log analysis isn't always a reactive activity, either, and it can be done proactively as well, such as using log output as an information source when running a general health check on key processes. On the whole, the logging configuration options fall into two categories—one for more static settings that are rarely changed and form the *normal* system configuration, and another set of configurations that are changed to help generate more detail for use in issue diagnosis.

## Enterprise Manager Extensions

Oracle Enterprise Manager is the single most important tool for monitoring and managing the complete Fusion Applications technology stack. As you'll see, it's certainly not the only tool, but it does offer many flexible and powerful features for use in almost all situations. We'll discuss specific use cases and related capabilities as we proceed; however, in this context, we'll take a brief look at a few application-specific extensions to the standard Enterprise Manager that can help with reliability management.

Although Fusion Applications is at the beginning of its evolution, it is already supported by several Enterprise Manager components designed for management success, such as the already mentioned Support Workbench feature that offers a rich and powerful method for incident and problem management. In addition, the Real User Experience Insight (RUEI) product has been specially extended to provide a Fusion Applications *accelerator* that offers a range of native features for investigating user-to-system interactions. The RUEI platform provides the following core features that can help the application manager understand where problems lie, calling up rich information to assist with the diagnosis and resolution:

- **Dashboards** One-stop-shop management pages whose regions can be customized to offer a wide range of performance indicators, data summaries (with drill-down), rich graphics, and powerful charts. Figure 6-6 shows an example.

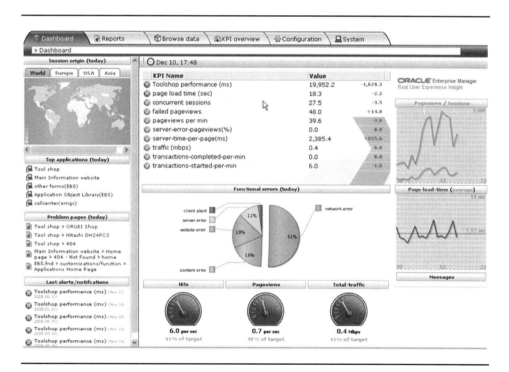

**FIGURE 6-6.** *A RUEI dashboard page*

■ **Diagnostic data** RUEI is based on the capture of full user session information every time the user interacts with the application, from initial login, to spawning child processes, to simply pressing buttons on a page. It brings together data from each running component to a single usable place for end-to-end analysis.

■ **Replay** This extraordinary capability allows you to replay the users' session activity, often all the way back to login. This is exceptionally useful for application managers who often find getting problem actions repeated by business users a slow and laborious process.

■ **Business transaction tracking** RUEI also singles out transactions based on their profiles (such as orders) and provides detailed monitoring and reporting, including both performance information and any associated failures.

■ **User segmentation** This feature allows the application manager to show user activity by standard (and custom) profiles, even including such variables as a user's geographical location. This can be helpful in spotting patterns in reliability issues.

■ **Comparative and automated analysis** A detailed history of user data is retained so that a wide range of analysis can be performed against past performance. RUEI can also monitor script-based *synthetic* users, often used for automated system testing. Again this is more data that can form a useful baseline for comparing against real activity.

■ **Technology stack support** RUEI provides full support for the Fusion Application technology stack, with native capabilities for tracking and reporting against WebLogic Server, the complete SOA infrastructure, and Oracle ADF.

■ **Service-level management** Using RUEI, you can translate the business service level agreement expectations and measures into a complete metric and threshold definition, and then use its full suite of alerting and reporting capabilities on top.

In addition to RUEI, another Enterprise Manager extension that provides the Fusion Applications manager with some useful resources is Oracle Application Testing Suite. This is covered in more detail in Chapters 10 and 11 where we'll look at testing and see what tools and practices can be adopted to streamline some of the work from this important area.

# Platform

We've looked at the tools and services available to manage reliability in the top two layers of Fusion Applications—so what's left? As you know, quite a large stack of technology components is what.  Many of these components have already been well covered by other system management books, therefore we'll focus on the core parts that offer the Fusion Applications manager some insight without including too much complex information and data. Of course, the Appendix includes expanded references for use should you want more specialized information.

## FMw Logging Frameworks and Reliability Utilities

All the components running inside Fusion Middleware have their own configuration and setup features and, likewise, their own native logging mechanisms. Figure 6-7 shows a small sample of the different loggers that exist within the underlying framework. Failures at this level clearly affect everything built upon it, so although this should form a stable, reliable base for the application, you should also be watching out for any potential issues.

Fusion Applications comes with a set of default settings for all the component loggers, although the profile and use cases of each specific instance will dictate how these should be set up. Although you can set up all manner of elaborate logging, the potential for performance and resource monopolization should be the overriding concern, and standard practice recommends that the implementation should be such that normal operations write the bare minimum while all serious failures are captured in detail. Often experience and careful testing is the only way to decide how that might be realized and set up for each specific instance.

This seems like a suitable juncture to mention tools for catching reliability problems—namely errors, exceptions, and similar symptoms and evidence. Although it's not the only tool for logging, Enterprise Manager's own log viewer is one of the best and easiest to use.

First, the search runs within a specific *context*, which is based on the technical architecture (Enterprise Manager targets) that exists within the overall deployment. As such, the search may entail viewing logs within several levels—the domain, the cluster, the WebLogic Server, or even one individual application deployment. You can also use Enterprise Manager's Grid Control to view logs across multiple domains, which is good for larger deployments and when you're viewing the complete Fusion Applications picture.

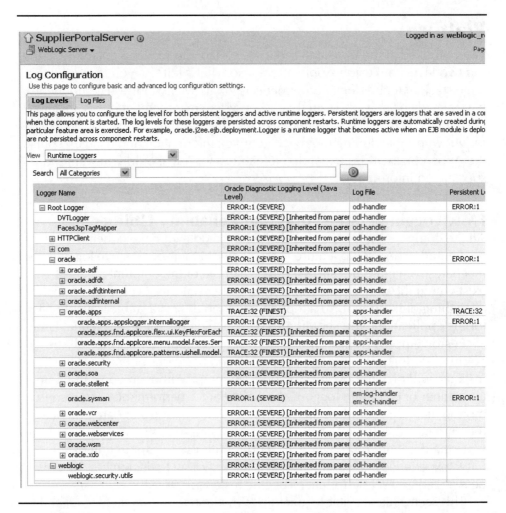

**FIGURE 6-7.** *Some of the additional platform loggers*

As shown in Figure 6-8, the following basic log search features allow details for reliability problems to be quickly identified:

■ Target selection that allows the log search to include and exclude the logs from certain components that exist within the context of the search.

■ Date ranges, specifying either a time interval (last 1 hour) or an exact *to* and *from* range.

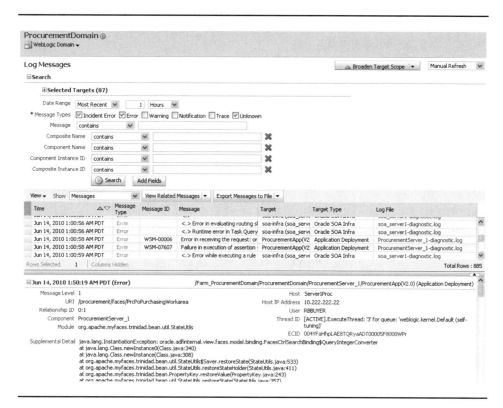

**FIGURE 6-8.**   *Viewing and searching logs through Enterprise Manager*

- Message types, which represent the verbosity of the logger(s) writing the output. This equates to the Log Levels configuration used in the Fusion Applications Diagnostic Log (mentioned earlier).

- Search logic that can include or exclude certain messages, as well as support the use of various wildcard search options.

- Add or remove searching by any of the fields in the ODL log content. This includes (and is particularly useful for) supplemental attribute data, such as the composite details shown in Figure 6-8.

- The ability to reorder, add, or remove columns from the results table.

- The instant display of full log line detail when selecting lines from the table of results.

- The ability either to show all messages or group them by Message Type or Message ID.

- The ability to view related messages either by time or the unique process identifier, ECID.

- The ability to export results as text, XML, or CSV format files.

## SOA Reliability

In a naturally distributed architecture, it is difficult to correlate technology stack component activity with the execution processing flow of one specific business user action. This challenge is well known, and fortunately Fusion Applications offers some great tooling help. Enterprise Manager manages and reports back on all the processing throughout the SOA infrastructure. As each *composite application* is instantiated upon request through business events, as shown in Figure 6-9, Enterprise Manager records a *Trace* with full details of all subsequent process execution, including Mediator messaging and Business Process Execution Language (BPEL) flows.

**FIGURE 6-9.** *The BPEL process trace in Enterprise Manager*

Enterprise Manager provides a detailed audit trail that includes any failures that may have occurred. It has several different views that help quickly identify the precise failure origin and all associated errors, data (payloads), and code objects involved. Figure 6-10 shows the graphical *Flow* view for a BPEL process, including *Audit* details for a failed step.

In addition to errors trapped by the SOA process, the *SOA-INFRA* J2EE application is also searchable in Enterprise Manager's log query tool. Look back at Figure 6-8 and you'll see that the composite search fields are available, along with the common ECID that is recorded by the SOA Audit Trail.

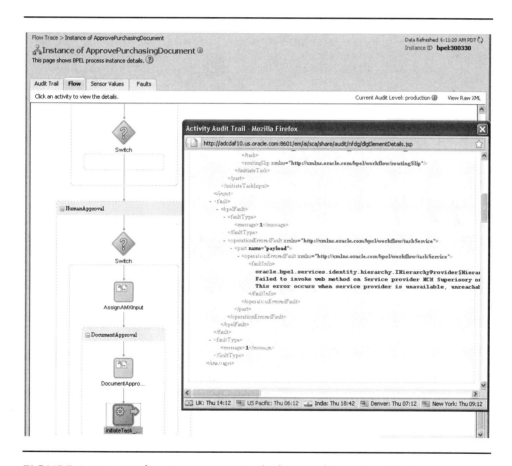

**FIGURE 6-10.** *Failure in process, including audit payload data*

Other Enterprise Manager features that can help investigate and monitor reliability problems in the SOA infrastructure are detailed in the associated documentation (see Appendix); however, key highlights include the following:

- A SOA Dashboard showing various summaries, including composite status and health

- Composite instance lists, with drill-down to the full audit features

- Tables showing all recent faults and rejected messages

- Clickable links to view associated logs

- Full payload and XML message visibility for all actions and activities

- Activity, variable, and fault sensor values for useful tracking of data

- A raw XML alternative view for all audit traces and flow displays

- Business event and subscription data, including implementation details, audit trail, and any failures

- A performance summary chart for each SOA engine component

## Enterprise Manager Management Packs

Although RUEI has been extended for Fusion Application specifically, several other extensions to Enterprise Manager are worth mentioning in terms of handling reliability in the technology stack. Although these additional tools may be used to great effect, they are not actually part of Fusion Applications, and as such, we'll not go into as much depth as we will for the Enterprise Manager features that require no additional license.

- **The SOA Management Pack** Extends the native SOA support, providing additional visibility to business transactions as they flow through the physical topology of the SOA infrastructure. This also includes support for advanced web service testing, security management, and detailed configuration, alerting and notification capabilities.

- **The WebLogic Server Management Pack** Provides multi-domain support for monitoring larger middleware environments, just like Fusion Applications. This includes extended capabilities in JVM diagnostics, transaction tracking, and patch and dependency analysis. It also offers dedicated configuration and compliance management features.

■ **The WebCenter Suite Management Pack** Offers a correlation between the abstract layers of the portal and WebCenter implementations across all underlying code objects and processes, enabling easy and accurate monitoring with reduced complexity.

■ **Business Intelligence Management Pack** Offers full failure and performance monitoring for all the Oracle Business Intelligence Enterprise Edition (OBIEE) components. Includes capabilities to embed SLA metrics and set up detailed reporting dashboards and alerting mechanisms.

■ **Management Pack for Identity Management** Offers full support for most of the authorization and security platforms used in Fusion Applications (including OID, OVD, OIM, and OAM), and offers full access to performance, configuration, and through-put information. It also includes capabilities for testing as well as SLA-based reporting and alerting, just like the other packs.

■ **Diagnostics Pack for Oracle Middleware** Provides additional tools for helping resolve issues found in the middleware architecture layer. It focuses on Java applications (of various types), the Java WLS servers, and JVM diagnostics. Like the other packs, it includes full reporting and alerting mechanisms.

■ **Database Management Packs** Includes a Diagnostics Pack, a Tuning Pack, a Change Management Pack, a Configuration Management Pack, a Provisioning and Patch Automation Pack, and a Data Masking Pack.

■ **Application Quality Management (AQM)** Enterprise Manager also offers a rich set of testing tools as part of its Application Quality Management (AQM) solution.

Many of these packs leverage the underlying capabilities in the Oracle Enterprise Manager Grid Control product, an extension to the standard Enterprise Manager Control, and a platform that provides a wide range of features and a more native support for larger system architectures (i.e., Enterprise Grid Computing mentioned in Chapter 2).

## ESS Reliability

As another core part of the architecture, the Enterprise Scheduling Service must be reliable to complete the process-heavy tasks passed to it. Just like SOA, the core administrative tool is Enterprise Manager (actually Fusion Applications Control), and the following is a brief list of the related features:

- An ESS Dashboard showing all recently completed and currently pending requests

- Statuses on the core *Dispatcher* and *Scheduler* components of ESS

- Deployment details and links to respective WebLogic servers

- Graphs and data on response, load, and performance

- Job details including the originating application, server, user, and any failures

- Work allocation and the purging configuration

- Links back to view detailed log output

In addition, because ESS tracks its execution in the database, simple queries can be used to get useful data. Two examples are tables **ESS_REQUEST_HISTORY**, which stores the job executions, and **ESS_REQUEST_PROPERTY**, which stores the input parameter values.

## Database Reliability Tools

As with all the tools described so far, Reliability Management is all about keeping a watch for symptoms that might result in disruptive problems. When they do occur, you must be able to drill-down easily to get to the root cause. The database, as Oracle's most mature product, has a substantial range of tooling available; we'll discuss only a few core areas here (see the Appendix for more information).

As anyone with any experience of the Oracle Database knows, two primary resources are used for investigating issues. First is the *alert log*, a log file that captures all activities, events, and failure information for that instance. Second, *trace files* are written upon request processing, outputting all the database statements executed and their associated metrics. As you may have spotted, which is highlighted in Figure 6-11, Fusion Applications supports turning on SQL tracing at the application user level, creating trace files for the processes and queries that result from that users' activity. Although commonly associated with investigating performance issues, trace data is also exceptionally useful in helping understand the interactions between processing and the underlying data objects, and therefore is a useful tool for validating data integrity and quality when investigating reliability issues. A host of tools handle alert logs and trace files (including ADRCI), and we'll look at a few in Chapter 8.

The database also has a dedicated Enterprise Manager Control (and optionally the Grid Control) instance, which provides similar powerful dashboard, configuration, and interrogation query features already discussed. Full detail on its capabilities can be found from the resources in the Appendix.

Oracle Database 11*g* is also used by Fusion Applications and comes with the DFw. This means all serious errors are captured as problems and incidents, and, as shown in Figure 6-12, the full toolset is available, including Support Workbench (and ADRCI) to facilitate reliability monitoring, alerting, and diagnostic data packaging for subsequent investigation.

**FIGURE 6-11.**    *The user menu for enabling SQL tracing and the PL/SQL Profiler*

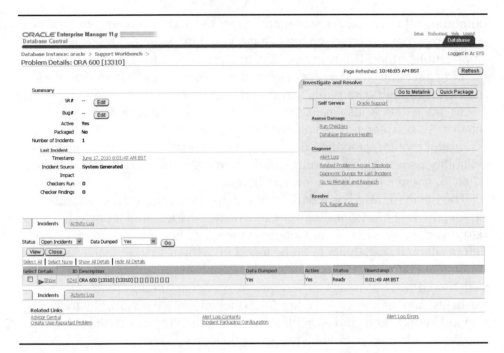

**FIGURE 6-12.** *The Support Workbench in the Database Control*

## Using Oracle Support Tools for Reliability

In addition to the capabilities built into the product and the supportability ecosystem built around it, Oracle Support has more utilities that work at the platform level that can be used to help ensure reliability. The broadest of such tools is RDA, which is somewhat similar in concept to OCM, but provides a wider aggregation of platform information for review and analysis, for use both reactively and proactively. RDA is a command-line tool and, as shown in Figure 6-13, the results form a set of indexed reports that provide drill-down capabilities to the configurations, versions, and general information for each component for which it is run (known as an RDA *module* and passed as an input parameter).

RDA modules include a large number of Oracle products (and some third-party products). The following list forms a small subset that is particularly pertinent to Fusion Applications:

- WebLogic Server
- Oracle WebCenter and Portal

- Universal Content Management (UCM)

- OIM (including Oracle Internet Directory [OID], Oracle Virtual Directory [OVD], Oracle Access Manager [OAM], and other security tools)

- Database (including RAC)

- Secure Enterprise Search (SES)

- SOA Suite (including Business Process Execution Language, or BPEL)

- Oracle Data Integrator (ODI)

- Business Intelligence: OBIEE (including Essbase)

- Java and JDBC

- Most operating systems

- Oracle-related networking products

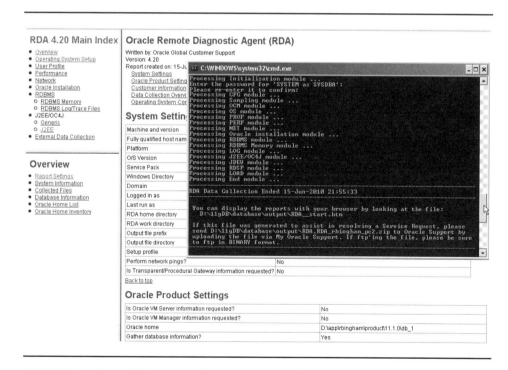

**FIGURE 6-13.**  *RDA execution and the resulting HTML pages*

RDA is also part of the DFw Incident processing flow, since as part of the IPS packaging process, the RDA tool can be run and the applicable output appended to the zip bundle for further analysis. RDA is run either generally or in the context of the incident type, using an internal mapping between a known list of problem keys (such as ORA-0600) and related RDA modules. Since RDA produces sets of files, they can also be manually added to incidents to ensure this rich source of technology stack information helps in problem resolution.

In addition to investigating reliability problems such as failures and errors, in lieu of a more complete configuration management tool, RDA can be useful for capturing a snapshot of the configuration for review and comparison as and when required.

# CHAPTER 7

## The Availability Management Toolbox

ou can probably easily imagine the kinds of tools that deal with availability, but let's just take a few minutes to clarify what we really want to accomplish regarding availability. You know about the reactive tools that should provide timely alerts to the occurrence of an outage, and, in contrast, the proactive tools that try to perform intelligent analysis and actions that help avoid such problems from occurring. Let's summarize a few key areas of concern and then look at the appropriate tools for use with Fusion Applications.

- **Service Continuity**  End user features and functions must be available, and all technical components must remain active and working together properly as processes execute.

- **Stability**  Where reliability and performance problems are frequent or severe, the resulting instability may cause full availability problems.

- **Resources**  Without sufficient resources, distributed according to up-to-date profile data and accurate plans, availability problems are much more likely.

- **Integration**  With its various distributed architectures (Service-Oriented Architecture, Business Process Management, Coexistence, and so on), Fusion Applications relies heavily on the fact that all integration points will be available as per the expectations set by the implementation design.

# Business Process Layer

If we take availability at its highest level, the Fusion application manager needs a good understanding and adequate tooling required to monitor the status and health of the core components that directly control end user features.

## Business Service Availability

Although the application as a whole might appear to be up and running, with a Service-Oriented Architecture (SOA)–based composite application with many module components (including Enterprise Scheduling Service jobs, BI Publisher reports, OBIEE charts and analytics, and standalone coexistence integration pieces), one of the many constituent features or processes could be unavailable. Similar to its use in troubleshooting reliability problems, the Diagnostic Test Framework (DTF) includes tests that act as health-checkers to validate that a process is in a suitable state for use. So although availability is usually categorized as a technical status of a server or component, DTF is one tool that can also assess the availability (and health) of business processes and features.

# Fusion Applications Control

Fusion Applications benefits from a set of high-level dashboards that offer general status information, provided at the pillar, the product family (Figure 7-1), and product levels. These pages form the heart of the new Enterprise Manager component designed specifically for Fusion Applications. They provide information including statuses, performance details, topology, and highlight any particularly long-running activities, such as Enterprise Scheduling Service (ESS) jobs and SOA instances. The pages are also useful for launching the log query tool (via the menu), since they set the proper context so that log searches include all appropriate files. Although they are

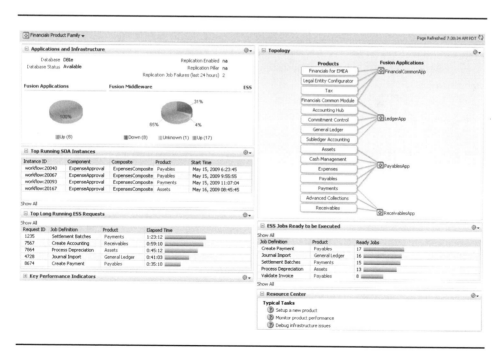

**FIGURE 7-1.** *Fusion Applications Control showing product family availability*

summaries, these top-level pages can be used to drill down into specific activities or the underlying Fusion Middleware (FMw) and database components.

## Service Testing

Many of the core business processes supported by Fusion Applications involve the use of Business Process Execution Language (BPEL) to invoke Web Services, and although it requires some basic familiarity with a products implementation, one of the most basic checks that the application manager can do is to verify that those Web Services operate as expected.

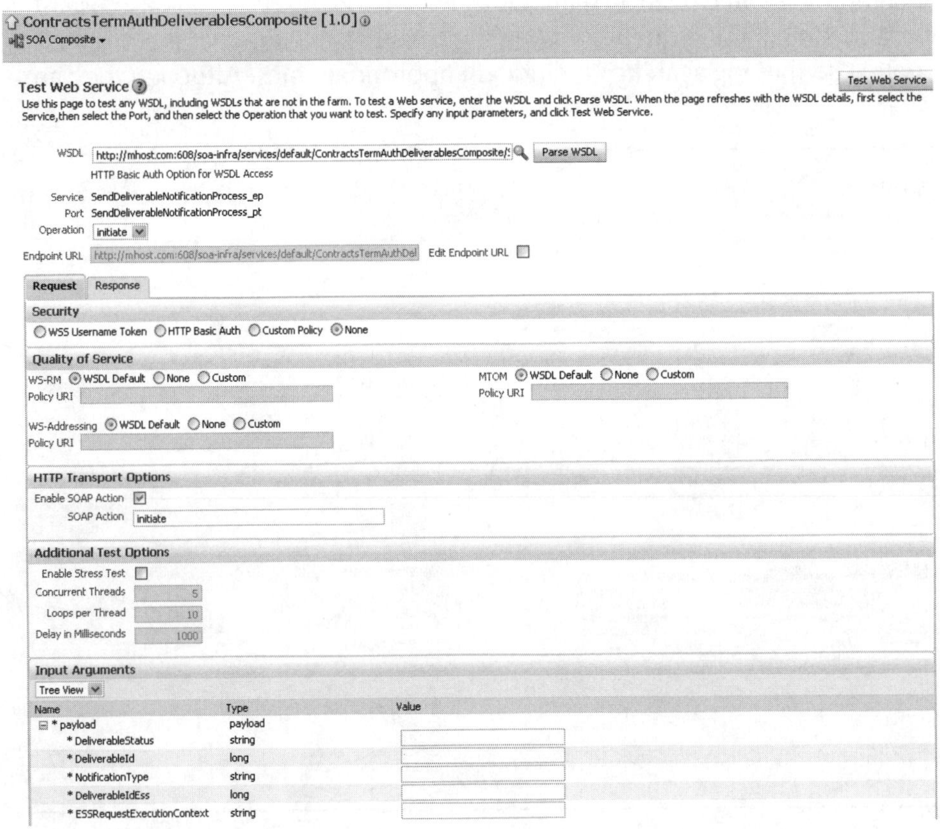

**FIGURE 7-2.** *Enterprise Manager FMw Control's service test*

Figure 7-2 shows Enterprise Manager's service testing feature that provides everything you need, from endpoints to input parameters.

Although these tests might seem a little low-level, for many features of Fusion Applications, they allow you to test the discrete modular components that form the building blocks of the features and functions to verify their availability. A good example is coexistence, and where the integration is based on discrete web service calls; should any be experiencing problems (and therefore unavailable), the whole process grinds to a halt.

# Applications Technology Layer

Any availability issues in the many pieces to the technology stack will significantly impact the features running above it as well as those running alongside it. For example, SOA, BPEL, ESS, Oracle Data Integrator (ODI), and Application Development Framework (ADF) all depend on one another, using the others' services commonly several times within one specific process execution, and should any one service be unavailable, the process will stall. Let's look at some core pieces and the tools for managing their availability.

## ADF

Each product in Fusion Applications is made up of one or more Java 2 Enterprise Edition (J2EE) applications. These are essentially individual deployments of Enterprise Application Resource (EAR) files that are made up of all the JavaServer Faces (JSF)–based ADF objects and resources needed to run the user interface, together with the SOA Composite code, as well as all other program files. As such, when deployed on each WebLogic Server, the ADF parts are themselves complete J2EE applications, and unlike many other Oracle Applications products, no separate server is responsible for rendering components like the forms and pages. ADF is therefore more about the development environment, since the deployed applications use the existing Java technologies available in WebLogic Server, most of which are open standards based. Deployments are shown in the context of their WebLogic container (server, cluster, domain, and so on), and their availability, health, and status is shown in both Enterprise Manager and the WebLogic Server Administration Console (shown later in Figure 7-6).

# Fusion Middleware Availability

Enterprise Manager Fusion Applications Control shows dashboards of basic availability for each of the main middleware components in use. This includes ESS, the WebLogic Domain (Figure 7-3), Clusters and Servers, as well as the full SOA Infrastructure (Figure 7-4).

Although these middleware dashboards are fairly basic, each offers a clear visual representation, links to performance data and charts, links to related logging, as well as the ability to drill down into detailed transaction or process level information. Adding the optional Enterprise Manager Grid Control provides many more capabilities, especially around alerting, historical reporting, configuration management, and SLA compliance.

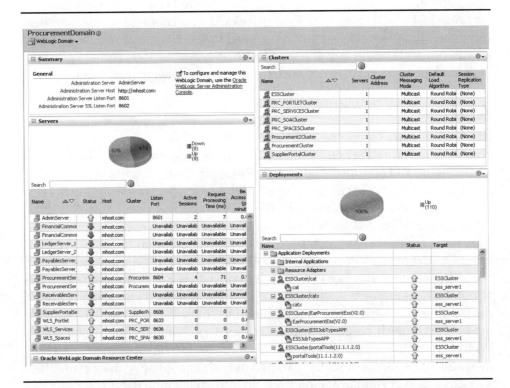

**FIGURE 7-3.** *The WebLogic Domain dashboard showing both server and deployment availability*

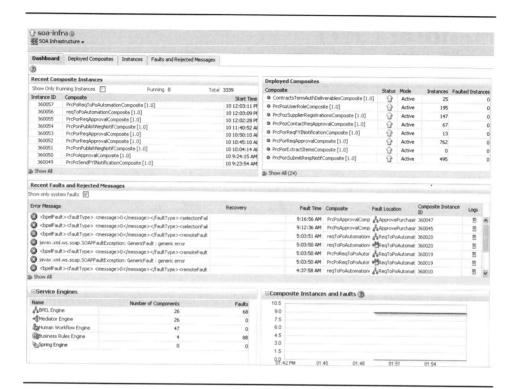

**FIGURE 7-4.** *The SOA Infrastructure dashboard showing composite status and availability*

# The MBean Browser

Fusion Applications includes a selection of purpose-built Java Management Extensions (JMX), implemented as Managed Java Beans (MBeans). These provide additional interfaces for reviewing and adjusting both configuration and runtime information from the system components. They are easily accessible through Enterprise Manager Fusion Applications Control and can be viewed using its MBean Browser within the context of either a single WebLogic Server, or one J2EE Application (essentially the same thing). Although these represent a key resource for advanced management, the current evolution of Fusion Applications will require additional work to create the extensions via custom coding.

# Platform Layer

Without a foundation, a house will collapse—and the same is true with enterprise applications. Let's take a look at how availability can be managed for the key components of the platform.

## Business Intelligence

For Fusion Applications, the Business Intelligence (BI) platform comes in two flavors, and as such two core components are used to monitor for availability.

The first controls all the standardized reports that the application creates, mainly used for record-keeping, printing, and other tasks. The *BI Publisher* component provides the engine against which each product feature submits its own data and predefined templates, either online or commonly via an ESS Job. Figure 7-5 shows the basic administration tool for BI Publisher.

The second BI component is the OBIEE Server that provides powerful and flexible tools for business users to analyze their operational data. Out of the box, most the basic analytical capabilities are embedded in the dashboards and pages of the ADF J2EE application itself, and as such its management is controlled by a OBIEE server component known as the *BI Presentation Server*. This provides the Oracle Transaction Business Intelligence (OTBI) features that supply a graphical view of the live data inside the deployed application.

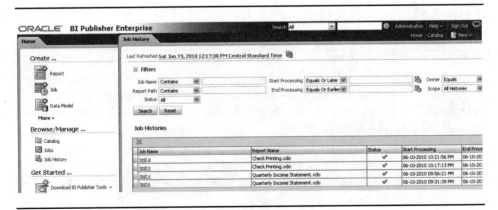

**FIGURE 7-5.** *BI Publisher's administration tool*

Fusion Applications also provides a prebuilt reporting capability with access to a wide range of additional reports and analytical content. This leverages the prepackaged OBIEE implementation known as Oracle Business Intelligence Applications (OBIA) features and works alongside the ADF context to ensure that relevant material and data are presented.

Finally, privileged Fusion Application users can also access report creation features (such as the Report Wizard) from the native OBIEE implementation and share results with other application users. This feature originates from the OBIEE Server directly, and therefore managing and monitoring availability depends on its configuration and the use of its administration tools. Along with Enterprise Manager Application Control's basic views on the health and status of the BI nodes, the OBIEE Server has its own dedicated integrated systems management console known as the Data-warehouse Administration Console (DAC). In terms of availability, the connections to the various BI Servers are intelligent enough to show disconnection type problems both to the end user and to the administrator, supplemented of course with dashboards and logs.

# Oracle Data Integrator

The ODI is the primary Fusion Middleware component used for transforming, moving, and synchronizing data from one instance to another (generally by an Extract, Transform, Load [ETL] process). It has various uses in Fusion Applications, from pillar replication, business intelligence, to various import and export features. It's also a tool for custom use, often for improving data quality and as a Master Data Management system.

Obviously, as a controller of business data, ODI's availability is important. However, it forms a discrete component in itself, and although it is leveraged by the product in a few places, it has little involvement in day-to-day operations.

Managing ODI is mainly an internal operation, since it has its own set of interfaces for designing and executing data manipulation. In addition, its tight integration to the database and middleware means the generic tools available in these components (mainly Enterprise Manager) would be the best place for more detail. The Appendix provides more detail, including specifics on the ODI system in the middleware stack.

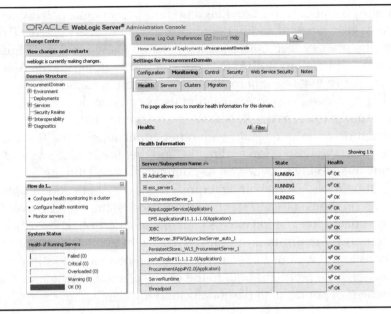

**FIGURE 7-6.** *The WLS Administration Console*

# WebLogic Server

Complementing Enterprise Manager's reporting and monitoring capabilities, the WebLogic Server (WLS) Administration Console is the central resource for configuring and deploying the application server components. We'll look at it in specific detail throughout these toolbox chapters, but for now you should know that it displays some basic availability information. Figure 7-6 shows both the top-level sidebar as well as the health monitoring page with the status of the domain, its servers, and all additional components.

# Fusion Middleware Availability

In addition to the Fusion Applications Control dashboards showing information for the pillar, product, and product family, Enterprise Manager supports the deployment structures used in WebLogic and provides equivalent dashboards at these levels as well. Just like the other dashboards, they show roll-up and summary information but also offer a quick drill-down into underlying detail to investigate problems or patterns observed. Figure 7-7 shows the top-level *Farm* dashboard, which includes access to its child domains, clusters, servers, and deployed applications simply by expanding the hierarchy. Availability information is also available from the Domain (see Figure 7-3), the Cluster, the Server (Figure 7-8), and Application deployment dashboards.

In addition to Enterprise Manager and the WebLogic Server Administration Console, the Fusion Middleware platform also provides a set of command-line tools to help you administer and configure all the core components. These are centered around the WebLogic Scripting Tool (WLST) that offers an environment for running prepackaged management utilities (including start/stop, interrogation, and configuration requests) as well as a language for developing your own custom tools.

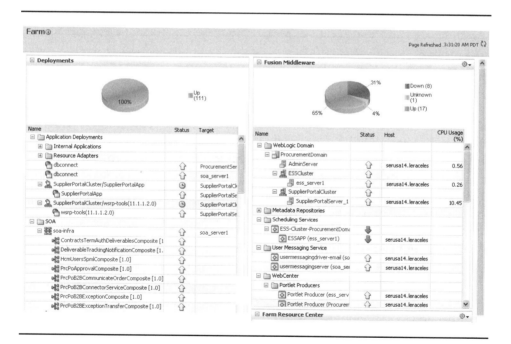

**FIGURE 7-7.** *The WLS Farm dashboard*

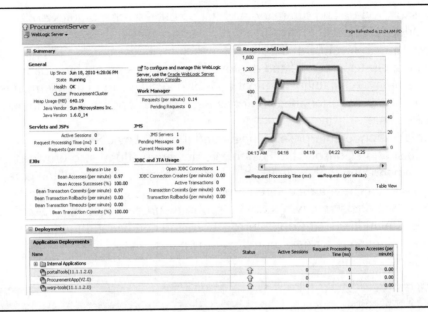

**FIGURE 7-8.** *The WLS Server dashboard*

Similarly, for those components that remain outside the WebLogic environment (such as the Oracle HTTP Server, Web Cache, and Oracle Internet Directory [OID]), the Oracle Process Manager and Notification Server (OPMN) also offers a command-line interface to perform similar actions.

Both these command-line interfaces are useful in helping you create standardized and reusable management utilities and scripts, something commonly important to traditional system administrators and therefore application managers. More detail on both of these can be found from the links in the Appendix.

Another FMw component is Oracle WebCenter. As the heart of many user interface features (such as dashboards, personalizations, and Web 2.0 features), this component needs to be available at all times. WebCenter has it own node in the WebLogic domain component hierarchy list in Fusion Applications Control and provides a basic deployment dashboard page showing availability and performance and configuration information, just like the other components.

One final mention in terms of FMw is the *Oracle Guardian*, which provides an additional diagnostic tool for managing the WebLogic Server environment. It's a generic tool that's not specific to Fusion Applications but helps to spot problematic configurations, missing patches and updates, and security and performance issues, helping avoid availability problems. It is seeded with hundreds of known problem *signature patterns* that are used to validate the system, with the results shown in its own client tool. Although this may be similar to Enterprise Manager and My Oracle Support Health Checks in purpose, its rich historical data and depth of detail means it remains a powerful source of diagnostic information for the WebLogic environment.

# Database Availability

As you've seen, the Oracle database under Fusion Applications comes with its own Enterprise Manager Control, and as such it has a dashboard similar to those provided for Fusion Applications. As shown in Figure 7-9, the dashboard displays the current database status and provides graphics and summary information on its general health and recent processing activity.

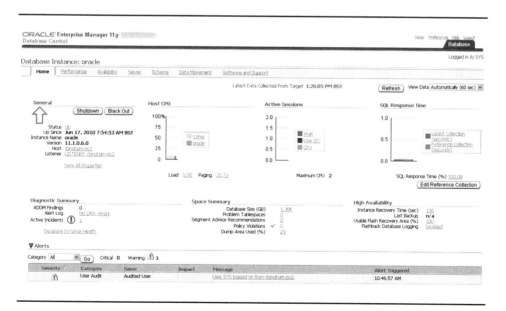

**FIGURE 7-9.** *The Database Instance Control dashboard*

Adding Grid Control enhances many of the basic features, with the enhanced alerting, reporting, and compliance very useful for managing database availability. We'll look at other detailed features in this tool as we drill into additional management sections in later chapters.

# High Availability and Backup and Recovery

Fusion Applications natively supports the Oracle Real Application Clusters (RAC) implementation of the database that provides a world-class multi-node, scalable, and fail-safe architecture. Similarly, Fusion Applications allows for the definition of multiple data sources in its WebLogic application server layer, and as such it ensures a safe and efficient switch of connections should any one specific database node fail.

As already described, the Fusion Applications middle tier supports the grouping and replication of WebLogic Servers into clusters, so that should one server hosting an application deployment fail, the others immediately handle the continued requests, causing little or no disruption.

Since Fusion Applications uses these core technology stack features, few additional considerations or factors need to be considered for high availability, and all the standard tooling (documented in the Appendix) can and should be used.

Backup and recovery is much along the same lines. The Recovery Manager (RMAN) is in the Enterprise Manager Database Control (and at the command line) and offers all the standard features required for database backup. For the middle tier, some capabilities exist in the WebLogic Administration Console and Enterprise Manager Control; however, much of the advice held in the Oracle Fusion Middleware Disaster Recovery Guide (see Appendix) is based on implementing a suitable architecture and topology, ensuring that database backups are taken, and properly managing a copy of all significant files from the file system.

# CHAPTER
8

# A Performance Management Toolbox

s the third *plan* in our Enterprise Application Management Lifecycle model, fast and responsive applications usually lead to happy, productive users and of course well-compensated application managers. Although we're used to web-based applications inevitably showing some network latency, broadband speeds are increasing such that it's often impossible to differentiate an application in an internal network from one that's provided through the Internet (about which cloud-based application providers like to brag).

Poor performance can lead to reliability and sometimes even availability issues, and tweaks and adjustments to performance actually fall under the optimization category. As such, this section is about information gathering—where to look for information about the current performance, to see if solutions or improvements are actually needed. Performance tuning is a large topic, and a substantial amount of specialist material is available for individual components (such as WebLogic and the Oracle Database), so the intention of this section is simply to illustrate the core Fusion Applications utilities and provide recommendations to help guide the applications manager in thinking in the most appropriate way, so they are aware of the basics, and where to look for more detail. Let's take a look at some of the tools in Fusion Applications used for managing performance.

# Business Process Layer

Although the performance of the application code, services, features, and functions is of course influenced by the underlying technology components, performance issues often occur due to causes unrelated to the tech-stack layers below, with the following as some common examples:

- Data model inefficiencies

- Data querying and manipulation bottlenecks

- Inefficient execution control structures used in code

- Unexpected load on specific parts of a process

- The misinterpretation of potential usage profiles and flows

- Incomplete or malformed functional structures and setups

# Product Performance

In addition to the dashboards mentioned so far, Enterprise Manager Fusion Applications Control provides corresponding performance summary information at the Product Family and Product levels, as shown in Figure 8-1, independent from the WebLogic Server or other technical components.

This transaction-based information shows how real processes are flowing through the system. As with the other summaries, the Metric Palette and Overlays allow for side-by-side comparison of performance, and in this case compare business transactions, features, and products, and not the technology components alone. This is an exceptionally powerful feature that allows end user problem reports to be immediately correlated with real system information.

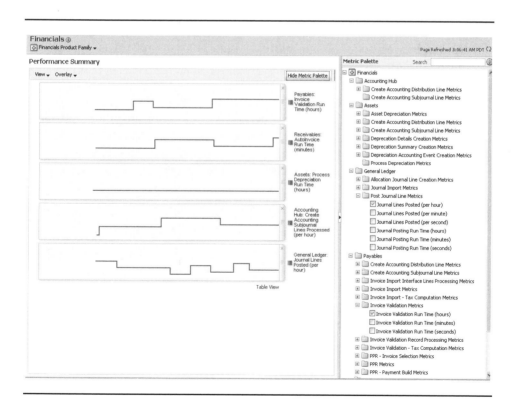

**FIGURE 8-1.**   *The Product Family Performance Summary*

Similar details are also used in Fusion Applications Control's Product Family and Product dashboards, showing their respective set of business performance information under the Key Performance Indicators. Although they don't provide huge lists or extensive reporting capabilities, it provides a window to look into the business efficiency of the processes and transactions, with examples (in addition to those shown in Figure 8-1) that include payroll runtime, sales predictor leads created, and order shipment line processing. This at-a-glance information helps to tie the software management system to its real-world business uses.

# Diagnostic Test Framework

Although the Diagnostic Test Framework (DTF) tests might not show performance information explicitly, when you're trying to understand how and why one specific application feature or transaction is performing slowly, you'll find that it often makes sense to check the high-level setup and any background data first. Transactions can contain spurious values, features can contain inconsistent configurations, dependent data may cause conflicts, and all manner of basic factors can result in an application performance issue.

For many people it's tempting to dive immediately into a technology stack investigation, especially when the system is as complex and extensive as Fusion Applications; however, when the issue is isolated, it's best that you not assume anything and that you check the basics first. In supporting applications, *framing problems* properly is vital, and the information and validation locked in the DTF tests are exceptionally helpful in doing just that.

# SOA and Business Process Execution

Many of the key business process flows in Fusion Applications are orchestrated using the Service-Oriented Architecture infrastructure (SOA-INFRA), and therefore being able to review and understand specific performance data quickly is vital, when, for example, users call to complain that a process is slow.

Each SOA-INFRA node in Enterprise Manager Control lists the composite applications that it hosts, and these directly map to the business processes, usually deployed as Business Process Execution Language (BPEL) flows. Choosing the appropriate SOA composite application instance that relates to a problem case will display several useful pages, and even the parent composite dashboard page shows average processing times.

The generic composite instance page shows a time-stamped trace of all activities that occurred. The first subpage is the mediator audit trail that shows time-stamped events, including all message transformations and communications. The second subpage is the BPEL audit trail that also includes the start time and all subsequent events (including partner-links/Web Service calls) time stamped as the flow executed.

In addition and shown in Figure 8-2, against each composite, the *Performance Summary* menu can be selected to show a graphical display of metrics. This includes both BPEL and Mediator data and offers a wide range of both standard and calculated metrics. It also allows additional metrics and graphs to be added via the *Metric Palette*, as well as more overlay datasets for comparing instances and processes on a single page.

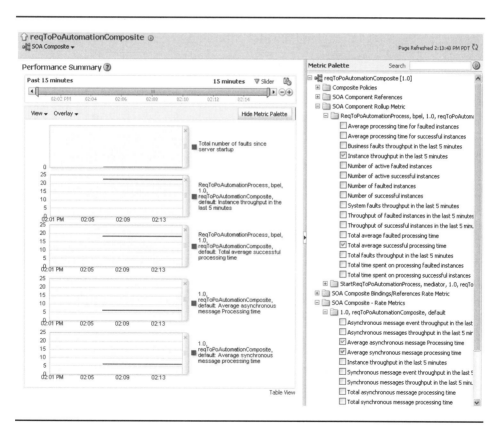

**FIGURE 8-2.** *The SOA Performance Summary*

Another important summary is the *Request Processing* page, available from the top-level SOA-INFRA menu. This shows several useful roll-ups of data, such as average request processing times, requests active and completed, and faults for each of the underlying engines that form the SOA infrastructure (that is, BPEL, Mediator, Human Workflow, and Business Rules). It also offers some interesting summary statistics on bindings, such as Web Service and Java Connector (JCA) performance.

In addition to composite and instance performance data, Event Delivery Network (EDN) performance is another vital check that helps you understand how business processes are flowing through the system. You can select the Business Events top-level menu item and then drill-down into the specific subscriptions and mediator instances of interest.

In addition, you can query some data outside of Enterprise Manager, as EDN maintains its own logs in the database, and using tables such as EDN_ LOG_MESSAGES, you can see additional detail. This kind of low-level access can be especially useful for inclusion in automated scripts and alerts.

## Business Activity

One interesting point to note is that Fusion Middleware, and the SOA Suite in particular, makes reference to Business Activity Monitoring (BAM) as the recommended method to analyze and monitor the execution of business processes. BAM offers fully customizable dashboards for viewing Key Performance Indicators (KPIs) in an intuitive graphical format. It shows business processes (mainly BPEL flows) using powerful reporting, analysis, and alerting capabilities, all based on real-time data that can be drilled into a fine level of detail when needed.

Unfortunately for us, this comprehensive tool is not fully implemented with Fusion Applications version 1.0 out of the box. So although it requires an additional effort to implement it, the usage of the SOA infrastructure all remains within standard practices and therefore all the Fusion Applications process execution data would be available for analysis in BAM.

We'll not go into more detail here, but the FMw documents in the Appendix provide detailed information on BAM and its capabilities. As an expert tool that is designed for this distinct purpose, heavy users of the BPEL process flows in Fusion Applications will no doubt reap rewards.

# Enterprise Scheduling Service

As a J2EE application itself, the ESS component is used to execute larger pieces of work either in the background of other processing or at a dedicated time, such as during a quiet period. This is similar to other batch-processing features in other applications, such as E-Business Suites' Concurrent Manager. ESS jobs are usually data-centric, querying and processing many rows, so clearly performance is a key concern. The ESS engine itself is merely a platform against which each product family can schedule the execution of its own processing programs. This means it's unlikely that performance problems will lie directly with the ESS engine, but will lie with the task it has been passed to launch.

Performance of ESS jobs can be reviewed using the Enterprise Manager Fusion Applications Control, and a dedicated dashboard provides an overview at each cluster level. This shows roll-up summaries of the longest running jobs, the number of jobs processed, the maximum and average processing time, as well as maximum and average wait times for pending jobs to get picked up. The line detail provides the request ID that can be examined to see the job definition, its source application, and the user who submitted it—all very useful for investigating performance problems.

The top-level menu also offers some *Performance Summary* reports, just like the other dashboards, and includes some extra details on current and historical activity. These same summary reports are available at the parent WebLogic Server (WLS) level, and this includes a link to access the page to query the time-stamped logs as well. Also, as shown back in Chapter 7 (see Figure 7-1), the exact same tables showing active and long-running ESS jobs are included in the Product Family dashboards, highlighting how ESS is crucial to many features and parts of business process execution.

One additional point to note regarding ESS performance is that since the content of the jobs are data-centric, standard tools such as the Database SQL Trace and the PL/SQL Profiler can be useful in getting a detailed record of the precise job activity and reconcile the observed performance with the executed code statements. As shown in Figure 6-4 in Chapter 6, both of these can be enabled by the user and will be used for all subsequent jobs they launch. (Obviously, enabling tracing can impact performance by its very nature, so this would be strictly used for troubleshooting only.)

In addition, ESS is used to schedule work that then runs in the context of one of the product J2EE applications via a callback process, and, as such, processing information such as logs and traces can be reviewed within the context of the application that hosts the work. Obviously, the ESS J2EE application itself will have its own time-stamped logs to review as well.

# Applications Technology Layer

With business features often running directly on core technology components, monitoring the performance of Fusion Applications tends to be either at the higher level, already described, or right down into the depth of each individual technology platform components. Despite this, let's touch on a few supplemental tools that can be used to enhance the performance of some of the processes at work in between.

## Business Intelligence Performance

Second only to transaction processing, the presentation of data to *information workers* is vital to the success of an enterprise application. Timely and accurate decisions cannot be made without timely and detailed information.

As mentioned in Chapter 7 (and shown in Figure 7-5), the various parts of BI in Fusion Applications have their own dedicated tools and utilities for monitoring and management. Although this is their main focus, of course they are manipulating database data; therefore, some of the other generic utilities and tools can also be useful.

Some of the Oracle Business Intelligence Enterprise Edition (OBIEE) pieces in Fusion Applications (such as OBIA and Report Wizard) leverage the underlying Essbase data-warehouse component as well. With its Extract, Transform, Load (ETL)–type processes of copying data from the transactional database tables into its own structures (such as cubes), its internal processes can demand significant time and resources. These parts are preconfigured out of the box, but they are customizable, and the application manager needs to monitor and perform optimization when required. As essentially discrete components working alongside Fusion Applications, more detail on BI Publisher, OBIEE, and data-warehouse/Essbase management is provided in the Appendix.

## SOA Performance Management

Oracle also provides additional off-the-shelf solutions for SOA management that may be of interest to apply in a Fusion Applications environment, especially for managing custom integrations and extensions to other specialist applications.

- **Oracle SOA Governance**    As you will see in Chapter 10, SOA governance tools help reduce risks and retain control of SOA development, deployment, and management. This includes support for rules, approvals, and policy management, as well as extensive configuration and change management.

- **Oracle Enterprise Repository (OER)**    OER helps manage and publish web service metadata for better control and reuse. OER is already part of the Fusion Applications technology stack.

- **SOA Management Tools**    Leveraging the acquired AmberPoint tools, Oracle will continue to develop these extensive visualization and performance-management solutions that work across the complete SOA environment.

- **Enterprise Manager Packs**    Solutions such as Real User Experience Insight (RUEI) have exceptionally powerful performance management capabilities, including Service Level Agreement (SLA) capabilities that help embed some IT Service Management (ITSM) best practices and concepts. Also, the SOA Management Pack includes tools such as Composite Application Monitor and Modeler (CAMM, originally acquired as ClearApp), a tool that provides extensive modeling and performance information for SOA.

# Platform Layer

If the platform is slow, almost everything that depends on it will be slow. This is not, however, a common reality. It's usually the pieces that sit on top of the platform that ask it to work in a way that presents a challenge, either by exhausting the resources it has available or by using conflicting or unsuitable instructions. Let's look at a few of the platform pieces and see how we can monitor and manage their performance.

# More Fusion Middleware Performance

We've already looked at performance for SOA, BI, and ESS. In a later section you'll learn about WebLogic Server performance. So what is left? Quite a bit, actually.

## The Web Server

The initial entry point for most requests is the HTTP web server, and under certain circumstances, it can run into problems that might degrade performance, both from unexpected high load and lack of efficient request processing. Fusion Applications Control (under the Web Tier folder) offers yet another dashboard and Performance Summary for reviewing the performance of the Oracle HTTP Server (OHS), showing request processing load and response times, throughput, as well as CPU and memory use.

Similarly Oracle Web Cache, which manages the reuse of pages and components, has a dashboard page in Fusion Applications Control with the same Performance Summary feature and its own set of metrics for adding and comparing.

## Application Development Framework

Because much of the basic application logic is closely associated to its ADF pages, let's review some of the performance options here as well. In the context of an individual application deployment on a WebLogic Server, Fusion Applications Control offers an *ADF Performance* menu item. The resulting page has two tabs, one showing performance data for the application modules (AMs) currently being used by the application, and the second showing the familiar Performance Summary charts, but for showing throughput and request processing time based on the active task flows. Although basic, when it's coupled with the detailed ADF log, this performance data is very helpful in diagnosing at which layer of processing a page performance problem may lie.

## WebCenter

Many pages also contain Oracle WebCenter components, and fortunately reviewing performance of this piece is similar. WebCenter is also associated with individual J2EE application deployments, and therefore Portlet Producer performance monitoring is the same as any deployed application would be, using the generic dashboard and the Performance Summary in Enterprise Manager features again. For WebCenter Spaces, however, the Application Deployment menu has an extra option to view Service Metrics. This provides a range of basic performance information for each of its features, including lists, notes, and instant messaging and presence.

## Security

Another important component of FMw is security, and it's vital that the solutions under Oracle Identity Management perform acceptably for use in Fusion Applications. Enterprise Manager's Fusion Applications Control contains the option to manage both Oracle Internet Directory (OID) and Oracle Virtual Directory (OVD) and offers the same Performance Summary feature with a wide range of Lightweight Directory Access Protocol (LDAP) metrics, including request and response times, processing details, and connectivity information, all accessible via the Metric Palette. This time, the information is available from the parent Administration menu since it applies to the whole of the FMw installation.

## Web Services

Although we've already seen a few metrics showing Web Services, for example, within SOA, it's worth explicitly mentioning that Fusion Applications Control provides several other methods to show performance information. These are viewable from the *WebServices* item in the parent menu (in the same place as the Performance Summary), and can be shown for either a WebLogic Server or for one individual application deployment.

Figure 8-3 shows an example for one WLS server. As you can see, the endpoints can be clicked to get more detail, an example of which is shown in Figure 8-4. You'll notice useful items including the Web Service Definition Language (WSDL) document, the implementation class, all Web Services operations, some charts showing faults and security violations, and the detailed configuration used. This page is especially useful because it also offers links to launch additional pages for further investigation, including message and diagnostic log searches.

As already discussed, by implementing Enterprise Manager Grid Control, you can find more features with highlights for performance regarding alerts and notifications, historic reporting, SLAs and service monitoring, and configuration management. Again, since it's not part of Fusion Applications out of the box, we'll not go into more detail.

⬆ ProcurementServer ⓘ
▢ WebLogic Server ▾                                                              Page Refreshed :2:54:48 AM PDT ↻

**Web Services** ⓘ
Attach Policies link to the right lets you attach policies to Oracle Infrastructure Web Services, ADF Data Connections, SOA Components, SOA Services, and SOA References.

| Java EE | **Oracle Infrastructure Web Services** | | | | |

| Web Service Name | Application Nar⇲ ▽ | Endpoint Name | Invocation Completed | Response Time (sec) | Total Faults |
|---|---|---|---|---|---|
| PurchasingNextUniqueIdentifierMigratorService | ProcurementApp(V2 | PurchasingNextUniq | 0 | 0 | 0 |
| ReqApprovalService | ProcurementApp(V2 | ReqApprovalService | 55 | 0.071 | 0 |
| PurchasingHazardClassesMigratorService | ProcurementApp(V2 | PurchasingHazardCl | 0 | 0 | 0 |
| SetupReqBuOptionService | ProcurementApp(V2 | SetupReqBuOptionS | 0 | 0 | 0 |
| WSRP_v1_Service | wsrp-tools(11.1.1.2 | WSRPServiceDescrip | 0 | 0 | 0 |
| ApprovalService | ProcurementApp(V2 | ApprovalServiceSoa | 82 | 0.028 | 1 |
| ReqToPoAutomationService | ProcurementApp(V2 | ReqToPoAutomatior | 171 | 0.002 | 6 |
| CreateReqService | ProcurementApp(V2 | CreateReqServiceSc | 10 | 0.119 | 0 |
| PurchasingUnNumberMigratorService | ProcurementApp(V2 | PurchasingUnNumbe | 0 | 0 | 0 |
| NegotiationNotificationService | ProcurementApp(V2 | NegotiationNotificati | 8 | 0.139 | 0 |
| WSRP_v2_Service | wsrp-tools(11.1.1.2 | WSRP_v2_Registrat | 0 | 0 | 0 |
| NegotiationTermsMigratorService | ProcurementApp(V2 | NegotiationTermsMi | 0 | 0 | 0 |
| SourcingCostFactorListMigratorService | ProcurementApp(V2 | SourcingCostFactorL | 0 | 0 | 0 |
| PurchasingDocumentStylesMigratorService | ProcurementApp(V2 | PurchasingDocumen | 0 | 0 | 0 |
| RegistrationsApprovalService | ProcurementApp(V2 | RegistrationsApprov | 0 | 0 | 0 |
| WSRP_v2_Service | wsrp-tools(11.1.1.2 | WSRP_v2_Markup_' | 0 | 0 | 0 |
| PurchaseAgreementService | ProcurementApp(V2 | PurchaseAgreement | 0 | 0 | 0 |
| PurchasingLineTypeMigratorService | ProcurementApp(V2 | PurchasingLineTypeI | 0 | 0 | 0 |
| WSRP_v2_Service | wsrp-tools(11.1.1.2 | WSRP_v2_ServiceD | 0 | 0 | 0 |

**FIGURE 8-3.** *Web Services performance summary information*

# WebLogic Server Performance

Just like the dashboards and performance information for the SOA infrastructure (see Figure 8-2) and for ESS, each of the clusters and individual WebLogic servers represented in Enterprise Manager has an equivalent dashboard. This is shown in Figure 8-5 and includes all the details of current activity within that server, including load, memory and CPU usage, and response times for all the various executing components. Like the other dashboards, it also shows Performance Summary graphs with respective Metric Palette and Overlay options.

In addition, the WebLogic Server dashboard menu has an option for showing Java virtual machine (JVM) performance, and, as shown in Figure 8-6, it provides basic detail on the health of the underlying Java platform. Charts of memory use profiles, along with details on the class loader and threads, provide a useful summary of performance. This page also includes the option to create a thread dump, again a useful tool for investigating current activity.

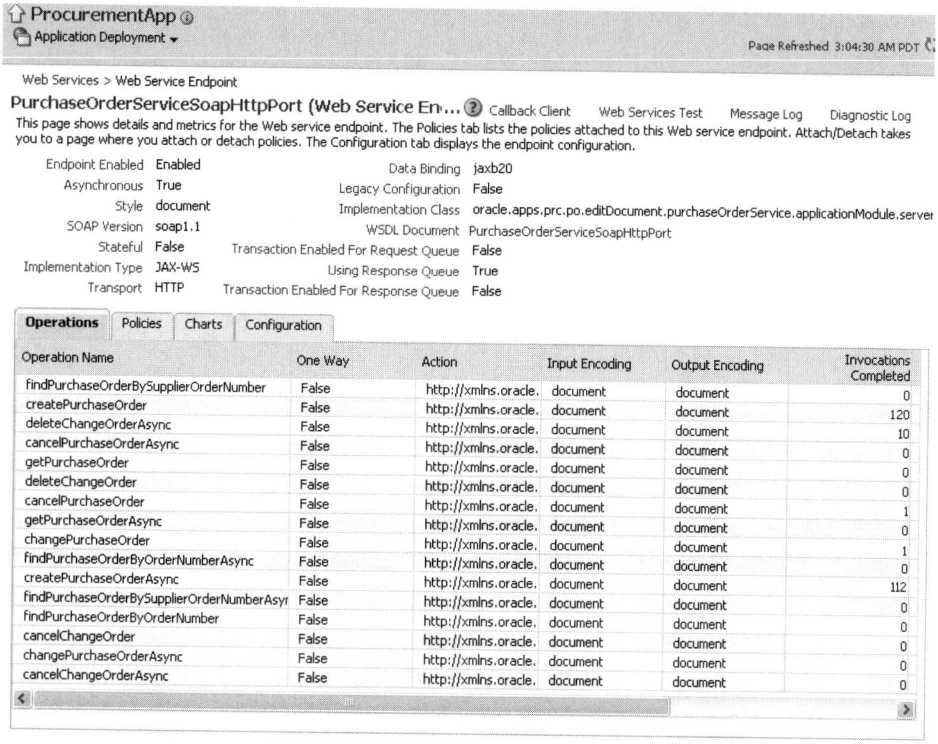


| Operation Name | One Way | Action | Input Encoding | Output Encoding | Invocations Completed |
|---|---|---|---|---|---|
| findPurchaseOrderBySupplierOrderNumber | False | http://xmlns.oracle. | document | document | 0 |
| createPurchaseOrder | False | http://xmlns.oracle. | document | document | 120 |
| deleteChangeOrderAsync | False | http://xmlns.oracle. | document | document | 10 |
| cancelPurchaseOrderAsync | False | http://xmlns.oracle. | document | document | 0 |
| getPurchaseOrder | False | http://xmlns.oracle. | document | document | 0 |
| deleteChangeOrder | False | http://xmlns.oracle. | document | document | 0 |
| cancelPurchaseOrder | False | http://xmlns.oracle. | document | document | 1 |
| getPurchaseOrderAsync | False | http://xmlns.oracle. | document | document | 0 |
| changePurchaseOrder | False | http://xmlns.oracle. | document | document | 1 |
| findPurchaseOrderByOrderNumberAsync | False | http://xmlns.oracle. | document | document | 0 |
| createPurchaseOrderAsync | False | http://xmlns.oracle. | document | document | 112 |
| findPurchaseOrderBySupplierOrderNumberAsyr | False | http://xmlns.oracle. | document | document | 0 |
| findPurchaseOrderByOrderNumber | False | http://xmlns.oracle. | document | document | 0 |
| cancelChangeOrder | False | http://xmlns.oracle. | document | document | 0 |
| changePurchaseOrderAsync | False | http://xmlns.oracle. | document | document | 0 |
| cancelChangeOrderAsync | False | http://xmlns.oracle. | document | document | 0 |

**FIGURE 8-4.** *Web Services performance detail information*

The WebLogic Server Administration Console contains a Monitoring tab for each server, under which the Health page shows details for each deployed application. This can be seen back in Chapter 7 in Figure 7-6. The information shown also includes clickable links that show even more detailed status and configuration. WebLogic Scripting Tool (WLST) commands can also be used to interrogate an equivalent list of performance metrics as part of command-line scripting that can be built into reports and custom tools.

One final WebLogic tool is Oracle Guardian, which contains substantial information and diagnostic content relevant to monitoring and troubleshooting of the WebLogic Server performance. The Appendix has much more detail.

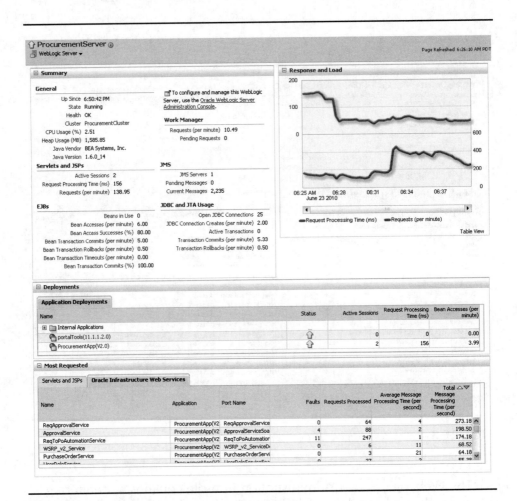

**FIGURE 8-5.** *The Enterprise Manager WebLogic Server dashboard*

# Core Java Performance

Although you've seen some useful J2EE performance metrics in Enterprise Manager Application Control, this is not the only source of information about how well this central execution environment is running the tasks it is asked to complete. Let's take a look at two more tools that can provide greater depth and detail, and although it might be argued that some of this might be somewhat beyond the scope of the Application Manager role, it's all useful diagnostic information.

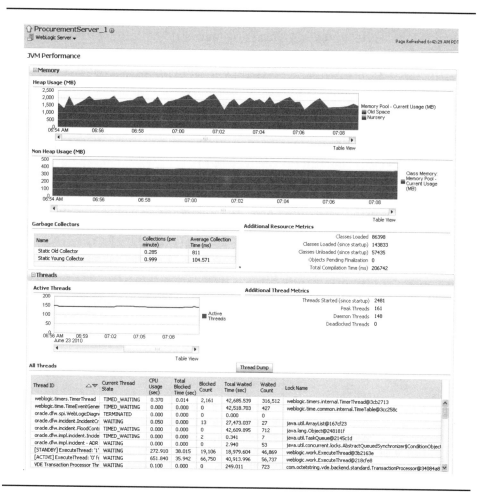

**FIGURE 8-6.** *The JVM Performance page*

# The Dynamic Monitoring Service

The Dynamic Monitoring Service (DMS) comes as part of Fusion Middleware, and therefore naturally part of Fusion Applications. This tool offers application developers a way to embed monitoring and performance metric collection within their product code and components, so that compliant applications are much more supportable. Although Fusion Applications product code itself is not actually using DMS, the components in FMw upon which they run (the technology stack) are DMS-aware, and as such substantial amounts of extra information is collected and made available.

The best (a.k.a. easiest) method for reviewing DMS metrics is to use the prepackaged servlet known as *DMS Spy* (accessed by adding */dms/Spy* to the end of your server's hostname and port number). This offers a very simple web interface for browsing tables of performance metrics. Figure 8-7 shows the wide range of available metrics in the left pane, including those specific to DMS, to WebLogic Server, and a combination of the two. The main pane shows a JVM summary, with specific information about the current status of ADF components, JDBC connections, and thread and memory use, all of which are vital for deeper performance analysis.

In addition, the same DMS metric table information is available through the use of Jython script commands. You can also dump (export) this data to a file, either using an explicit Java API or Enterprise Managers' Support Workbench, since DMS metrics are included in packaged Diagnostic Framework (DFw) and Fusion Applications incidents (see earlier). More details on using DMS is provided in the "Oracle Fusion Middleware Performance and Tuning Guide" listed in the Appendix.

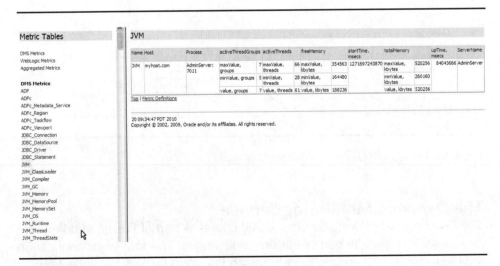

**FIGURE 8-7.** *The DMS Spy metrics page*

## JRockit Mission Control

The second Java-specific tool originates from the WebLogic/BEA technology stack and is especially designed to offer superior management for the high-performance JVM distribution known as JRockit. The tool is known as *Mission Control* and, along with JVM monitoring, it offers focused diagnostics for reducing both memory leaks and application latency. One of its key benefits is that it is architected in such a way as to be nonintrusive, meaning the overhead of running it is very small, making it suitable for use in many production environments.

Mission Control provides not only real-time information as top-level dashboards, with graphs and gauges to help you spot trends and exceptions, but it also offers a range of capabilities that allow you to drill into more and more depth when tracing through one specific component or data point, right down to the methods within a class. It also lets you capture data via a *flight recorder*, meaning that the full metrics and activities for a specific time period can be saved to a file and then imported again later for detailed diagnosis.

Although it is not natively part of the tools bundled with Fusion Applications, JRockit Mission Control comes with either the Enterprise Manager Diagnostics Pack for Fusion Middleware or standalone as part of the larger WebLogic Management Suites.

## More Java Tools

Although I said I'd mention only two tools here, it would be remiss not to mention at least two more helpful utilities. The first, Real User Experience Insight (RUEI) (see Figure 6-6 earlier), was mentioned in terms of SOA performance; however, this tool also includes lower level JVM and networking information as well, and these metrics can of course be used in its advanced tracing and alerting capabilities.

The second tool is one we have not mentioned so far. The *Oracle Application Diagnostics for Java (AD4J)* has pretty much the same purpose and provides many equivalent features of Mission Control. On the surface, it's perhaps not quite as feature-rich as Mission Control, and it's also not JVM-specific and includes more focus on linking information across tiers, particularly to/from the Oracle database.

Clearly, many of these tools are add-ons to the existing performance management capabilities already included in Fusion Applications, however their exceptionally powerful and comprehensive capabilities make them popular. It could be argued that the majority of use cases for these tools involve tuning home-grown applications, and a prepackaged application should already be optimized, but the flexible nature of Fusion Applications in terms of deployment architectures and usage options mean these tools may well have a place at the center of many management implementations.

# Database Performance Management

Enough material has been written about this topic to keep even the most fervent DBA happy. As such, we'll briefly cover a few core tools and resources that are especially relevant for checking database performance within Fusion Applications. None of these tools are actually Fusion Applications–specific, since although each leverages many of the advanced capabilities of the database, it does so in a standard way, allowing all existing knowledge and tooling to be applied.

Figure 8-8 shows the Performance tab in the Enterprise Manager Database Control, which provides substantial amounts of real-time information on throughput, performance, and resource utilization. Highlights here include the top-level CPU and active session graphs that can be compared with logons and transactions, and even disk I/O, parallel processing, and internal service execution. It also includes a range of links, with useful things such as viewing blocks, hangs, and locks, plus more general information such as the Top Activity page that shows active sessions, the most expensive queries, and the most active modules, clients, actions, objects, and PL/SQL.

In addition to basic real-time information, the 11*g* Database contains two core elements that work together to provide detailed performance diagnostics. The first is the *Automatic Workflow Repository* (AWR), a source of performance information that the system itself collects and maintains, with very little overhead or manual interference required. Working with this is the *Automatic Database Diagnostics Monitor* (ADDM), an analysis tool that has in-built intelligence via its *classification tree* and works to spot performance concerns early and to offer solutions with enough detail to show the precise benefits from their use. These almost self-diagnostic capabilities also extend to Real Application Clusters (RAC) implementations, where the wider complexity and detailed configuration are often prime candidates for fine-tuning.

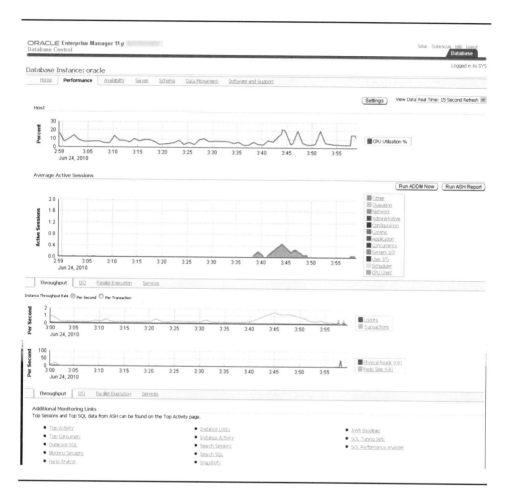

**FIGURE 8-8.**   *The Performance tab in Enterprise Manager Database Control*

Another performance tool that stores its data in AWR is the *Active Session History* (ASH) sampler. This data has a corresponding diagnostic report that shows details for all active sessions over a specified period of time. Information such as SQL identifiers, object-file-block numbers, wait identifiers, and module name are helpful as reference information that can be used to dig deeper. ASH is especially useful when you're analyzing transient performance issues that relate to one session, or while performing detailed analysis of one short time slot. Figure 8-8 also shows two buttons for immediately launching ADDM and ASH, although they also form part of the automated performance diagnostic capabilities available (see the Appendix).

Many more tools are available in the database to measure, analyze, and diagnose performance (such as Real Application Testing), but we're discussing this in the context of a prepackage application that should have its SQL already optimized. Many of the more detailed tools are intended for debugging custom written SQL and data manipulation code, and whilst useful for customizations they fall outside the scope of managing Fusion Applications.

# Logging, Tracing, and Other Utilities

The various dashboards, metric collections, and diagnostic utilities available to support Fusion Applications often support only the more traditional need to collect and analyze system output. With so many moving parts, each spooling output of one kind or another, it's not always easy to pinpoint the best information sources. Although Enterprise Manager's log query feature includes many data sources, let's run through a few more basics resources, with particular reference to performance.

- **The WebLogic and ADF logs**   Enabling additional logging verbosity for these components provides more execution process detail that can be used to track execution speed.

- **Fusion Applications Diagnostic Logging**   Similarly as applications code logs more lines, the ODL time stamp can be used to track the execution flow between code objects and spot slow areas.

- **SQL Tracing and PL/SQL Profiler**   Turning on SQL Trace for application user sessions (via the menu) creates trace files that are rich with performance information for all subsequent data manipulation. The PL/SQL Profiler offers a performance report of database activity over the time period for which it's enabled.

- **Trace analysis**   At the lowest level, the raw data in trace files can be used by various diagnostic utilities to expand the resulting reports to provide more depth of information in a format that is more consumable. Examples include the *TKProf* program and *Trace Analyzer* script (trcanlzr.sql), as well as utilities to diagnose individual statements such as the *Enhanced Explain Plan* script (sqltxplain.sql).

- **Operating system tools**   All enterprise operating systems come with tools and utilities for monitoring the performance of the services they provide, and most are more advanced than the simple yet effective **TOP** command used in UNIX/LINUX systems. We've already seen how some of this information (such as CPU use) is offered in tools such as Enterprise Manager, and indeed some of this depth might be closer to the system administrators' areas of expertise; however, access and use of basic platform information must be available so the applications manager has a complete performance picture, and so that his or her first action is the right one (even if it's just calling the SysAdmin).

- **Hardware and networking tools**   In the same way that operating system performance basics should be available to the applications manager, he or she should also be able to interrogate the health of the firewalls, proxy servers, switches, routers, and all other equipment (both hardware and software) that sit between the application host nodes and the end users. Without this, great amounts of time can be wasted searching for application issues when a simple network bottleneck is the cause. When all members of the IT department play nicely together, everyone wins.

# CHAPTER
## 9

# An Optimization
# Management Toolbox

s discussed in Chapter 3, optimization management involves three core goals: better productivity (do more), more efficient operations (cost less), and new business insights (improve). The achievement of these is based on several tasks, including process improvement and development projects, configuration and customization management, and improved resource and supplier administration. So how do these goals and the tasks to achieve them result from using tools to manage Fusion Applications? Let's take a look.

# Business Process Layer

Optimization, like the others plans before it, can be accomplished at the various levels of Fusion Applications, starting with this highest level, the one that's closest to the business operations themselves. Optimization requirements frequently stem from this level, since the needs of the business and its end users originate many of the demands the application manager faces. Although some of these demands will be technical in implementation—faster response time, for example—many more will be concerned with extending and adjusting features so that they better support the organization's business tasks. As such, Fusion Applications sits at the center of the business and it's contribution can be greatly enhanced by a range of tools, services, and built-in capabilities that support all types of optimization.

Although the following items are not necessarily supported by tooling, the Application Manager should establish clear targets, processes, and procedures for the following types of optimization:

- **Business process execution**   The most important and most used processes should be regularly reviewed to ensure that they are as efficient as possible. This should include the development and implementation of any requested extensions, enhancements, and improvements to those processes.

- **Application and IT management process**   Most organizations regularly change and adopt new management capabilities and best practice methodologies (such as Information Technology Infrastructure Library [ITIL]) and this needs careful monitoring as an improvement project. The application manager may be involved in a detailed project or may simply be required to ensure his or her part of the IT operation is fully compliant.

- **Implementation adjustments**   Commonly, the implementation of an enterprise application contains aspects that, when finally applied in the live production operation, produce results that are unsuitable or not quite as intended. As such, constant fine-tuning will occur, and although most post-production changes fall into the category of Change and Configuration Management, some reference back to the implementation model is required to ensure that the same mistakes are not repeated.

# BPEL and BPM

The Oracle Business Process Management (BPM) Suite is the overall set of applications and capabilities for modeling and deploying business process flows, implemented as Service-Oriented Architecture (SOA) Composite applications in Fusion Middleware. Its integrated BPM Studio tool offers a complete development environment, fully compliant with JDeveloper, and using open standard Business Process Modeling Notation, BPMN 2.0. Here the building blocks for processes are constructed and these can be arranged in a collaborative fashion with business domain experts using the BPM Process Composer, a web-based process editing environment.

Although Fusion Applications v1.0 does not come with BPM Suite as standard, it is easily set up to extend and enhance the standard process flows either to match existing requirements or deliver additional business capabilities. Obviously, you should be careful to ensure that invasive customizations do not add much management overhead; however, since BPM Suite natively uses the Metadata Services (MDS) repository for implementation, all extensions can be made to comply with the appropriate Fusion Applications recommendations (see the extensibility guide mentioned in the Appendix).

# Oracle Enterprise Repository

Although process flows might be adjusted using the BPM Suite, fully extending the features and functions available usually requires additional programming. It's recommended that you compliment the existing architecture by using Web Services for such additional programs, and to help, Fusion Applications comes with the Oracle Enterprise Repository (OER), which acts as a registry for all existing services and related information. This resource promotes the reuse of existing code when and where appropriate, and in many cases, existing services can perform the operations and actions needed in new business process flows, meaning less coding, cost (time, money, effort), complexity, and ultimately management overhead.

In addition, as previously mentioned, the OER solution offers a source of information that is invaluable in creating integrations to and from Fusion Applications, and again making this work easier, simpler, and therefore more effective. Figure 9-1 shows examples of the kinds of information available, including Web Service Definition Language (WSDL) location, code files, method details, and features to search for and graphically display related services.

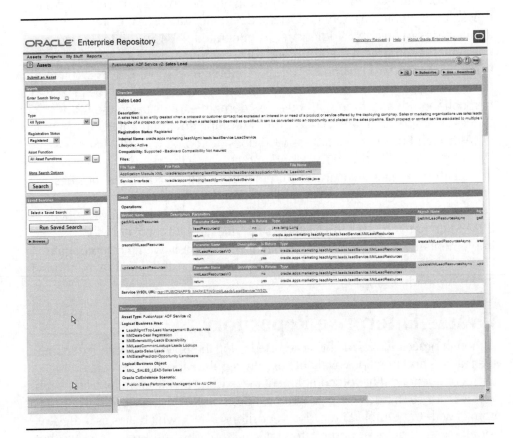

**FIGURE 9-1.**   *The Oracle Enterprise Repository*

Organizational resources are used more efficiently thanks to the information and features in OER, and process improvements are more effective and easier to manage. The OER runtime that can be used to add custom objects is also available as a configurable plug-in for JDeveloper, Eclipse, as well as other common Java integrated development environments (IDEs).

# Configuration and Data Optimization

A couple of tools are worth considering (and revisiting) in the context of optimization management, because they provide you with simple and effective ways to access and review both the configuration and core transactional data in use in the application.

## The Diagnostic Test Framework

Although the Diagnostic Test Framework (DTF) tests might not immediately be categorized under the heading of optimization, their use in certain recommended practices can provide beneficial results. Consider two simple examples that illustrate the point. (Every organization works in different ways, and, as such, there may well be even more circumstances in which they're useful.)

First, many of the processes within Fusion Applications are used to manage daily business operations, such as reviewing the demand and supply of products and services. Although, hopefully, the majority of this works seamlessly, at some points in the organizational lifecycle, significant events require the execution of processes that are outside the routine, and these are usually exceptionally important but also commonly large and complex. Simple examples might be inventory counts (stock-take), financial period end reconciliations, and mergers and acquisitions. Although Fusion Applications supports all of these events and tasks, it is recommended that you perform due-diligence on the system setup and its data before such significant sections of work are initiated, and this is where DTF tests can be exceptionally helpful. I have often seen how expensive downstream problems could have been avoided by some basic initial validations. Indeed, the DTF architecture itself even permits the registration of home-grown tests that organizations can develop to meet any of their own unique requirements.

Second, in efforts to optimize process flows (such as order capture), DTF tests can be used to provide the information that is needed to analyze precisely where adjustments and improvements might be made. Configuration tuning is common in general software management, but for enterprise applications it's also important that organizations engage in focused efforts to review business process setups as well, since this helps drive optimizations at the higher level too.

### Functional Setup Manager

Along the same lines, in addition to DTF tests, Functional Setup Manager provides another useful tool to allow you to review the application setup looking for optimization opportunities. This offers two useful insights—in understanding the relationships and tasks involved in a business process or product implementation, and in actually being able to review (and export) the actual values in use. Adjusting and comparing values is therefore made much easier and the productivity of such optimization work is much higher.

## Proactive Support

We have already mentioned a few parts of the Oracle Support service, such as Oracle Configuration Manager and My Oracle Support's Health Recommendation features, and although it's easy to dismiss these, their sole purpose is to provide information that is either an advisory from Oracle or, most valuable of all, from the experience of other organizations using the exact same products. Many of these features are based on product and process setups, and they ensure that the configurations used are complete, accurate, and roughly fit-for-purpose, although for flexible enterprise applications this can depend wildly on each implementation.

In addition, the My Oracle Support tool provides other information sources that should be regularly checked for optimization opportunities. This comes in many flavors, but it's generally good practice to keep abreast of alerts and articles and also make sure the following published items are not missed:

- Solutions to common mistakes and known problems

- Patch advice and recommendations, based on OCM data

- FAQs and usage recommendations

- Details on new and forthcoming features, updates, and patches for use in planning

- New and updated tools for gathering key information, such as Remote Diagnostic Agent (RDA)

- New Oracle services that may resolve serious issues or offer improvements that significantly outweigh the costs. Advanced Customer Services (ACS), Oracle Consulting, and Oracle OnDemand are constantly offering new services, many of which can be tailored to suit individual needs.

In addition, a large proportion of valuable knowledge comes in the form of documentation, training, and notes with hints and tips on management, monitoring, extending, and even on optimizing features and processes.

Finally, using information and services from Oracle helps you strengthen the ties and relationships with this key supplier of IT infrastructure, and although some shy away from dependency, with a close understanding of its vision, goals, and future directions, you can make suitable provisions so that plans are somewhat synchronized, productivity and specialization maximized (such as outsourcing), and the value returned from the investments are continuously strengthened.

# Applications Technology Layer

So how can the applications-specific technology components be optimized? Unlike the pieces in the platform below, it's not only about pure configuration and resources; however, it's also not quite as simple as applying specific tools, as with most business process optimization. Similar to all of these toolboxes, the applications technology sits between the two and its optimization is logically a mixture of tools and configurations.

## Extending Features

Many (if not all) organizations will want to adjust and extend the standard features in Fusion Applications. As already mentioned, the existing flexible configuration options are certainly the first place to look for potential improvement options; however, sometimes the scope of what's possible as standard still doesn't quite meet the need. Fortunately, Fusion Applications provides tools and architectures to ensure that extensibility and customization is more straightforward and manageable than ever before.

## Personalization

At the top level, the application itself has many capabilities of which end users should be aware, and it may be up to the application manager to share this information. There are basic features within personalization, such as saved searches, where with just one click the user can save a useful query helps them avoid having to rekey complex combinations of criteria in the advanced search pages. Even simple things such as resizing regions and page components, hiding frames and portlets, and setting up standard preferences can result in significant productivity improvements for frequent application users.

## WebCenter

At the next level down, Oracle WebCenter provides many of the advanced user interface features in Fusion Applications, and it has its own set of development, configuration, and management options. WebCenter Composer is the development environment, offering declarative and easy-to-use page customization capabilities in a friendly browser-based tool. WebCenter itself runs as a set of J2EE applications and as such its management is done through Enterprise Manager Fusion Applications Control. Each of the WebCenter WebLogic servers (portal, spaces, and services) can be reported on in terms of configuration and performance, for their own potential optimization.

## Metadata Services

As described in Chapter 2, the implementation of most extensions is accomplished through the services provided by the Metadata Services (MDS) repository. This uses the layering approach to apply all custom changes over a stable version of the original standard product. The MDS platform exists in the context of a WebLogic Server domain and its data is stored in the database into a specific *partition* (that is, schema) using a tool known as the *Repository Creation Utility (RCU)*. The Enterprise Manager Fusion Applications Control offers tools for creating and administering the MDS repositories and partitions, although these are set up automatically during installation and provisioning and shouldn't be changed without expert assistance. As an internal system component, the RCU should not require great amounts of optimization; however, where customizations seem to slow performance, you may need to investigate RCU and MDS further.

Troubleshooting problems related to extension can be done using multiple sources, including the Oracle WebCenter Composer and items such as database performance information, the configuration and use of MDS caching, and the use of MDS purging. In addition to these, some general utilities have extended support for MDS, including some WebLogic Scripting Tool (WLST) commands, some Java MBeans (available via Enterprise Manager's MBean Browser), and the Dynamic Monitoring System (DMS) used by Fusion Middleware to provide tuning and diagnostic information.

For some Fusion Applications products (CRM, mainly in version 1.0), extension and personalization play a big part, and as such some tools actually exist within the application itself that help create, implement, and manage new features. Customization Manager is a component that allows application-specific extensions to the task and process flows of the application, without resorting to using the generic development tools that for many users and requirements is simply overkill. This allows business users to embed their expertise and knowledge into the product itself and much more easily optimize its performance and productivity, instead of having to wait for nonbusiness software developers to translate and code-in sets of complex requirements. The other obvious tool that is provided for working with MDS is JDeveloper, and using its dedicated role (Fusion Applications Customization), you can apply custom changes and remove specific MDS layers, providing an effective way to determine the impact of personalization and customization.

# Business Intelligence

Apart from improving the performance of reporting and of its graphic-based business analysis tools, you can also optimize Fusion Applications by extending its reporting capabilities. Fusion Applications provides various Oracle Business Intelligence Enterprise Edition (OBIEE) and BI Publisher tools for both adjusting embedded and integrated reporting, as well as the Report Wizard for full custom report creation.

Clearly, for effective use, the application manager needs to make sure the appropriate people have suitable access, suitable tooling, and of course the right skills. This is an exceptionally important opportunity, since with the right ingredients, significant business insights can be derived from application data, and it's often up to the application manager to put the right tools in the right hands from both the business and IT to make it happen.

## Applications Configuration

Although we mentioned this earlier in the context of the DTF, the components and services that make up the application features can be tweaked and adjusted to try to squeeze every last drop of efficiency out of them. Normally, it's not recommended that you change too many of the default settings for an out-of-the-box Enterprise Application environment, but I know the outside world works slightly differently. Firstly, I know all DBAs, SysAdmins, and application managers will be interested in all the settings that exist within the application and its technology stack, and they will spend time tinkering in test instances to see what happens when the dials are turned (the same curiosity used in taking a toy apart to see how it works when you were a child, albeit hopefully less destructive this time). Secondly, Fusion Applications is a lot less of an application-specific technology stack than its predecessors, with most components running fairly independent of each other, and as such they can occasionally be tweaked without unforeseen impacts. With diligence, testing, validation against certification, and similar prudent checks, you can make some significant optimization, especially for those implementations that differ from the expected standard (such as those that are especially large or distributed).

In terms of tools, for the majority of these, Enterprise Manager Control offers the easiest way to review the configurations being used, and it includes some basic configuration capabilities for such things as the Enterprise Scheduling Service (ESS). The primary configuration tool for the Fusion Applications middleware environment is the WebLogic Administration Console, and as shown in Figure 9-2, the number of configuration options (tabs) is very broad. Specific configurations can be adjusted at various levels, including the server, cluster, and domain, and even for individual application deployments.

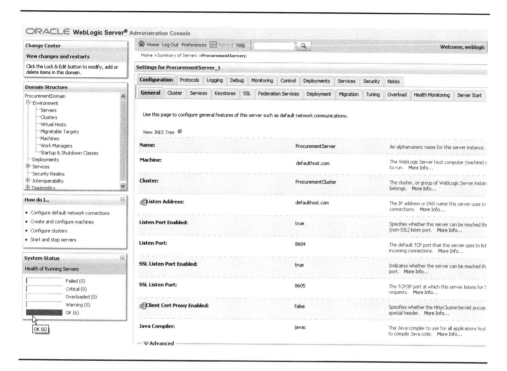

**FIGURE 9-2.** *Detailed configuration in WebLogic Server Administration Console*

# Platform Layer

The goal for optimization is to deliver contributions that help achieve organizational objectives and improvements. You've already seen how improving business processes can immediately affect the application users, helping to reduce complexity and increase capabilities, productivity, and business insights. In addition, the core parts of the software platform can also contribute in their own way as well. It's important to always bear in mind the overall objectives, since technical experts often dig into complex software systems without a clear vision of what they're trying to accomplish and how that affects the actual business operation. The applications manager must marry these two sides together to ensure technical work adds business value that is very clearly highlighted.

An interesting work redefinition occurs when we consider optimization at the platform technology layer. With complex execution and processing systems involved, and the introduction of engineering disciplines from related hardware components, all the optimization efforts (tweaks and adjustments) can be categorized under a new name: *tuning.* Since performance represents a significant area for potential optimization at this level, this certainly does seem an appropriate term.

# Database Optimization Tools

In addition to being the central repository of transaction data, the database also holds business intelligence data, metadata such as MDS, and code objects such as PL/SQL packages. As such it understandably represents the most common target for application optimization. Let's take a look at some core areas for consideration.

## Data Management

How can we optimize the actual data in the system? Obviously, the database has its own tools and processes for indexing and maintaining internal system metadata (such as the data dictionary), and part of the basic care of the application would be to ensure that these tools are either automatically run or regularly reviewed and acted upon as needed.

Recall the Chapter 4 discussion of the Information Lifecycle Management (ILM) model that helps organizations improve the effectiveness of their data storage, with a view toward cost reduction. Tools such as Master Data Management (MDM) applications can be especially useful in this area, and even the standard archive and purging features within Fusion Applications should be effectively employed to ensure that data storage is properly optimized.

In addition to transactional data, large sets of data are copied to secondary OLAP-type repositories (e.g., Essbase) via the Extract, Transform and Load (ETL) process for analysis and reporting. This workload is another optimization candidate, since it can include huge volumes of data and as this scales out, the resources required to refresh such data sets become significant. In addition, sometimes the value added for each new data field becomes negative, since too much data can actually dilute important values, trends, and patterns, making the end result actually more difficult to consume and interpret. Carefully reviewing this with stakeholders from the business operation ensures that just the right amount of data is used.

## Optimizing Database Configuration

Chapter 8 discussed various performance tools for the database and how these can be used to get a good picture of its current operation. Obviously, this is just one step away from actually making an appropriate change based on what is observed—that is, actually performing the optimization. Clearly, you need reasonable expertise to know how to translate any evidence of suboptimal (or untuned) performance into an effective adjustment. The following areas represent a few of the most common topics for database optimization consideration:

- Control files, system dictionary metadata, and initialization parameters

- Data files and processing configuration (redo and archive logs, rollback segments, and so on)

- Backup and restore policies

- Alerts, metric collection, and monitoring

Fortunately, a wealth of help on this topic is available from various sources, including the built-in *Advisors* and *Checkers* in Enterprise Manager Database Control, various training courses and books (see the Appendix), My Oracle Support–based knowledge documents with tips and hints, and even expert services from Oracle and other providers offering tune-ups and health reviews.

Again, as a prepackaged application that comes with detailed documentation to support its implementation, the Fusion Applications database shouldn't require extensive reconfiguration; however as part of the cyclic review process of our lifecycle (Chapter 4), database optimization should certainly be addressed.

## Database Resource Optimization

In addition to pure performance, optimization extends to the effective use of available resources, and the application manager must not only ensure that the database has the capacity it needs to provide acceptable performance, but that consumption and efficiency is optimized as well. This takes a very careful eye and at the least should include establishing baseline tests and benchmarks to help set expectations accurately. On top of this, metric collections can be implemented so that utilization rates can be captured and carefully monitored. Enterprise Manager Database Control offers the tools to do this.

## Database Security Optimization

The final core element to database optimization for Fusion Applications (but is by no means every possibility) is improving security. As you'll see when we discuss governance in the next chapter, although much of the product security (authentication, authorization, and so on) is handled at the middleware level (via Java Authentication and Authorization Service), ensuring that standard security recommendations have been implemented on the database is essential and should not be overlooked. This again is a well-documented topic, and since there is nothing specific to Fusion Applications per se, the Appendix offers material that contains recommendations and tools to use.

# Middleware Optimization Tools

We've already mentioned how WebLogic Server provides the ultimate tool for implementing application server configuration changes to optimize both itself as an execution environment as well as the components it runs. In addition to basic configurations, the WebLogic Administration Console provides several other tools that can aid optimization efforts.

### The WebLogic Server Diagnostic Framework

A few WebLogic diagnostic features are worth quickly mentioning and are related to the context of this discussion. The first two are *watch rules* and *notifications.* Together these provide a system in which user-defined metrics, events, or logs can be set to generate alerts and activities of various types, including passing diagnostic data out to Java Management Extensions (JMX), Simple Mail Transfer Protocol (SMTP), and Simple Network Management Protocol (SNMP) client applications. Being aware of system activity, and especially anomalies, is the first critical step to optimization.

The WebLogic Diagnostic Framework provides support for adding custom code to applications to expose monitored performance metrics through standard JMX interfaces. This allows metric data to be carefully tracked during execution and offers very fine-grained health information. Although this is overkill for standard Fusion Application deployments, it may be useful for critical, transient, and illusive issues, or for use in supporting custom or integration-related code.

Finally, WebLogic *work managers* allow rules to be defined regarding how pieces of a process are executed by the server. These pieces are then available for monitoring and can help you better understand large and significant execution, and therefore potentially create opportunities to introduce optimization.

## DMS Metrics

As discussed, the Fusion Middleware components such as WebLogic Server use the DMS service to capture comprehensive metrics on system activity. This raw data should be screened and filtered and the results fed into detailed analysis and reporting. This work should not only focus on problem identification, but opportunities for optimization should also be identified and actioned.

Again, optimization of platform components should center on the efficiency of various factors, and in middleware this includes resource consumption (such as connection pooling), processing throughputs (such as caching) and usage and request profiles (such as load balancing). The exposure and use of DMS metrics are dependent on which parts of the application are used since they invoke only the technical components required. For example, Purchase Order creation may use the online ADF application pages, or may be automatically triggered as part of requisition approval and processed by a back-end Java engine. Same functionality, but different technical processes involved.Hopefully, the principles and intentions are clear and the application manager, through analysis and subsequent liaisons with business users, will determine the precise areas where DMS can be used in optimization.

## Oracle Guardian

As another source of expert advice for improving the health of the middleware (and WebLogic in particular), Guardian embeds proven solutions and improvements into the product management and offers immediate and quantified advice. Optimization is about improvement, and although many features of Guardian are about problem avoidance and resolution, it also contains recommendations and performance advice. The system will be improved and therefore optimized even simply by the introduction of Guardian and the establishment of process and procedure to ensure its frequent and systematic use.

## Middleware Security

Similar to database security, the optimization of this layer occurs within the security components themselves, mainly Oracle Identity Management (OIM), Oracle Access Manager (OAM), and Authorization Policy Manager (APM). That said, adjusting the detailed security component configuration and implementation of a prepackaged application is rarely necessary, and any identified improvements should be validated by Oracle Support before implementation. Rather than reconfiguration, simply scaling up the capabilities and resources available for the security components can often lead to marked improvements in authorization processes, especially as the user base grows.

**NOTE**
*Review the detailed material in the Appendix, and reconcile advice given for Fusion Applications with the options and capabilities available in the tools involved. We'll look a little more at some of these as we discuss governance in the next chapter.*

# Hardware Optimization

Also important for optimization are the physical machines used for hosting Fusion Applications. This often involves multiple devices for each instance to support the distributed topologies that are required for better performance, better security, redundancy for fail-over, and general load-balancing needs. Between these hosts are various physical network components (firewalls, proxies, routers/switches, and so on), and these are also strong candidates for potential optimization. We'll not go into too much depth here and will stick to discussing a couple of general recommended principles.

## Component Lifecycles

As mentioned in Chapter 3, the physical system components (hardware) have a lifecycle of their own, and every piece will ultimately require repair or replacement at some point to remain certified and supportable. With careful attention, this overhead should be integrated with other planning so that optimization efforts all coincide between hardware, software, and business operations. This is crucial, because when these elements fall out of sync with each other, synergies and opportunities can be missed and more often than not serious problems can occur (for example, business changes and the associated system expectations are not coordinated with separate, unrelated technical adjustments).

## Resource Consumption

Just as with the middleware and the database, along with general performance guidelines it's important that you assess and monitor how efficiently resources are being consumed. Although the hardware offers resources to the layers above it, clearly it also has its part to play in how efficiently those resources are distributed and scaled based on demand.

For example, every SQL query will be made as efficient as possible by the Cost Base Optimizer inside the database; however, the actual response time the end users see will vary depending on the resources, capabilities, and health of each physical machine (and the connections between them). Where resource consumption is high (after all, the goal is to have a well-used Fusion Applications instance), even slight latencies can quickly scale up to become rather noticeable by end users.

The pursuit of hardware optimization is rarely a pointless task, and although it can require significant expertise, it shouldn't be ignored. All hardware vendors offer tools to help (many are provided within operating systems), and once set up properly, these can help you spot simple patterns and beneficial opportunities.

# CHAPTER
## 10

# A Governance
# Management Toolbox

hapters 3 and 4 described our governance plan in a broad manner, essentially boiling it down to ensuring that each feature and data object is of high quality and is available only to suitably authorized users. More specifically, the chapters looked at aspects of security, data quality, information management and audit, and change control. Remember that it's vital that governance plans focus on adherence to all kinds of measures, targets, and expectations, and that they should be easy to enforce and execute. This chapter again brings real tools and activities into play and should help get the Fusion Applications manager on the road to success.

# To GRC or Not to GRC

Two options are available for implementing the governance plan: adoption of the full Governance, Risk, and Compliance (GRC) product set, or relying on a few specific tools to manage related tasks.

Fusion Applications comes with the GRC product set that offers many capabilities and tools to help you successfully create and execute a governance management plan. Because it is purpose-built for governance, it is the preferred option and even extends into areas that, although possibly outside the normal remit of the application manager, offer insight and important tools for others in the organization. Here is a brief summary of some of the capabilities in the GRC product family:

- **Security** Automate and enforce the provision user identity and authorization using segregation of duties security across all systems (Figure 10-1).

- **Configuration** Enforce the adoption of automation in regularly used administrative setups and configurations across and between systems, as well as ensure change management is controlled and monitored.

- **Audit and regulatory compliance** Tools for testing, performing assessments, and archiving of data and reports required to meet the requirements of most of the well-recognized official bodies.

- **Risk management** Powerful analysis and reporting tools that provide parameters for risk analysis against live and historical operational data (see Figure 10-1).

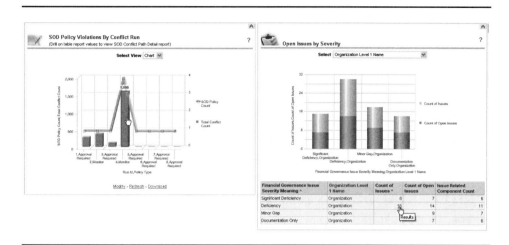

**FIGURE 10-1.** *GRC reports showing segregation of duty policy conflicts and financial governance open issues*

- **IT control** Tools to record and evaluate project proposals and selection criteria, including integration with standard frameworks such as Information Technology Infrastructure Library (ITIL).

- **Policy and procedure management** Detailed management of content related to policies and procedures, including the incorporation of legal, regulatory, and best-practice compliance.

- **Data management** Tracking of key metrics that control Fusion Applications business processes, including reporting and alerting on any policy and compliance violations.

- **Extensions** Comprehensive dashboards and custom analytical options for deeper business insights.

Clearly GRC offers some fantastic capabilities for optimizing business operations, as well as reporting on what has already taken place, however there are several other tools available for specific tasks in governing Fusion Applications.

# Business Process Layer

At the top of the stack, the features and functions that expose information and data to end users represent significant areas for the application of governance. We'll look at the obvious candidate, security, in the next section, because although the displayed content and features in the user interface is subject to strict control, the security process is applied in the applications technology layer. As such, several other high-level tools can be applied to areas that fall under our definition of governance.

## Functional Setup Manager

As a central resource for functional configuration data (via export), or simply as a method to understand the dependencies therein, the Setup Manager offers the applications manager a simple tool for use in controlling changes and performing basic auditing tasks.

Although it is not totally intended as a fully-fledged change-control solution, as might exist in other tools, Setup Manager is easy to use and offers comprehensive coverage for functional configuration for Fusion Applications version 1.0. This simple but useful resource shouldn't be overlooked in the search for something more compete.

## Master Data Management

Fusion Applications includes a couple of tools that help application managers ensure that the data in the system is clean, distinct -and not duplicated, free from redundancy, suitably archived, and of general good quality.

The first are core parts of the application suite itself, and like GRC they offer dedicated, fit-for-purpose features that are intended for use within a reasonably narrow focus. One good example is the Product Information Management (PIM) Data Hub that forms part of the Supply Chain Management product family. This application allows inventory and product specialists to manage, control, and maintain their product item data carefully, to ensure that transactions are completed based on the most up-to-date information about products and services. Similarly, the Customer Relationship Management product family contains the Trading Community Hub applications that ensure that customer records are properly managed and maintained, improving data quality and information clarity to drive efficiency and effectiveness.

In addition, features that process significant amounts of data usually come with their own maintenance routines, and again these should not be overlooked in the search for a dedicated tool. Good examples are within Enterprise

Scheduling Service (ESS) jobs and Service-Oriented Architecture (SOA) Human Workflow, where the purging of old redundant data often improves SQL query execution time. This is because day-to-day processing of attribute data can often run into hundreds of rows for each execution, and therefore with complex processes invoked many times a day, resources can quickly fill up. It's not practical to provide a full list of such features here (there are just too many); however, each well-used application and feature should be reviewed for such options and appropriate use should be encouraged.

# Fusion Applications Patch Management

Although a core part of the Fusion Applications Management role, we have so far avoided much discussion of patching. This has been deliberate, for a couple of reasons. First, *patching* is a verb, a "doing word," and as such is a layer of abstraction lower than much of the higher lifecycle planning discussion thus far. During our efforts to look forward, discussions about patching would make us look downward at specific activities and tasks, and this can make us lose sight of first creating a proactive management plan. It's better to have a purpose first and then consider how to achieve it.

Second reason is that the details of patching are well covered by the existing Oracle product documentation and as such require little or no repetition in this book (see the patching guide in the Appendix). Also, a reasonable amount of additional material has been written about patching best practices that cover when and how to do it so that it has maximum benefit with minimum disruption to end users and the social life of the application manager. So while some material is available, we discuss this area of patching in the context of managing application health in the next chapter.

We'll just mention a few of the  key features of the Fusion Applications Patch Manager and its associated utilities, such as OPatch, AD Control, and AD Admin:

- The ability to monitor patch progress and status, with features for aborting and rolling back patch application attempts

- The verification of success, including patch application logging available at various levels of verbosity

- Online and offline modes, reducing need for server bouncing (called near-zero downtime)

- Preliminary version, dependency, and prerequisite checking

■ The merging of multiple patches into one for increased efficiency

■ Detailed patch reports, including lists of those applied, patch contents, and detailed impact analysis, which is useful for audit records and change management purposes

One final word on patching: Because Fusion Applications is tightly integrated with Enterprise Manager, it also makes available a comprehensive set of patching tools for managing technology stack updates. The Database Control component comes with the Deployment Procedure Manager for checking patch prerequisites and a prescheduling application, and the central Patch Advisor offers integration with My Oracle Support to bring the latest and most pertinent patches directly into the tool for their application. Similar capabilities will no doubt exist soon for the middleware components.

## Diagnostic Test Framework (DTF)

Again, strictly speaking, the DTF isn't intended as a governance tool, but because the tests it contains provide reports on the health and status of the data and processing in the system, it can prove useful.

The obvious candidate is in audit, with which, for example, the output from DTF reports can be stored as records and snapshots of system information, for retrieval at a suitable later date. Keep in mind that this is not the intended purpose of these reports, and you shouldn't rely on them without validating that the content meets your requirements and is archived appropriately.

In a similar manner, data quality can be also verified using DTF tests, because they offer an easy-to-use window into the transactional and setup data and help you determine the need for any remedial action. DTF's common use is as a proactive validation tool, executed before running significant system events, and it exemplifies its use in data quality management.

## WebCenter

As part of Fusion Middleware, and in addition to related Enterprise Manager pages, the WebCenter application contains a couple of its own interesting tools designed specifically for reviewing user activity, and therefore potentially useful in executing governance plans.

The *WebCenter Analytics* feature provides detailed intelligence to report precisely who is doing what with which WebCenter feature. Because WebCenter controls all significant personalizations and collaborations, this feature can be very useful. And as an additional option, the *WebCenter*

*Activity Graph* feature offers a detailed analysis and recommendation engine that records user activity and carefully calculates what related information or features each user might like to see. Although powerful and potentially very useful, this is a separate feature and requires significant effort to integrate with the first release of Fusion Applications.

# Applications Technology Layer

Three elements of Applications Technology governance are discussed here and the remainder of the technology stack is covered later in the "Platform Layer" section. The three sections discussed here are most closely related to the functional features of the application, influencing (governing) directly how they operate and what information they have available.

## SOA Governance

SOA governance is a relatively new topic introduced as a result of general confusion and failure to design, build, and implement effective SOA-based enterprise applications. With the flexibility and power of Business Process Modeling, together with the open and independent nature of Web Services, many organizations struggled to build consistent and well-architected, large-scale integrated applications. As such, a set of recommended practices was established to make sure SOA projects limit complexity by following clear standards and good practices. This is implemented through the use of sets of enforceable SOA governance policies. Clearly, with Fusion Applications being a prepackaged application, SOA governance has already been applied, but with customization and extension work fairly common for integration needs, a few of the detailed tools available for SOA governance are worth mentioning here.

The Oracle Enterprise Repository (OER), discussed in Chapter 9, forms the library for all the Web Services within Fusion Applications. So although it's immediately available as a reference to help promote object reuse and reduce redundancy, the OER is also available for the registration and discovery of custom services and program artifacts, and it offers several features that can be rolled into SOA governance plans. OER offers lots of basic metrics and analytics regarding use and performance of the objects it contains. It also offers the policy creation and management functionality that allows the control of the SOA assets throughout their lifecycle. Finally, it comes with various built-in templates, samples and metadata, and impact analysis details that can significantly help promote best practice use.

The second tool, Enterprise Manager, is Oracle's primary tool for SOA management, and with extra tools such as those in the Management Pack Plus for SOA, significant extended capabilities are available. Indeed, combining the various other generic solutions available for SOA management (such as the Oracle Service Registry and Oracle Web Services Manager) with the acquired AmberPoint capabilities, Oracle offers the opportunity to build a complete and flexible solution for almost any and all SOA governance needs.

# Testing Suite Tools

Enterprise Manager 11*g* includes some powerful add-ons for managing the work that accompanies making changes to the application—such as retesting by checking for problems with features and data. This task commonly falls to the application manager, and tools and mechanisms that help you better manage and control existing test processes should not be ignored.

These testing tools fall under the umbrella of *Application Quality Management* (AQM) and form part of the overall Oracle solution known as the *Oracle Application Testing Suite*, which includes five parts:

- **Oracle Load Testing** Provides performance and stress testing of both user interface and direct Web Service calls. It can simulate thousands of concurrent requests at one time, created and run through an easy-to-use tool.

- **Oracle Functional Testing** Offers the automation of basic and complex functional and regression tests. It contains a powerful scripting and execution capability together with detailed reporting and analysis features.

- **Oracle Test Manager** Provides overall project management for application testing. It offers features to capture requirements, manage scripts and test execution progress, and track the resolution of all issues encountered.

- **Oracle Data Masking Pack** Provides a tool that prevents sensitive or confidential data from being displayed when datasets are copied or cloned from one system to another, commonly known as *obfuscation*. It contains easy-to-use masking templates and complex capabilities to ensure that the right values are hidden. This is all done with referential integrity and limiting any performance impact.

- **Oracle Real Application Testing**   Offers the replay of application workload on a changed system. The captured result is then compared with performance data taken before the change for detailed comparative impact analysis. Although it is primarily concerned with SQL performance, it offers some interesting capabilities in analyzing significant changes such as database upgrades or patches.

Functional testing and load testing both include special *accelerators* (prepackaged solutions) for Oracle Fusion Applications, as well as detailed reporting and analysis integration with Enterprise Manager, WebLogic Server Console, and Real User Experience Insight (RUEI).

# Security Governance

Governance and security go hand-in-hand. Whether it is user authentication and access control, data protection, or aspects of integration and physical security, the Fusion Applications manager must have a good understanding of all areas. To build an effective and executable security plan, the manager must have accurate and up-to-date knowledge of the related tools. Although some aspects might be important enough to warrant the purchasing or development of new tools, it's logical to use existing tools whenever possible.

Four main tools are used for Fusion Applications security management, each with its own specific uses and capabilities. These tools make up the Oracle Platform Security Services (OPSS) solution. Security is well covered by the Fusion Applications product documents, so we'll only touch on a few key features of each tool here. Proper training and material should be used to ensure that features are appropriately used.

*Oracle Access Manager* (OAM) provides centralized authentication processing, including access policies, single sign-on capabilities, and extensive custom and regulatory reporting for audit. Its Administration Console offers application managers full access to review and adjust configuration options, as well as enable and disable the various extra features.

*Oracle Identity Management* (OIM) offers similar consoles for managing user accounts: one for user self-service profile management, and another for more detailed administrative work (creating new accounts, expiring old accounts, and so on). OIM offers powerful reporting as well, including a large set of precreated reports for detailed auditing, including validating compliance with most of the major regulatory standards.

*Oracle Authorization Policy Manager* (APM) provides application managers with detailed access to the standard job roles, their duty roles, and the lowest level policies that are provided with Fusion Applications. This pre-seeded dataset is commonly referred to as the Fusion Applications *Security Reference Implementation* and can be adjusted to meet specific custom needs using the APM tool. Figure 10-2 shows the process of editing the lowest level security policies that are granted within the Payables Invoice Processing Duty role. You'll also notice the Data Security tab that allows the editing of the privileges under that role.

Finally, the Oracle Web Services Manager (OWSM) tool provides open-standard Web Services security policy management for explicitly managing and securing SOA composite-based applications. For Fusion Applications, this capability comes as part of both Enterprise Manager Control and the WebLogic Server Administration Console and offers a set of standard access policies to help enforce governance across all SOA resources.

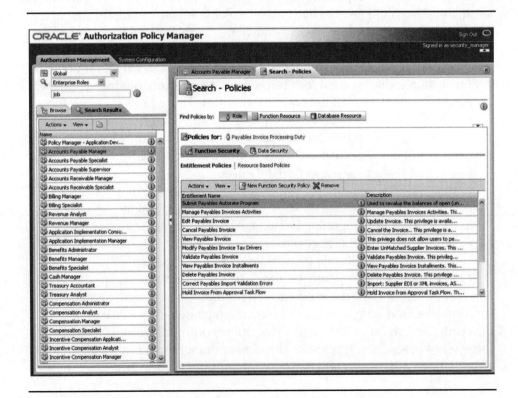

**FIGURE 10-2.** *Authorization Policy Manager*

# Platform Layer

The base platform for Fusion Applications offers some key tools for managing and enforcing governance. With core components of both middleware and database running here, your ability to control the resources, capabilities, and information is crucial. Although the layers above offer many key governance capabilities, being able to apply controls at the finest level of granularity ultimately means everything above it will inherently meet the same criteria. Let's look at a few examples.

## Enterprise Manager Compliance

Enterprise Manager Grid Control offers a specific *compliance* capability that emulates some of the GRC type features but focuses purely on the governance of the technology stack components. It promotes the adherence of various measured components to a user-defined set of criteria. It focuses on security elements in the main, but it also offers some support for control of both configuration and storage information.

Similarly to other features mentioned, it involves the creation of policies that define the thresholds (known as evaluations) for various metrics and supports most of the Enterprise Manager targets, including Host, Database (including RAC), WebLogic Server, Oracle HTTP Server, and Web Cache. The alerts and reports available as the outcome of violations contain detailed information for the application manager follow-up.

## Information Management

Although the security discussed so far has focused mainly around the access and authority to perform tasks within the application, in Fusion Applications this is only one side of the role-based access control (RBAC) implementation. Data Security, the other side, controls which data slice the user can view, create, update, and delete; and as mentioned, if this is not working as intended, it can mean a forced system shutdown.

### Data Management in the Database

Fusion Applications implements its own functional implementation to set up data security for users, commonly based on Enterprise Structures (such as business units) and function assignments. However, the applications manager can also use some lower level tools to help enforce governance. The most obvious example is the audit features available in the 11*g* database. These powerful features by default allow the tracking of any spurious activities, such as unexpected user creation, the use of system objects, configuration changes, and changes to database objects (Database Definition Language [DDL]). In addition, auditing can be criteria based, so that should values for fields conflict with user-defined values, an audit will be fired and key information captured. Figure 10-3 shows how custom audits can be set up to capture use by object, privilege, or statement, as well as offering a set of standard audit trails.

Finally, Database Audit also offers capabilities to track system activity such as network and connection issues. This feature can serve many purposes, such as regulatory compliance, general performance analysis, and usage profiling, as well as investigating suspicious activity. Note that a low-level audit should be undertaken with care so as not to overwhelm either the system with extra work or the applications manager with too much information. Formulating a clear and justified audit strategy first is essential.

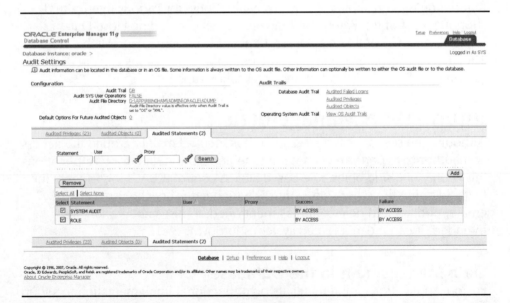

**FIGURE 10-3.** *The Database Audit settings page*

## Content Management

Another information management tool is the Content Server associated with the Oracle Universal Content Management (UCM) system that stores the unstructured data for Fusion Applications, such as supplemental documents that get uploaded as attachments. The Content Server contains various administrative and reporting tools that allow the applications manager to track and control detailed information storage. Some examples of useful features are the Content Analyzer that offers information about the health of the UCM components, the Repository Manager that offers a set of diagnostics and management functions, and the Archiver that allows stored items to be reorganized based on use. In addition, audit reports and security features also exist in the Content Server administration interface (actually known as the tray), offering more fine-grained governance capabilities.

# Configuration and Change Management

This, like several topics before it, warrants a complete book on its own, because it forms a critical part of delivering effective application management. It's a well-known fact that unplanned configuration changes are one of the most prevalent causes of unplanned system downtime.

Configuration management and change management are grouped together here because the related tools available for Fusion Applications mostly provide both capabilities together. We've already discussed the tools used to manage functional type configuration and setup, so let's now take a look at managing the same for the technology stack and controlling any changes made therein (although change management is not related only to configuration).

Enterprise Manager already offers Change and Configuration Management Packs for Oracle applications. Unfortunately, at the time of writing, this does not yet extend to Fusion Applications, but it seems sensible to expect this to come. Although this solution is not immediately applicable, the application manager should be aware of the existing capabilities because they offer valuable insight into recommended practices.

In the middleware space, Enterprise Manager and WebLogic Server offer complete and clear management of configuration, and although no dedicated tools are devoted to managing change, the existing audit and reporting capabilities, as well as simple things such as application deployment versioning, can be adopted and adapted to suit of the change and configuration management needs.

For the database, additional packs are available to extend Enterprise Manager's capabilities for both configuration and change management. Although not Fusion Applications–specific, they do offer features to fix a gold standard baseline configuration and to then manage it over time, identify and compare any variations, and migrate that baseline to and from other instances.

Two other tools that have significant capabilities inside the configuration and change management parts of a Fusion Applications governance plan are *Oracle Configuration Manager* (OCM) and *Remote Diagnostic Agent* (RDA). OCM offers detailed collection of configuration data for the entire software stack, and through its integration with both Enterprise Manager and My Oracle Support, it allows detailed comparison, change notification, and historic reporting. RDA is more reactive in nature, being explicitly executed to gather extensive system information and store that in a static set of reports for later analysis. Although missing some of the utilities of OCM, the RDA data is rich, and as a static snapshot of complete system information, it can have a great many potential and flexible uses to suit an individual governance management plan.

So that's our toolbox. Let's now look at how, where, and why we can use it, together with some general good practices that can be used to create and maintain a healthy Fusion Applications system.

# CHAPTER
## 11

# Getting and
# Staying Healthy

I t's one thing to be a technical whiz, dashing to and fro, putting out fires, making improvements, and avoiding near misses. But effective Enterprise Application management has a more subtle side to it as well, which is about adopting the right approach to the role, and making sure the right personal skills are used to complete all tasks properly. In addition (and not instead of), an application manager should have a clear appreciation of the fact that regularly taking a step back and adopting a more holistic view can also bring insights and a targeted focus that can otherwise get lost in the daily hubbub.

We're fortunate to be able to discuss this topic just at the start of the life of a new Enterprise Application. Fusion Applications, like its predecessors, will be with us for many decades to come and everyone implementing it has an opportunity to start from scratch and accomplish the things they now wished they had done with their existing Enterprise Applications. This kind of opportunity is indeed rare. Although adoption of Fusion Applications may be incremental, the best management building blocks must be in place from the start, and not bolted on in a hodgepodge fashion in an attempt to quell the effects of poor system management visibility and capability.

This chapter looks at the concept of the *health* of an Enterprise Application, and although Fusion Applications is the basis for the discussion, many of the concepts can be applied elsewhere. We look in detail at specific areas of the application that require health validation and use a logical structure to ensure we're not missing anything obvious. We'll also try not to repeat anything discussed already, regularly referring back to items from the toolbox chapters to provide specific examples.

The last three sections of this chapter cover even more practical advice, although this time the focus is on the approach and personal skills instead of specific tools or system capabilities. We'll look at the task of supporting the application itself, helping users resolve problems and get the most out of it. Application support requires a specific set of abilities that is often overlooked and is obviously an area in which I have a lot of experience. Next we look at the support environment, commonly called the *helpdesk*, although we'll consider more than just the creation and management of a call center. In the final section, we'll look at some recommended methods for ensuring that the application and its management remains healthy, again based on my experience of working with hundreds of organizations over many years, coupled with insights from Fusion Applications itself.

# The Principles of Application Health

You can think of application health as the reality or consequence of applying good application management. Health can be seen as a measurable assessment across the whole of the application. It's really an attempt at understanding how well the application is performing so that you can help it excel at what it's supposed to do. Good health indicates that all the components involved in completing a specific process or action are operating so that the results consistently meet or exceed expectations. Obviously, poor health is the opposite.

A health snapshot can be taken at several levels. At the start is the complete picture, which helps you adopt the aforementioned *holistic* type approach. Next down is *relative* health, comparing the system against other existing applications or systems to look for interesting differences and similarities. Finally, because the information is available, you can review a very *fine-grained* level of detail by drilling into the health of one or more specific capabilities or activities.

System health (and not limited to IT) is usually a *balance*, where the fastest system is usually not the one packed with thousands of features, and the most capable system is not always the quickest. This balance must be acknowledged and addressed in a formal manner, and although users will request specific features to be faster or richer, you must consider the system as a whole. Sometimes tough decisions have to be made, and maintaining the balance means not everyone will get everything they think they want. With some careful manipulation of expectations and some clever and inventive solutions (and communications), you can help each side (commonly business vs. IT) achieve a win, even if the result is actually a compromise.

Application health also includes the health of the software. Clearly the software programs need to be running properly for good health, but much of this is governed by the application data (such as transactions and reference data) and the application setup (such as Enterprise Structures) against which the software is running. The flexibility inherent in modern enterprise applications, especially Fusion Applications, means that although the program code may be working fine, what is being asked of it may stretch or exceed its intended limits, and as such can cause all manner of additional health problems. Spurious data values imported from external sources, unanticipated usage of functions and features, and incomplete or contradictory setups are some examples that are often to blame for health problems.

# Health in Four Dimensions

Let's consider four ways in which we might look at analyzing application health. We'll start by reusing one of the categorizations we use in both our overview in Chapter 2 and in each of the toolboxes: technology stack levels. Although this could represent many levels and divisions, we already used a very simple differentiation between business functional items, application-specific technology items, and pure technology platform items. This seems a fairly logical approach, and reviewing each of them this way allows the use of appropriate tools that specialize along the same lines. Obviously, a formal review of each and every component's health would be quite exhausting and complex, although would probably be the simplest method.

An alternative approach would be to adopt a more business-centric approach and try to plan the health assessments based on business process. In Fusion Applications, most of the features, the supporting help documentation, and the training are based on using the application to complete a distinct business process, rather than simply using features within one or more products. An example might be the order-to-cash flow, where key parts of the process are monitored and assessed to measure and verify its overall health. Although this might seem intuitive and far more meaningful to the organization than just managing software, it is not actually that easy to do. A functional business process will be implemented to use whatever parts of the software stack are required for its completion, and some processes are quite extensive, depending on almost every technology component in the stack. Although some of this could be avoided by breaking down the more complex processes into more manageable chunks, it still requires a detailed knowledge of how a particular process executes; with thousands of business processes tasks available, this is difficult to implement. A recommendation would be to use business process as an attribute for some of the key sources of health information, so that, if required, a key business process could be analyzed. Figure 11-1 shows how the Managing Payments business process could be represented as attribute A, and its health review can be based on information available from the setup within the Payables application, from within the processing flow for invoicing, and from data related to bank accounts.

The third dimension, one going back to preceding chapters, allows the application health to be reviewed based on each of the five tenets of Enterprise Application management: reliability, availability, performance,

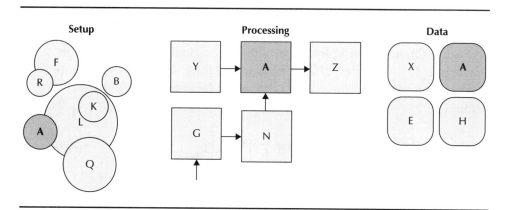

**FIGURE 11-1.**  *Business process as an information attribute*

optimization, and governance. This fits with our Fusion Applications Lifecycle Model from Chapter 4, where we designed a flow that includes review cycles to ensure that plans and capabilities are adjusted as the product, environment, and usage evolve. It's interesting to consider how again the balance factor exists here; Figure 11-2 represents the fact that effective health comprises a mixture of all of these areas.

A last possible approach to measure application health is to consider time explicitly. As the business changes, the expectations of the enterprise

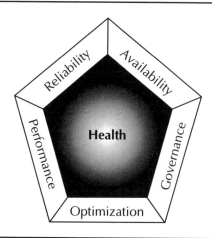

**FIGURE 11-2.**  *Health as the outcome of effective application management*

application will change and the assessment of its health should change accordingly. Again, it's similar to the lifecycle processes discussed in Chapter 4. Obvious examples of such shifts could include the adoption of new applications features, changes that affect internal business structures (such as mergers and acquisitions), and new integrations to internal or external partner systems.

## Importance: Business Health vs. System Health

Ongoing health can be considered in two ways. As mentioned, obviously the application manager needs to ensure the software system is healthy, making sure the technology is run according to predefined targets and expectations. The performance dashboards of Enterprise Manager, as mentioned in Chapter 8, are a good example of how to review this kind of information.

In addition, and again hinted at by the business process attribute used in Figure 11-1, the application must facilitate business health—in other words, the application must ensure that all business tasks can be completed according to targets. Specific examples of sources of information include the embedded analytics and Business Intelligence reports available across Fusion Applications, as well as many of the tests provided within the Diagnostic Test Framework (DTF) Dashboard.

Rather than view this as an either/or decision, you can attempt to integrate a solution that applies the best of both system and business approaches. The ideal approach would be to start with the most critical business processes and prioritize the technical components that hold the key to their health, across the stack. Poor health and failure of any individual technology component usually represents a serious issue; and by linking it to the business processes helps prioritize and focus on the issue. Using this process also helps ensure that core business processes are reinstated first. The same principle can be applied to improvement efforts as well, so that even small technical adjustments create the most positive downstream business impact.

## Monitoring, Monitoring, and More Monitoring

I have always wondered how common it is for people to go to the doctor for routine check-ups. I appreciate that certain jobs (and insurance policies) require that a person meet specific levels of physical and mental health, but it seems only those with genuine health concerns (or obsessive personality traits) actually get regular check-ups. In an ideal world, a regular health check would make sense, because many serious diseases can be cured if spotted early enough, and the warning signs are sometimes noticed too late. Unfortunately, we don't live in an ideal world, and although health is a priority, our lack of time, the cost, and the general effort required to get regular check-ups keep us from doing it. In application management as in medical health, just waiting for problems to occur is not the best approach.

## Monitoring Infrastructure

Although we discussed and demonstrated a few monitoring tools in the toolbox chapters, the application manager needs to build his or her own infrastructure to check the health of the system on a continual basis. As mentioned, automation is a key ingredient here, since being notified of activities that are starting to stray from an optimal measured range is much more productive and manageable than having to execute tasks and review results repeatedly.

Unfortunately, like most architectural feats, most of the resource cost (time and tooling) of this has to be made up-front, with the benefits revealed later as the system continues to perform as it should. In fact, even when a health monitoring capability is in place, it can be difficult to measure its benefits. A lack of costly mistakes and incidents is not really quantifiable, especially in terms of savings, since predicting failure rates and what the downstream effects might have been are vague estimates at best. Most organizations are aware of this, but few are really able to commit to the significant extra costs required without a clear definition of risk and its measurable impacts. Although we all know problems and service interruptions do occur, it can be difficult to explain that these are to be expected and that you must plan for them, especially when you're implementing a brand-new, best-in-class application.

On average, 70 percent of IT budgets are used for maintenance and operations, and only 30 percent is spent on innovation-type projects. Some organizations have even recorded closer to 90 percent of their costs attributable to the work required to deal with system problems. Indeed, the one lesson this book repeatedly tries to teach is that of *the six Ps*, that *prior preparation and planning prevents poor performance*. It costs little (money anyway) to review the application carefully, including the business processes and technical architectures in use, to learn about the embedded and complementary management tooling available, and finally to pull these together using an intuitive and practical approach that makes sure all key capabilities have some health monitoring in place.

# One Last Lifecycle

System health needs to be engrained in every part of the application management approach, because change is inevitable, and building a static and rigid infrastructure might work and resist for a while, but unless the principles and foundations include a flexible framework then shifts in implementation and requirements will require a costly tear-down and rebuild.

The following basic lifecycle flow—setting objectives, creating a strategy, planning, implementing, maintaining, and evolving—has been well proven in many areas as a solid outline to follow.

## Setting Objectives

Objective setting is traditionally approached in an informal manner when it comes to IT management; however, with the advent of IT Service Management (ITSM) models and tools such as those inside Oracle Enterprise Manager, things are changing. Objectives should be defined at a higher level than simply performance thresholds and monitoring targets, and setting these requires taking a few steps back to look at where we are now, where we really want to be, and creating a joining path based on realistic constraints. This needs to be at either the whole system level, or perhaps just one level lower down, based on a logical business separation, such as the Fusion Applications business process level 1. Setting health objectives is important, because all the time and effort spent in proactive research must be clearly directed toward a goal. Without this the purpose and priority gets lost in the huge array of time-draining subjects and activities passed to the application manager, coming from various business departments, IT departments, and all manner of suppliers and partners.

## Creating a Strategy

Strategizing involves outlining how the objectives will be reached. This is not each and every detailed activity, but a broad overview of the basic steps that may be involved in reaching the objective. Reaching a particular fail-over implementation objective, for example, could require an analysis of components involved and their high availability capabilities, an analysis of network and hardware, procurement of additional equipment and software, and the process of implementation, configuration, and testing.

## Planning

Once the key stages of the strategy are clarified, including the order in which they will be addressed, it's down to the application manager to form a detailed plan. The preceding chapters covered planning and many of the related tools available for use in creating a health monitoring infrastructure.

## Implementing

After planning comes implementation, as discussed in Chapter 4 in terms of setting up the application management infrastructure. Complementary to this is the fact that a healthy install is absolutely essential. The foundation of the software application needs to be rock solid, verified, and validated from all angles before it is approved for use. This extends beyond simply operating systems and hardware, since a healthy install and provisioning of each part of the application technology stack will inevitably influence later success.

The application manager must ensure every last task, action, process, and validation-check is completed and 100 percent successful, which requires diligence, perseverance, patience, and often the involvement of specific experts. A skipped task, assumption, mistake, or ignored piece of information can (and most likely will) have compounded detrimental effects later on. Worse still is the fact that going back and fixing implementation problems is often all but impossible, and usually involves significant costs in rebuilding and reimplementation.

Another part of implementation that needs unwavering attention is the migration of configuration, setup, and business data into the new system. Often this is also a great opportunity to revisit, cleanse, and rationalize legacy structures and models, and re-implement areas of the application in a manner that better meets the current needs of the business. Obviously, risks are involved in performing this clean-up; however, the risks of taking no action can cause more serious issues, since old, unsuitable data is regularly found as the root cause of application problems.

The final part of implementation is testing. From conference room pilot and proof of concept, to full system and acceptance testing, a significant management effort is required, in which the earlier plans are verified as accurate. As the old proverb goes, the proof of the pudding is in the eating.

## Maintaining

Just as with the ITSM lifecycle models discussed in Chapter 3, after implementation is complete, the focus of the application manager turns to system maintenance. Here the objectives, strategy, and planning accomplished earlier are put into practice and the subsequent infrastructure is used to manage the health of the application. This has been discussed throughout this book and it is mirrored in the execute node in our Fusion Applications Lifecycle model. As a reminder, this is not, however, a static point, and the lifecycle model has regular review cycles to ensure that activities constantly meet expectations, that work is based on accurate and relevant information, and that plans are synchronized with related stakeholders from the associated IT and business teams.

## Evolving

The final phase ensures that the application manager makes time to understand and appreciate lessons learned from the previous activities and uses this information to improve and redesign capabilities accordingly. Feeding information and knowledge right back into the objective setting and subsequent execution helps ensure that progress is rooted in reality. Although it shouldn't inhibit optimism, creativity, and aiming for auspicious targets, it promotes fine-tuning, continuous improvement, and taking smaller achievable steps on the road to something bigger.

# Be a Superhero, Not a Target

Because the application manager sits at the gateway between business users and the IT department, he or she should be seen as the go-to person for various areas and should at the least facilitate passing requirements and solutions back and forth. Take the opportunity to be that person who listens to what the business needs, translates that into actionable solutions, and initiates and manages the backroom IT work.

Obviously, this process could work negatively too: business users can complain about every last problem or challenge, and IT's constraints and stresses can be offloaded to the application manager. But with some initiative, the right outlook, and positive communication, you can make sure this doesn't happen. Much of this chapter is devoted to this precise goal.

# Mind, Body, and Soul = Business, System, and Process

So what areas are the best to focus on when considering the health of the enterprise application? Let's look at this in more detail. The application health needs to encompass the needs of the business (the mind), the performance of the systems in and around the application (the body), and of course all the reliant approaches, processes, and procedures in terms of executing application management (the soul).

## Business Process Health

You know that the enterprise application exists purely to serve the needs of the business, whether that's to optimize inventory and complete orders, reconcile financial information, or keep employee records up to date. IT is a facilitator and servant for the business, and the focus must always come back to that. It's all too easy to treat IT as an exciting and fashionable area, always having the potential to create a system that revolutionizes the way the organization works and provides improvements in capabilities and potential profits. Although recent economic events have forced businesses to limit investments to areas in which tangible benefits are all but promised, the evolution of software has continued at such a pace that the market remains flooded with cool new technologies that have great "potential." The enterprise application manager should serve as an advocate for the more significant opportunities borne out of technology, produced as a result of rationalizing and analyzing all forthcoming concepts for their potential impact on the business operation.

As you saw in Chapter 1, Fusion Applications is built around a business process model, and the health of this models execution needs constant review and potential optimization. The enterprise application manager should be constantly liaising with all business stakeholders, including data entry clerks, business development analysts, and senior management to understand precisely how well the core business process are enhanced (or impeded) by the application. This formal process can also be used to verify the expectations placed upon the application and to prioritize additional efforts in many areas of its management plan, especially in performance, optimization, and governance.

Another important element of business process health is that is helps to facilitate a better understanding of business objectives, strategies, and plans so that IT activities can be made to complement and support them as things evolve. Without this, a disconnect occurs; actions performed on each side lose coherence, and instead of offering complimentary synergies, they become disconnected; activities and resources become unrelated; and at worst they begin to conflict with each other.

# System Health

System health encompasses many aspects, and almost all of the toolbox chapters are related to enhancing the application health in one way or another. Let's cover a few of the areas that are particularly important in managing application health.

## Tuning and Performance

Response time is key, be it for opening pages, updating regions and graphics, submitting transactions, importing external data, returning search results, or generating reports. Clearly, different actions require different resources, and most users will have slightly different expectations. These expectations result from other applications they use on a day-to-day basis, and the difference between unconscious acceptance and intense frustration may be a matter of milliseconds depending on the task being performed. Consider, for example, opening a page for simple data entry: it's logical to expect this to be faster than opening a page that contains lots of detailed data and perhaps a graphic or two. If the data entry page isn't relatively fast, then it seems odd (also note that the expectation here is a fast-opening entry page and not an especially slow report page).

There is a huge range of business-related application activities that need to be hooked up with system performance dashboards, log data, and analysis reports that are available from the different technology components running underneath. Although expensive in terms of time and effort, a monitoring infrastructure should contain a prebuilt mapping to business process flows. Tracking a user's report of a problem to what happened across the whole system at that time can be difficult and time-consuming. Fusion Applications helps with this by providing the Diagnostic Framework (DFw) to create ad-hoc incidents to capture system diagnostics and logs, and then by including in the incident package business process diagnostic information from related DTF test reports.

Powerful pure technology tools such as the Enterprise Manager dashboards show recent activity for each technical component and provide Performance Summary pages for core parts, such as the Service-Oriented Architecture (SOA) infrastructure and WebLogic. Going further, other tools, such as Real User Experience Insight (RUEI), offer even more dashboards based on transactional, business-like information, including an instant drill-down into the constituent technical components to help you understand why something happened the way it did.

## Base Hardware and Platform Systems Health

A consistently healthy underlying server system upon which the applications, middleware components, and database run is clearly a necessity. These servers, commonly running some enterprise version of Linux, UNIX, or Windows, are normally well equipped with their own monitoring, reporting, and health-checking tools. The application management infrastructure must include the use of these platform tools, and they all should be well understood and lead to actionable steps in case of problems.

These components also come with their own supplier services as well, including technical support. This should be well understood, and proper resources and procedures should be created so that a resolution is never too far away. Each vendor is usually readily able to demonstrate the features of its various post-sales support services.

An enterprise application cannot exist in isolation, so the network around it needs to be as healthy and responsive as the host servers themselves. There is little point in having a fabulous system if its environment makes it seem problematic. Slow and severed connections, interruptions, and capacity issues all cause user dissatisfaction, and in a fully distributed topology, problems can even effect the internal application transaction processing itself.

These days, access to an enterprise application can be very complex, with wide area networks and users located outside the corporate network, using point-to-point secure connections. Consider, for example, Windows Remote Desktop or Citrix, in addition to the complexity of VPN-type connections, where the origin of user requests is either other networks or the Internet itself. For a web browser–based application with a rich user interface, the nodes in the network path must be tested and regularly verified that they're up to the task of delivering the range of requests and responses.

The flexible deployment architectures of Fusion Applications support many standard network topology best practices, so that the right model can be used for each organization's needs. This can range from single machine installations for test and development systems, to production instances that are set up for full database and middleware high availability, using the clustering of all key server components for load balancing and fail-over, full physical machine redundancy, and multiple firewalls and proxies forming complex DMZ's between the network nodes.

Where the platform infrastructure is extensive and complex, the management burden should fall to dedicated specialists, though the application manager still needs to plug into the implementation and be aware of health status and monitoring tools. Although specialists might focus on certain details, other areas remain important for accessing the enterprise application. Consider, for example, that network administrators commonly like to block non-standard traffic, but the enterprise application is often integrated with remote systems that generate messages not registered with the network filters but still represent essential business features. A real-world example might be the transmission of remote data such as that used in refreshing supplier product catalog details.

## Health Resources

The application manager needs to understand well the resource requirements of the system. These are usually calculated based on past data, current consumption and performance data, and the future plans and projections. For a new application, this isn't so easy, because although historic data might be derived from similar legacy systems or from basic benchmark data, the actual knowledge will come only for real live experience.

Resource planning is also closely related to the lifecycle models discussed earlier, since it involves changing and adjusting the management of the system over time, as it evolves together with the environment within which it operates. The Fusion Applications lifecycle includes the Optimization and Performance Plans, and these both inherently include scope for input into resource capacity planning.

**Capacity Planning**    The goal for a capacity management plan is to minimize the discrepancy between underutilized resources and unsatisfactorily fulfilled requests. Effective capacity planning is not just about the ability to justify a stockpile of resources just in case, but it includes cost-effectiveness by optimizing consumption rates without affecting performance, while simultaneously meeting both short- and long-term changes in the system.

This means that, along with simply adding more of the existing resources, you can optimize a system to increase capacity by changing or introducing new techniques, processes, and components. In the traditional manufacturing world, capacity planning methods include the following:

- **Lead strategy**   Resources are added in anticipation of a future increase in demand.

- **Lag strategy**   Resources are added only after the requirement for them has been realized and a constraint (a problem) is proven.

- **Match strategy**   Resources are added quickly and incrementally as changes are observed.

**Resource Profiles**   It is important that you factor in the time it takes to acquire and implement additional capacity and resources. This might be automatic for some items, such as the auto-extend tablespace feature in the database, while for others it might be more *hot-pluggable,* where after making a change perhaps only a refresh or at most a component restart is required (such as with most hardware). However, for some resources, such as adding application servers or changing security and network capabilities, adjustments might require more extensive configuration and post-implementation testing. The approach taken in the capacity plan should reflect the implementation profile of the resources in question.

**Service Usage Profiles**   In addition to changes in the demand for resource capacity, the *utilization rates* need to be monitored and accounted for. Changes in the use of the application are often the cause of problems.

As new users are added to an application, it can be helpful to qualify what kind of overhead each one will represent. An invoice processing clerk who mainly creates transactions, for example, will have a usage profile different from that of a sales person who occasionally pulls contact details and submits a few orders, and his user profile may be different from that of a business development manager who runs many detailed reports and uses complex ad-hoc analysis tools. Although overhead can be difficult to quantify with much accuracy, some attempt to be aware of this and understand its impact will help bring significant benefits and reduce costly oversights.

Changes in the application features and the business operation are also important considerations. As features are implemented or existing features are used in new ways, the resource utilization can change significantly.

With some of the advanced capabilities in Fusion Applications, such as Customer Relationship Management's (CRM) predictive modeling features, together with potentially huge user-base sizes (that often include external customers and suppliers), usage profiles can be dramatically varied and have a real effect on resource consumption.

Your first mitigation strategy should be to look at improving resource *consumption efficiency*, rather than just throwing more costly resources at a problem. This is not always easy to do, and it takes discipline, effort, and most of all time. This work can be exceptionally technical in nature and may involve specific skills or experts. The application manager must help identify candidate areas for review and then use his or her overall system and business knowledge to help simplify process flows, since this is often the most effective method of improving throughput.

**Capacity Forecast**   How can resource requirements be predicted to negate potential exhaustion? There is no silver bullet here, especially when it comes to something as complex as Fusion Applications with all its features, options, configurations, and flexibility. However, a few simple tried-and-tested techniques can help you formulate a sensible approach.

It's important that you meet with business management and carefully go through the business plan and related projects, so that details can be understood in enough clarity to be interpreted and extrapolated to envisage both the requirements from and influences upon the enterprise application. In addition, and somewhat similarly, the IT management must be consulted regarding general service planning so that infrastructure and system changes can also be accounted for in the application capacity plan. This often affects the availability of resources rather than the need for them.

Finally, capacity can be estimated as a result of benchmark testing using automated load and performance testing tools, such as those that exist in the Oracle Applications Testing Suite. These include the setup and execution of standard scripts as well as the various ways to make requests to the system, including virtual users. The resulting hard data should be used in quantitative analysis and as key input into recommendation and planning calculations.

This approach is also reflected in Information Technology Infrastructure Library (ITIL version 3), where capacity management is viewed as having three core elements: Business Capacity Management, which ensures that the focus remains on fulfilling business goals; Service Capacity Management, where the ITSM approach to the provision of IT is used to ensure the agreed upon capabilities and performance is maintained; and Component Capacity Management, where specific technology pieces are validated as having optimized resource availability and utilization rates.

Using these items as inputs, you should attempt a *risk analysis*, looking at the impact of the best- and worse-case scenarios and considering appropriate mitigation strategies. This should result in a range of problems and matching solutions and include a general agreement on the most probable outcome and an appropriate plan.

In addition, you can create a *contingency capacity plan*, in case a severe situation arises due to unforeseen circumstances. These predictions are best guesses most of the time, and although testing and trials are ideal, the nature of many resources means that there is often a lack of opportunity, capability, and enough accurate information to do any detailed tests. This backup plan might also include some tolerance ranges as well, where specific scenarios can be weathered up to a point, after which other activities are set to kick in. This kind of preparation and planning can be very useful when you're trying to implement capacity management automation, such as load-balancing and fail-over.

**Cost-Benefit Analysis**    Review the potential gain against the corresponding costs. Now more than ever, effective application management needs to involve *cost-efficiency,* and technical resources (along with power and salaries) form the core expenses. You already know that 70 percent of IT is spent on maintenance, so if money can be used wisely, better application management can result.

## Healthy Application Setup

Beyond technical setup, an effective enterprise application must be set up to run its functional features properly and over time it's not unusual for this setup to creep away from its original definition, eventually causing conflicts and problems. Consider the flexibility within the Enterprise Structures available in Fusion Applications; they provide more than enough rope to hang yourself with. Most good implementation consultants and project managers go for simplicity to ensure manageability long before they introduce the complexity involved in trying to satisfy every last non-critical requirement.

Although we'll not go into specifics here since Fusion Applications has such a broad range of setup options, suffice to say that application managers must engage closely with system integrators, consultants, and of course business managers to ensure the following:

■ Project targets should include health-related processing and measurements.

■ System setups should be complete and kept within the thresholds defined in the original designs and plans.

■ Major reconfigurations, extensions, and customizations should be fully understood, tested, and carefully recorded.

## Healthy Application Data

You know that governance and optimization management plans should include the data in the application database as a key focus area, both as a valuable resource that should be carefully controlled and as something that contains potential opportunities for operational improvement. The Master Data Management (MDM) solutions available for Fusion Applications were mentioned in Chapter 10, and you know that by utilizing these, quality and health of both reference and transaction data can be realized.

## Integration Health

Many parts of the application accept, process, and send data internally through application-to-application (A2A) integrations as well as to the outside world through business-to-business (B2B) integrations. For Fusion Applications, this primarily comes in the form of A2A coexistence, and you should consider how changes in external systems and environments can introduce problems. External changes would normally include simple alterations to remote system processes or technology stacks, but can also be related to data changes as well as shifts in the requirements of and expectations from the integration.

For Fusion Applications, the Oracle Enterprise Repository (OER) tool offers some basic reports as well as some failure handling that may occur within the application itself (such as DFw incidents).

On a non-technical level, it's essential that you maintain a good working relationship with the owners and managers of all integrated systems and maintain communication so that any upcoming changes are prevalidated as not being detrimental to any integrated systems' health. We'll discuss managing partners and suppliers later in this chapter.

# Healthy Processes and Procedures

Now that we've looked briefly at the parts of the system that are most sensitive to health, you can see that, as in most jobs, it's not just the machinery that needs to work, but also the complete operation that supports it, its inputs, running environment, and what happens to its outputs.

## Security and Governance Health

Security and health are front-and-center when it comes to application management, because the corporate data it holds is often a vital asset. Unauthorized access (or conversely incorrect restriction) to features and data can cause severe impacts, all but halting normal operations. Security can also apply to the technical setup as well, with one simplistic unhealthy practice being that the passwords are sometimes configured to reset too often, resulting in users having trouble remembering unique values.

The application manager needs to run checks periodically to make sure all is as it should be, and not simply sit and wait for notification that it is not. This should be part of the standard application management process, where regular reviews with security and audit teams allow tweaks in the infrastructure design based on concerns, improvements, and any changes to requirements and expectations. Any adjustments should be okayed by all the stakeholders involved, with the end results and capabilities (such as reports and dashboards) accessible to everyone concerned, again reducing the burden on the application manager.

## Approach

Effective application managers must be very well organized, because of their wide-ranging responsibilities. Unless they are clear about what needs to be achieved and have the discipline to stick to it, it's easy for hours and days to pass just maintaining the status quo and rarely making any new developments or measurable progress toward objectives and goals.

Although much of this is general good advice, it applies especially to the application manager, who sits at a pivotal position in the organization where the means demands from both the business and IT worlds meet.

As such, the application manager must be very clear about all objective setting, the associated child sequential strategy, milestone targets and deadlines, and detailed activity and work plans. He or she must also be aware of the availability of resources, not just those around technical capacity, but also in the associated environment such as the availability of dependent personnel and systems.

Another obvious but common challenge is distraction. As the central go-to person for many teams, the application manager can rarely afford to burn bridges and turn people away. That said, prioritization of work is essential, and the manager must occasionally focus on certain tasks, sometimes at the expense of other requests. The careful scheduling of periods of time dedicated to specific types of activity is a simple but useful method to employ to get things done.

Finally, the application manager should remember that reactive work (such as the examples later in this chapter) should ideally be accomplished by exception and not by rule, and the automated monitoring and health validation setup in the management infrastructure should be centered on supporting this mantra. Without this, or some powerful delegation skills, all attempts to improve and optimize can get lost in the barrage of incoming questions, requests, and problems.

## Sharing Information

For too long, the differences between the business users and the IT department has isolated the two sides and prevented information sharing, resulting in incomplete or unclear business requirements, ineffective IT solutions, and general frustration. The potential benefits of IT often ended up as significant additional costs. With adoption of ITSM and similar approaches, these walls are finally being torn down. It's now generally recognized that IT is subservient to the business requirement for it, and it must satisfy both immediate and long-term business needs. And because the application manager sits at the forefront, he or she must understand, translate, and re-convey information to and from both sides, and to do this they must possess a kind of *multilingual* ability.

The modern consumer IT landscape has come a long way since the enterprise resource planning (ERP) systems of old. Today's Generation-Y workforce expects a wide range information to flow efficiently to them based on a very small amount of personalization and filtering effort. It's about *visualization*, meaning that data and information must be represented in a way that is immediately consumable, highlighting any anomalies, peaks, trends, or patterns, just like the embedded intelligence capabilities of Fusion Applications.

Not only should this kind of infrastructure exist for the application manager, but a subset or distilled version of it should be shared with the users of the application so they are aware of the health of the tools to run the business. The status, activities, and general goings-on in the IT department have always been a black hole of information in the eyes of the business users, but just because some technologies contain underlying complexity doesn't mean that general information cannot be shared. You don't have to know how a Ferrari works to be able to appreciate what it can do. Do many Facebook users know exactly how it source code works?

Sharing information has another huge benefit: it reduces workload. Providing a layer of information and related tooling between the application manager and the business users (or any similar consumers) acts as a huge cushion that absorbs many incoming questions, concerns, and requests. Information that is updated automatically facilitates many basic needs and by adding helpful utilities and additional guided processes, it can help to eliminate substantial amounts of reactive work. I have found that the more you try to automate a job, the more you can focus on improvements and optimizations, and the more valuable (and enjoyable) your work becomes.

Consider the following examples, which could be considered for inclusion in an application management public dashboard–type solution.

**Current Status**    This would obviously include the availability of the application as a whole, plus for Fusion Applications, it might be further broken down into specific pillars, their component applications, and even status and known issues in the individual WebLogic servers that are running them. It may also include other common components that might affect only certain features within the application, such as the health of integration connections, the status of processing engines such as in Service-Oriented Architecture (SOA) and Enterprise Scheduling Service (ESS), as well as the reporting services from Oracle Business Intelligence Enterprise Edition (OBIEE). The application manager often sends outage notifications to all users when serious problems occur, and these could include links back to the dashboard page for more detailed information, such as expected up-time and basic investigation and resolution information.

**Performance**    Rather than adopting a simple "up" or "down" status report, we can do better. Using some of the basic metrics readily available, you can give users an at-a-glance view of the *relative* state and performance of the application at any one point in time. This need not be hard data, and Figure 11-3 shows how data (the top line) can be derived from such things as CPU, memory, and network metrics that might be simply mashed together to provide a combined performance metric that offers an overall picture of system health. You might ask, Why would a user want to see this? In my experience, most users will not look at this until they have a problem; however when they do, it shows them both that the issue is recognized—reducing frustration and effort duplication—and, when accompanied by resolution detail, it shows that the problem is being addressed. This all goes to provide confidence and reassurance. In addition, using dashboard features and actions, users can quickly and easily report problems that may have slipped through automated monitoring and alerting.

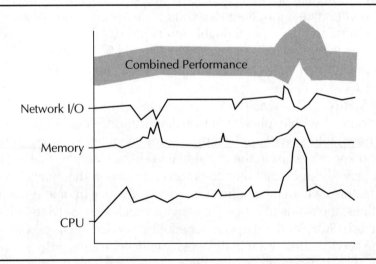

**FIGURE 11-3.**    *Performance chart showing use of a combined health metric*

**Improvements**    As part of the work defined in the optimization plan, the Fusion Applications manager will be looking for opportunities to adjust, fine-tune, and generally improve the application, and some of this could be shared with outside parties. Business users (like any user of computer systems) take for granted normal operations and tend to focus feedback on problems and difficulties. As such, sharing improvements represents a PR-type effort that when clearly illustrating significant adjustments made to *their* system, it helps buy some slack should problems occur, and fosters a more positive and constructive relationship. Examples could include performance and health improvements, benefits from implementing new features and upgrades, throughput workload (since users are normally unaware what others are doing in the same system), and even simply the patches that have been applied proactively to avoid known issues.

**Upcoming Maintenance**    A mandatory part of the job is planning and reminding business users of when the system will be unavailable due to maintenance work, either regularly or on an urgent basis. Rather than initiating the annoying blanket e-mail reminder a day or two in advance, send a short notification to a limited set of subscribers, but make sure the status dashboard page shows the upcoming schedules and perhaps provides a brief summary of the work planned—focusing particularly on its benefits.

   As mentioned, the architectures such as near-zero downtime patching that exists in Fusion Applications aims to minimize the disruption to business users, allowing more maintenance work to be carried out even when the applications are running and this is important for today's always-on international organizations. That's not to say downtime will not be required, but, hopefully, the outages will be significantly shorter and less frequent.

**Changes Coming**    Similar to improvements, changes to the system will occur, and the earlier and clearer these are shared with business users the better. These might include the results of investigations and projects whose purpose is to alleviate shortcomings or problems known to business users, and as such they provide yet another way of offering good news. With enough lead time, sharing detailed plans can allow users to offer feedback about concerns and interpretations on the planned actions, and this often reduces the risk of unforeseen impacts.

**Poll**    As a communication channel that is surrounded by accurate and up-to-date contextual information, the dashboard page can offer a route for questions, input, feedback, and concerns, often as an alternative to the normal support helpdesk. This requires tight controls to avoid misuse, but with the right approach, it can be a valuable source of optimization ideas, as well as a method to validate the application manager's own plans. With modern Web 2.0 collaborative tools finding their way into most corporate networks and services, many different options are available for providing broadcasts, capturing and processing feedback, and channeling responses of various types.

**More Information**    Finally, the dashboard can provide business users a method to access what they need to fulfill nonstandard tasks. Examples might be providing access to extra reporting tools such as the Fusion Applications analytic OBIEE components for creating ad hoc custom reports. Another example might be a listing of company training resources, such as reference material, tutorials, classes, and even contact information such as mailing lists, online forums, and specific subject matter experts.

# Day-To-Day Health

Let's looks at several key tasks that traditionally constitute the bulk of the application manager's time, specifically in relation to Fusion Applications. This includes various recommendations to help you make sure that the most amount of time is spent on items that achieve the most meaningful results.

## Patching

Chapter 10 outlined the Fusion Applications patching tools and pointed to the patch guide listed in the product documentation for fine detail. We'll therefore not discuss specific tooling here, but will instead consider what it takes to outline a healthy patching strategy.

At a high level, patching is of two types, mainly categorized based on need. The first, *reactive patching*, occurs when something isn't working as designed and a fix is needed so that business users can continue to use a feature in their work. Although commonly an urgent problem, it also might involve just a simple inconvenience or the use of a temporary workaround.

The alternative to this is proactive patching, for which solutions to one or more known problems are bundled and scheduled for application before any of these issues are actually experienced by users. This type of patch is commonly recommended by software vendors to ensure that any reported problems are not side-symptoms of already fixed issues. It also helps to ensure that any additional fixes needed are made on the latest code line, and a reduced complex dependency analysis to ensure backward compatibility.

In the real world, the applications manager has to adopt a patching strategy that is a blend of these two types. They preschedule the adoption of bundles of patches with known problems for the products in use and make provisions for emergency patching during either regular maintenance windows or as special one-off activities. Creating an adequate combination of the two patching types is clearly advisable because neither one alone represents a practical operating process.

In addition to determining exactly what to apply and when, some other traditional challenges to patching Enterprise Applications include the following.

## Patch Awareness

It can be difficult to be immediately aware of any and all new patches that are important to specific key business areas. The application manager must spend time reading alerts, notifications, and web pages, looking for items that are especially relevant to them, and this can be tiresome and ineffective. Fusion Applications, and the technology stack underneath it, provides a couple of significant improvements.

The *Patch Advisor* tool integrates Enterprise Manager and My Oracle Support to offer lists of patches that can be immediately validated and applied within a single tool. This also works with Oracle Configuration Manager's *Health and Patch Recommendations*, which shows patches (and other solutions) that will resolve known issues identified as applicable in scanned systems. Even the My Oracle Support portal contains a range of features (complex saved searches, recommendation lists, alerts, patching plans, and so on) to help you identify a specific set or types of new patches and verify their suitability for use.

## Handling Dependencies

Complex prerequisites and relationships often exist between the files contained in patches, and even with versioning it often causes extreme confusion and costly mistakes. Significant improvements have been made in the patch application tools, such as the validation of dependencies and prerequisites, as well as ad-hoc termination of a patching process. Improvements have also been made in both the documentation of complex patches and the better bundling of consolidated aggregate patches that include all dependant files. In addition, several new tools can help verify patches against the system before their application, such as the Fusion Applications Patch Manager **validate** command and its *Patch Impact Analysis* report, as well as the aforementioned *patching plans* in My Oracle Support, as shown in Figure 11-4.

## Resource Consumption During Patching

Some larger patches can require significant resources, such as large periods of processing time and occasionally disk space, CPU, and even memory. With the adoption of more efficient patching, where larger sets of patches are consolidated and released together as a roll-up bundle, the application of larger patches appears to be an increasing problem in terms of resource

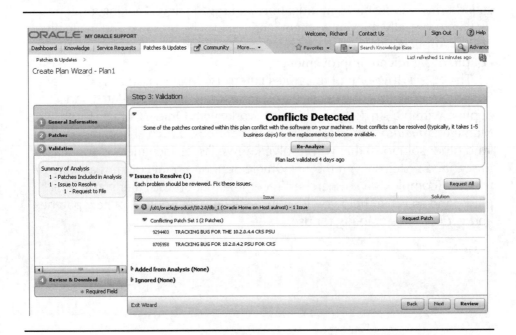

**FIGURE 11-4.** *My Oracle Support's patch plans, with validation capability*

requirements. The truth, however, is that by looking a little deeper, the savvy application manager will know that loads of individual patches are more complex to control, more likely to introduce dependency problems, and take significantly longer to apply than one larger bundle. Although some fixes in the bundle might seem extraneous, applying these fixes is never a bad idea, especially since Oracle's own experts have verified that these do need to be grouped together.

## Fixing Patch Problems

In the past, it was difficult to know what to do when patches were applied in error or when they failed and couldn't be restarted. This usually involved complex and risky restores from backups. Although not a common requirement, historically there was no clear and foolproof way to reverse the effects of application patches. Thankfully, this has changed, and modern patching tools such as Fusion Application's *Patch Manager* include various safety features that allow resume on failure, reapplication, and reverting of the system changes made. That said, there is still (and will always be) a place for backups, because not every eventuality can be handled by management tools alone.

## Patch Progress Monitoring

Although progress information is shown in the console where the patch is being applied, it was traditionally very technical in nature, related to the patch code execution, and rarely easy to interpret into meaningful progress or estimate a time of completion. Many variables are involved here, and most consumer IT systems (such as PCs) are much more friendly, hiding the complexity under the hood and showing more meaningful details such as a full progress bar, a time left estimate, and a few summary statements about what it is currently doing. These same features are used in the *Oracle Universal Installer*, and unlike its predecessors, Fusion Applications leverages this component in several places to provide a rich monitoring console, although it retains detailed logs should include more granular information be required. In addition, while keeping many of the features of the proven patching tooling (such as ADPATCH and ADCTRL), a rich layer of Application Development Framework (ADF)–based management pages are now provided to improve the general patch application and management experience (enhancing the command line interface).

## Patch Level Management

Although most modern enterprise applications offer features that provide some patch management information, such as lists of version numbers and patches applied, these were usually fragmented as the output of scripts and reports, and were often found only in expensive add-ons. In addition, the application manager usually had to undergo a multistep manual process to check whether a missing patch was actually suitable for application, including parsing code files for fine-grained version information, opening patch files to compare the versions, and trying to reconcile the fix description details with the reported user problem.

Fusion Applications addresses this by leveraging Oracle Configuration Manager (OCM), which allows you to compare detailed system information with complete patch information, all in My Oracle Support tool. This allows for easier management of both the current patch details and the identification of additional suitable candidates, including those suggested via its automated *Patch Recommendations,* as shown in Figure 11-5.

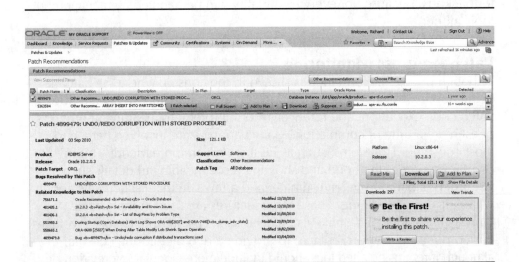

**FIGURE 11-5.** *My Oracle Support Patch Recommendations*

# Patch Expertise

Although the topics mentioned so far address some of the larger patching issues, let's take a brief look at some recommendations regarding how to take the task to the next level and deliver substantial improvements on the experiences of the past.

## Getting Patches

In the past, Oracle applications patches were released based on a rather subjective decision as to whether or not the need was urgent. Often, whether you received the patch immediately or had to wait until the next patch set or bundle depended on how well you could state the business impact. Clearly, this approach didn't scale well and usually resulted in a huge amount of work as you maintained hundreds of separate code versions. This has changed in the last few years, so that individual patches are provided on an exception basis, only for those rare issues that truly leave the system inoperable. The vast majority of patches are bundled into regularly released patch sets, often also referred to as roll-up patches. These roll-ups have various benefits, including the fact they include all co-dependencies and are validated as a whole, eliminating the possibility of conflicting code.

The effective application manager needs to understand the patch release process and base their planning and decision-making around this. This also applies to setting expectations with business users as to the resolution of noncritical issues (next patch set) and, when critical issues (marked as *Severity-1*) occur, making Oracle aware of the detailed background, true impact, and the cost of the issue so an immediate fix can be made available. Working with this process is the only option—and in my experience, trying to work against it or circumvent it normally leads to more problems than solutions.

**Backports**    Another factor involved in patch availability, particularly after a product has begun its lifecycle with different active code releases and versions, is the matter of *backporting*. Code fixes normally occur on the latest branch (version) of the code, and if the application manager is running a slightly older version, he or she must decide whether to apply the update—and absorb the cost of extensive testing—or to ask Oracle if a fix can be made (backported) on the older version of the code being used.

As a rule, it doesn't make much sense to work on older code when fixes are already available in newer releases. That said, occasionally the fix can be backported, although normally this is for only the most critical issues. You need to clearly understand the cases in which a backport request may be required and (again) work with the process, providing all the detailed and relevant information to get the solution that is most applicable in each case.

**Data Fixes**    On some occasions (hopefully rarely), a problem has caused the data in the system to contain mistakes—from a single value, such as a bad description, incorrect amount, or a incorrect status field, to the corruption of a record that breaks design constraints and causes processing failure, such as orphaned records or missing parts of a transaction. Although the products are built with many fail-safe components and specific validations to prevent such problems from happening, upon critical failures (such as a hardware failure) or perhaps usage that's outside the design (such as manual data import), it can happen. On occasion, Oracle does provide *data-fix patches*, scripts that correct the data in the system by changing, adding, or removing values so that normal processing can continue.

To make working with data problems a little easier and solutions more effective, think long and hard about when and how something might have happened in the application that could have led to a data problem. Most of these kinds of issues are caused by the following five reasons; spending time reviewing for these can save you hours and days of work:

- **Bad data**    Unbeknown to the application manager, small amounts of problem transactions or reference data can be sitting in the system, sometimes for years, and problems resurface only when this data is used. Checking for similar problems in the past can help you find transferable solutions and can confirm a pattern of occurrence that means the cause can be corrected as well. Some of the Master Data Management (MDM) type solutions in Fusion Applications can help find these bad records as well. In addition, similar problems can be created by the import of external data by using badly designed import routines or if the source data contains mistakes. Carefully checking for the occurrence of recent data imports and validating their activities can save you huge amounts of time later on. Oracle supports only the import routines that it provides, and by using the reports in the DTF of Fusion Applications, you can analyze most significant setups, transactions, and reference data for potential problems.

■ **Bad manipulation scripts**   Data can be updated en-mass using custom scripts—such as when a corporate merger or takeover requires that users' e-mail addresses use a new domain value (john.doe@old.com becomes john.doe@new.com). Standard practice is for Oracle not to support these nonstandard update scripts; however, some circumstances can make this all but impractical to avoid. Problems usually occur when data update scripts used successfully in the past are not validated fully against the current version of the application and therefore hidden inconsistencies are found when the updated data is used for actual processing. Obviously, the products and their data models evolve over time, and where the product features themselves cannot support the required adjustment, any extension or custom solution must be fully reviewed to ensure that it remains appropriate. Fusion Applications, adherence to implementing Web Services and the Model-View-Controller architecture (especially View and Entity Objects) means that data updated in the database is actually filtered through a layer of processing that can catch mistakes or inconsistencies before they are finally committed. These solutions should be reused and leveraged whenever possible, because they can prevent many costly mistakes.

■ **Bad customizations**   Apart from data problems resulting from bugs in custom code, when the base product changes, the custom code written on top of it must be reviewed and adjusted to support those changes. A great way to avoid this is for the application manager to help development teams implement the custom code in a modular way to facilitate its comparison with the base product components, since a side-by-side comparison is much more effective (and can be automated) than code written in a complex "spaghetti" fashion that becomes difficult to correlate and compare. The application manager can also directly make sure the change and customization management process includes enough detail to facilitate detailed customization analysis. In addition, and probably the most important factor, thorough regression and acceptance testing are critical in managing custom code. (We'll discuss testing later in this chapter.)

■ **Serious failures**  When code is running and updating records, and something catastrophic happens (such as a severed network connection, sudden unavailability of a technology stack component, or the total consumption of resources), the code can fail part way through its processing, causing incomplete data updates. Thanks to today's modular coding techniques and transaction-controlled updates, this result is fairly rare; however, application processing is not normally just one single update, and even an incomplete multistage process (such as those in BPEL) can be difficult to reinitiate from the user interface alone. For this reason, occasional data-fixes may be available to complete a partial processing run.

■ **Unintended usage**  As mentioned, the range of features and flexible implementation options available increases the possibility that something might be used in a way that differs, even slightly, from its intended use. With Fusion Applications provided as a cross-industry solution, one company's operations can be wildly different from another's, but the same features and code are being used by both. Although rare, some features can be used outside the scope of their original design, and this can sometimes affect the data. The most obvious example is storing data that is beyond its original purpose, with the subsequent processing failing to support it properly. Another example might be where some fields are actually displaying correct values, but their intention is misunderstood by users. This situation can be quite common for values in reports as well as some of the more complex calculated fields, although with good documentation and suitable training it should be limited.

Data fixes vary in their origins, and by understanding the most common problems it can improve your ability to get to the root of a problem and resolve it in a timely fashion. By considering the following recommendations, you can ensure that data fixes are fast, accurate, painless, and complete.

First, you should ensure that the data in question is fully understood. DTF tests can help with this, in addition to documentation such as the technical reference manuals provided for previous Oracle applications. The Oracle Enterprise Repository (OER) contains equivalent detailed information on the objects and data models involved for Fusion Applications. Although the applications manager cannot be expected to analyze all the thousands of internal structures, a good overall appreciation can help him or her ensure that fixes are well understood, get a reasonable picture of what it's going to change, and interpret the net result.

Second, using the various application instances available, the problematic data should be replicated in one or more additional environments so that all investigation and fixes can be safely tested and validated. This instance replication can take time and effort to set up but should not hold up the resolution of any important data-related issues.

Third, where data problems do occur, the application manager should make an effort to liaise with the business users and translate the investigation and progress so that sensible decisions can be made to prevent live business transactions getting stuck in extended periods of limbo. By knowing the real situation, business users can decide whether a temporary (or permanent) alternative solution should be implemented to alleviate intense operational pressures.

Finally, the application manager must ensure that where a data fix is issued and applied, the root cause of the issue is well understood and that the appropriate steps have been taken to ensure that this does not occur again. This is often a two-step process: First the data is corrected so that one or more stuck transactions can resume. Then, once the heat dies down, diligence and determination must ensue to assure that the root issue is fixed—after all, the data problem is only a symptom. This can be difficult to maintain, and can require that you track back through change and configuration management records, data activity archives, implementation and project information, and complex code reviews. Without proper diligence to fix the problem, it can resurface months or even years later and cause problems again.

**Language Patches**    Most enterprise applications can be provided to end users in their language of choice, and when fixes are made that affect the display of text to end users (that is, beyond just processing code or data fixes), a patch must be applied for each of the installed languages. Historically, this has been an arduous task, and although the application of base patches along with language equivalents can be grouped (merged) together, the administrative tasks such as downloading, validating, and recording are often repeated. The application manager needs to recognize the impacts of language support (not just limited to patching) and should ensure that the costs are well understood by all parties and, when possible, minimize administrative steps through process standardization and automation. Although a few useful utilities might exist in the patching utilities themselves, improvements often involve creative use of the application manager's existing guidelines, tools, and resources.

## Scheduling Patches

Regarding scheduling the application of the different patches—from individual patches, to roll-up patch sets, to full upgrades (or anything in between)—consider the following points.

Every patch comes with a full listing of the problems it fixes, many of which are also covered by other documents, such as My Oracle Support articles that explain in detail each issue. Although these can be laborious to go through, you can partner with business users to identify key changes and decide on suitable scheduling. For example, it would be dangerous to apply a patch set that includes significant changes to a currently stable general ledger system just before the period-end reconciliation is processed.

These articles can also help you add steps to patch application to form a more complete solution; for example, they can point to related patches, highlight post-install steps, offer information on verification and testing, or offer links to addendums. They also include certification advice to help you ensure that all components stay within the supported versions for the complete application, avoiding incompatibilities while reducing the requirement for too much full in-application testing.

Other organizations using the same application features will come across problems, and the application manager needs to keep a watchful eye out for solutions. My Oracle Support's alerts and newsletters can prove very useful in this regard.

Finally, remember that working with business users is key to effective patch management. This is because yet-to-be-fixed issues require using temporary solutions that seriously impact productivity and this can stimulate a negative feeling toward the system (and even the application manager). As such, it can be tempting to offer them temporary solace in a false or unvalidated final resolution date, but patches are rarely delivered early, and expectations should be set properly with clear explanation as to why the wait may be longer than hoped for (reasons such as awaiting dependent fixes, patch creation effort, and detailed quality assurance and testing).

## Managing the Patching Environment

Although patches are obviously applied to all the system components, the patching tools often require a certain amount of administration and organization to ensure that they are running and managed successfully. The patching environment consists of many different things, such as dedicated file system directory structures, specific operating system versions and components, and administrative user accounts with suitable access privileges and resource constraints. This is in addition to basic items such as supporting files, utility scripts and programs, and the availability of change management and tracking systems. This should all be in place and correct setup verified before patching begins.

**Test Instances**     In addition to the detailed bits and pieces that make patching easier, each patch should be initially applied in a test system. The key to success is making sure the test system used is as close as possible to the production system, in terms of its setup, code versions, and dataset. This must also include any customizations, extensions, or anything else that exists in the production environment. In addition to complete patch failure retesting could bring up a few more negative outcomes: the patch may not resolve the issue, it might fix one issue but cause another, or it resolves nothing and creates more issues. Clearly any of these outcomes should not be experienced first in the production system.

**Workers**     In terms of resourcing patching, one of the key aspects is ensuring that the patching processes (known as "workers") run as efficiently as possible, and parallel processing helps ensure time to completion is as short as possible. To facilitate this kind of processing, the system needs to be instructed precisely how parallel it should run. Although it will make a recommendation based on some basic resource identification (commonly number of CPUs, operating system, and database configuration), you can override this to expand or limit processing. Usually the default is acceptable, but tweaking it can be useful to help fine-tune patch processing.

**Environmental Variables**   Somewhat similarly, the patch processing makes use of system capabilities, and utilities, and uses environmental variables to locate these across the technology stack and deployed topology. As mentioned, ensuring that the environment is properly set up is critical for success, especially in new instances or where patching tools are associated with particular system accounts. Similarly, changes in administrative user passwords, often regularly required for governance compliance, need to filter through to patch management.

**Detritus**   Patching commonly leaves behind original patch files, temporary backup files, records in tables (especially from incomplete attempts), and log files. Although these files are not immediately detrimental to the system, it's good practice to keep a clean and well-organized work area, and as such the last stage of a patching process should be a simple clean up. Some things can be removed, closed out, and deleted, while others such as logs might be moved into offline archive storage for a while first.

## Patch Utilities and Handling Failures
In addition to the standard practices, let's look briefly at a few more handy methods for making patch application a minimal consumer of the application manager's time and effort.

**Special Modes**   Most patching tools, including those in Fusion Applications, include some optional input parameters that can be used to suit a particular situation; these can improve both the productivity and affectivity of patching routines. Here are some examples of the more commonly useful options, most of which are simply yes or no–type switches:

- **APPLY**   The patch process can be almost entirely completed without actually applying the changes to the system. It's a useful quick and dirty test.

- **PREREQ**   Controls whether or not the patching tool should check the system for the existence of the predetermined prerequisites for this patch.

- **FORCE**   Either the whole patch or specific actions can be made to execute, overriding default controls that might prevent it. Useful when reapplication of a patch is required.

- **SILENT MODE**   Patches waste a lot of time printing information to the console and this can be eliminated, although, of course all activity is still captured in the logs.

- **LOG**   It's also possible to explicitly control both the name of the patching log file and how verbose the output is. For simple but laborious groups of patches, reducing the log output can help reduce the overall completion time.

- **SECURE**   For some activities and systems, patching may represent a security vulnerability and as such extra secure modes can be used to ensure all passwords are explicitly requested and key system details are hidden from the log output.

**Reducing Administration**   We mentioned how effective it can be to group or merge related patches into bundles for simultaneous application. A couple of other techniques can help limit the amount of manual intervention required for patching.

You can pass a parameterized file into the patching execution and have it pick up all the input values it needs from this file. This is much more effective than halting the execution and waiting for user response, and it also reduces the likelihood of mistakes since input parameters can be standardized and prevalidated with just one or two small adjustments for any one patching run.

In addition to using canned input files,  patching processes can be run as background sessions (such as using UNIX's **nohup** command), so that the application manager doesn't have to maintain a bunch of running sessions as each patch runs.

Finally, to validate results of patching, a bunch of scripts can perform standardized checks to confirm the right changes have occurred (such as file version increments) as well as check for unwanted changes (such as uncompiled objects). Using scripts to compare system information before and after patching is a simple but very useful technique.

**Understanding Input and Output**   To understand failures, you need to have a good grasp of what patching does and exactly how it does it. More than that, the terminology and processes used in patching form a vocabulary of their own, and your fluency here can pay dividends when problems occur.

Patches consist of two main elements, code files, or scripts that change the system so issues are resolved, and a list of instructions on how these should be applied. The instructions, sometimes known as *drivers*, are written in a kind of scripting language that the patching engine understands, and it's helpful for the application manager to be able to identify what these activities are really doing since progress statements, logs, and even failures will often use this internal verbiage.

Because patches are coded internally, few references or training materials are available, but you can simply observe patch execution and its log output to get a feel for what is really happening.

**Failures**     Two types of patch failures occur. First, one specific activity (or worker) inside the patching application fails but the patching engine itself catches the failure, reports it to the output (screen and logs), and safely suspends all activity to allow a manual solution to be applied. For example, an expected application object is missing or is in an unexpected format or status (such as uncompiled). Invasive customizations are also a common cause for this kind of patch failure. Once any manual intervention is complete, the tools provided allow the patching process to be restarted from the point of failure and hopefully run to completion. The only unique skills here are in spotting exactly what the patch was trying to do at the point of failure and understanding how the error message can be resolved.

The second failure type is more severe and hopefully more infrequent, and it represents a complete unexpected aborting of the patching process. Here the patching engine itself encounters an error that prevents it from continuing any further and brings the whole attempt to an ungraceful stop. This might occur if serious system-wide issues such as depleted resources, severed connections, or even hardware failures occurred. In these cases, more often than not the backup taken before patching is used to restore the system to its previous state, since trying to undo a myriad of different activities is usually impractical and often error-prone.

# System Testing

After any major system change, most commonly upgrades and patches, the affected features must be fully tested to ensure that they still operate as expected and the day-to-day business operation is not affected. The application manager is traditionally responsible for several parts of this process, although he or she is not usually the one actually performing functional testing.

## Translation: What to Test

Firstly, the application manager must verify and publish which parts of the functional system (and hence business processes) will be affected by the system changes, so that the appropriate resources from the business are aware, prepared, and made available for subsequent testing. This often requires a translation of the details in the patch, upgrade, or customization into a meaningful outline that can be applied by nontechnical staff across various organization-specific business processes and departments. Although the task is rather laborious, having the right people understand and support system changes is essential for creating and maintaining a positive application user base.

## Testware: How to Test

Next, the application manager will be required to help organize the steps to be taken to test the implemented changes adequately. Although this involves liaising with business users, it should also involve the use of existing test material, often known as *testware*. Testware should be a library of previously used *test cases* that allow any user to run through a basic process quickly and accurately, validating the expected results as they come up. This type of material is often created during the initial application implementation, during various testing phases, most commonly during User Acceptance Testing (UAT). Reusing this material ensures consistency and accuracy, although a few updates might be required as processes and features evolve.

One key point here is that the data used in testing, especially for script-based testware, needs to be standardized, and some kind of reference dataset should be made available for this purpose. Although purely business data, importing or adjusting database content is clearly another area that benefits from the application manager's help.

With these manual testing processes, the results must be carefully captured and where any kind of problem, failure, or inconsistency is detected, the feedback needs to be detailed and become part of a clear resolution process. Again this process (as well as resolution) is an application manager's task.

Taking scripted testing one step further, where tests are fairly simple and easily repeatable, the steps can be replicated within an automated testing system and then launched and executed without the involvement of a user.

Automated testing is notoriously difficult to implement fully, and results can lack depth, but most organizations successfully employ it to some degree, especially in areas where repetition is common. One other benefit of automated testing is that it allows for the easy creation of load, volume, stress, and security testing, ensuring that the stability, reliability, and performance of features remain within acceptable levels.

### Testing Tools: Facilitating and Enhancing Testing

In our Governance Management Toolbox (Chapter 10), we looked briefly at Oracle's Application Testing Suite of products that can be readily employed to facilitate testing, with special capabilities within test automation and analysis. These tools are also very flexible and can be used in many scenarios. One example is in a requirement to complete integration and compatibility testing. The Oracle tools excel since they natively understand the entire stack and all related standards-based technologies therein, so they can support both the standard Oracle Applications features as well as extensions, customizations, and even completely external systems with which it may collaborate.

Choosing the right testing tools is dependent on the history, resources, and focus of each individual organization, and although Oracle and third parties offer extensive and flexible suites, the application manager needs to invest considerable time and effort to select the right solutions for their needs.

## Proactive Health

Let's take a minute to revisit and add some aspects to help us seek out potential problems even before they have serious effects. Some of the topics and tools here are similar to those in Optimization Management (Chapter 9) and Governance Management (Chapter 10); however, this discussion covers a day-to-day approach to the related core tasks.

### Configuration Management

Oracle Configuration Management Pack (a plug-in for Enterprise Manager) and its embedded Application Configuration Console (ACC) tool provides a configuration management database that stores, standardizes, and allows analysis of configuration data across the stack. Although not yet explicitly extended for Fusion Applications, it is flexible and powerful enough to be able to support many parts of the infrastructure around it (database especially), and it seems sensible to expect a dedicated solution in the future.

Previous chapters discussed a few other tools around configuration management, with two items of special focus being Oracle Configuration Manager (OCM) that integrates features with the My Oracle Support portal, as well as the basic information collection process in Remote Diagnostic Agent (RDA). These, along with Functional Setup Manager as well, are essential support tools that can be run frequently so that key information is properly reviewed and archived. Although these tools are somewhat limited in their native form, the applications manager should be able to leverage them, together with some creative (or third-party) additions, to create a basic configuration management solution.

## Change Management

As part of governance for a healthy system, the application manager needs to have a good grasp of past system activity and events in enough detail to include all results and outcomes.

Currently, Oracle offers Change Management packs for E-Business Suite and the Database products only, but this will grow to include more technology stack components and hopefully Fusion Applications. In addition, the Governance, Risk, and Compliance (GRC) product suite itself contains change management capabilities that can be leveraged.

Change management solutions are often discussed; however, frequently a complete and practical infrastructure for recording and recalling actions becomes so complex that the tools become fragmented and are not kept up to date. For example, one system is used for patch management, another for hardware, several for platform components (database, middleware), and even more for the different business components of the application itself (such as Finance, Human Resources, Manufacturing). Bringing all the activities and types of changes possible across such a broad area is a real challenge, but it is vital to control and manage it as a single complete system. Simple solutions include the unification and standardization of control and reporting systems, as well as creative tricks such as placing a visualization layer (such as a portal) across different change management systems so they appear and seem to operate as one.

For the most part, both change and configuration management help the application manager in the following three key tasks, themselves part of the system health:

- Understand where they are right now, so that all future planning is based on an accurate picture. This might be uptake of upgrades, capacity planning, the implementation of new features for business users, or even simply tracking system evolution over time.

- When sudden problems occur, allow the tracking back of activities and data to check for potential causes. This can also include an easy comparison between systems.

- Audit requirements so that should governance problems surface full investigations can be undertaken. This is where the GRC capabilities come in.

## Customization Management

Customizations bring the solutions that business users say they need, but at a price that is historically very high, and a well-used statistic says that software maintenance costs increase by about 70 percent when customizations are involved when compared to the same products used out of the box. Indeed, it never fails to surprise me that a mature enterprise application that is riddled with customizations rarely has a clear and up-to-date repository that anyone can point at to give a decent amount of basic detail about them. Even simple information such as where customizations are, what form they take, and why they were deemed critical in the first place is rarely available. At best, customization design documents are passed around, but they are usually written by developers for developers. This means they give little detail on the true extent of their effect across business processes and even more rarely include any built-in mechanisms for their management going forward. All too often, customization work is done by consultants who come in, deliver the code, and leave, with a less-than-ideal handover to the existing IT staff.

As discussed, Fusion Applications offers many capabilities, architectures, and easy-to-use features that make customizations significantly less impactful and easier to support. We discussed the Metadata Services (MDS) architecture that is prevalent throughout the application, and how for most custom object definitions, they are reapplied at runtime over the top of a locked-down gold standard definition, allowing patches and upgrades to change the base and for customizations to be simply overlain. Although the architectures are present, how can the changes by managed?

First, we'll look at existing, proven tooling that can help you manage customizations. For Fusion Applications, most of this is done in JDeveloper, where a specific customization role exists for designing, creating, and implementing changes within the context of an MDS layer. Although this relatively low-level tool is not exactly a system management tool, the manager of extensive custom code would be well-advised to understand it.

Oracle WebCenter Composer represents another significant, purpose-built tool that can be used for creating and managing user interface adjustments. The leap from JDeveloper to WebCenter is quite broad because the focus moves far away from customizations to business logic in ADF Business Components (ADFbc), business processes through Business Process Execution Language (BPEL) , and even the database design. Fusion Applications, especially Customer Relationship Management, identifies this gap and offers some intermediate tooling with a design framework backed up by another graphical composer feature, so business objects and underlying code can be manipulated in a way that is application-specific and therefore fully compliant.

To be perfectly honest, at this early stage, although the platforms for customization are well-defined, little specific tooling is dedicated to tracking and managing nonstandard custom code. Even so, effective management solutions are possible. To make a reasonable job of this, the application manager needs just two vital ingredients.

The application manager needs good organizational skills to chart the detail of customization projects and ensure that all the results of design, development, testing, and implementation are available for reference. Much of this should correspond to the general management of the appropriate instances being used, where the development instance is associated with design documentation, the test instance has records of applicable testware and results, and the production instance has the patching records associated with implementing the custom code.

Second, and perhaps most important, the application manager needs to be involved in the customization work. From the outset, he or she must ensure that supportability and manageability are embedded into the solution and help verify that the requirements truly justify the proposed extension by working with developers to scope out the ongoing management overhead and potential risk in introducing the nonstandard code. This material is valuable during the implementation process and again is an essential reference for later use to facilitate management success.

One interesting thought to consider is that the usual approach is for IT systems to be made/bent to meet the needs of the business. Based on a great many people's experience (my own included), in reality, to get truly effective return on investment and the most efficient and fluid processes, the business can often be changed so that it better fits with the IT services available. IT, including the enterprise application, forms part of the business infrastructure and as such can be literally viewed as a *facility*, just like a factory plant. In the same way that retooling machinery to meet idea-world requirements is prohibitively expensive (or often not even possible), for an application to be effective it must be allowed to run as designed. The traditional view is that software by its very nature is so flexible it can be molded in any way possible, but in the reality of high volume, always-on business operations, it's often more effective to adjust processes around the software than to start messing with the software itself. One of my favorite quotes of all time (source unknown) is this: "The fastest way of doing something is not to do it at all." For customizations, you can make it "fastest, cheapest, easiest, and most manageable."

## Resource Management

The application manager, like everyone, has finite resources (time, staff, equipment, budget) and must decide the most effective way to allocate them to achieve the most important goals. As shown in our Fusion Applications lifecycle, the range of goals is pretty wide, from critically important and often urgent tasks such as those in availability and security, to goals in performance and reliability that are more subjective as to how urgent and important they are, and finally to governance goals that are rarely urgent yet are often important. Keeping an eye on a task's urgency versus its true importance is one way to help assign resources.

A good understanding of priorities is key to effective resource allocation, and as such the targets set with the various stakeholders within application management must be divided carefully and appropriately provisioned. That said, just like the capacity management of the application itself, things change in both the short and long terms, as sudden emergencies appear, the business operations evolve, and applications progress through their natural lifecycle. Being able to flex with these changes is a key factor in building the management operation, so that the health of the system can be resourced no matter what occurs, from power outages and security violations, to performance degradation or configuration-based errors. In reality, this means that very few resources should be tied completely to one set of tasks, and although clearly utilization should be high, many resources (time, people, and their abilities, or tooling) must be flexible enough to be redirected to new priority areas at a moment's notice.

## Managing Service Definitions

As discussed in Chapters 3 and 4, the ITSM approach to managing the IT infrastructure is based around the management of a range of services that are provided to business consumers. Each service, such as a set of enterprise application performance targets, has to be identified, its contents designed around achievable expectations, and then implemented using the appropriate architecture and tools. Services also need to be supported by clear methods to measure actual results against targets, and a clear process by which outcomes can be reviewed and necessary actions agreed upon must be in place. Normally, business users are available for collaboration, but they are obviously focused on their day-to-day jobs and it is likely the enterprise application manager will be expected to do much of the service management work.

In terms of proactive health, once services are set up, implemented, and running as part of a complete management solution, they form an effective way of bringing together IT resources around goals that are truly important for the health of the business. Indeed, the very provisioning of an ITSM-based process can help focus and monitor key system performance areas that might otherwise be taken for granted, addressed only when they cause significant pain and costly productivity drops for business users.

At a high level, the nature of both Fusion Applications and its management is naturally SOA-like, consisting of many discrete components operating independently, but brought together to work as a unit in the support of a standardized set of business processes. From application components such as the database, the middleware, and the business intelligence, to the management functions such as error handling, performance management, and configuration data management, the need for both a broad range of skills with simultaneous expertise and specialization is a challenge that needs a clever solution. The most common analogy used for software support is the medical profession, where the work is comparable to diagnosing and treating health issues. Indeed the overall management infrastructure is a lot like a hospital, where some general skills are used in places like the emergency room, however, different wards also specialize in especially complex and acute problems. We look at this more in the next section.

Enterprise Manager supports incident and problem management, and, through its various extensions (especially Grid Control), supports the implementation of SLAs to aid the tooling around ITSM methodologies. These extensive monitoring, alerting, and notification capabilities are well suited to implement approaches such as Information Technology Infrastructure Library (ITIL). The Enterprise Manager features also provide a ready-to-go integration with Oracle Siebel Customer Relationship Management (CRM) Call Center application (or similar solution, such as BMC's Remedy product) so that the tools available can be implemented across the IT Infrastructure.

# Reactive Health

Although the areas mentioned so far (and many more) are concerned with general good practice in managing and improving the enterprise application, another realm of tasks occurs in response to one or more particular events, to ensure that appropriate reactions benefit system health. It's easy for the application manager to get bogged down in this type of fire-fighting work, but a few tips and tricks can help avoid this and maintain the balance.

## Technical Support

A significant proportion of the application manager's resources are spent handling and resolving problems in the day-to-day operation of the application system. As discussed in Chapters 5 and 6, these problems might be system-generated, automatically detected as soon as they stray outside defined thresholds (such as performance and resource consumption), or simply problems reported by end users that are not currently being monitored (such as data issues and bugs). Another alternative source of reactive problems comes as a result of detailed system analysis where some of the proactive time spent around optimization (Chapter 9) identifies problems that need immediate action before they turn into major issues.

As you may recall, I have spent more than a decade in the trenches of Oracle Support, and even before that I was on the other side of the fence as an application manager working closely with vendor support teams and consultants in implementing and managing complex environments. I will attempt to offer some insights on how to get more effective results from Technical Support. Some of these may seem rather obvious, and certainly some professionals already use most of the techniques and practices discussed here, but, in my experience working with thousands of application managers and their staffs, more often than not some big assumptions are made and important techniques glossed over, with the results reflecting that. Even as an exceptional professional (which I am sure you are, and the fact you are reading this book is a sign of that), you still should be able to glean a few insights and reminders that can be used to make improvements.

**Problem Identification**     In dealing with software problems of all kinds, you'll see some up-front basics that many people skip over in their haste to delve into the details and hunt for solutions. Although enthusiasm and tenacity are definitely important skills for an application manager, huge amounts of time are wasted chasing red herrings and going down avenues of investigation that drift away from the original problem itself. This happens the most for business user–reported problems, where very technically focused staff jump into the complex analysis of the problem without truly understanding what the problem is, where it is, and even why it represents a problem. Before even considering potential solutions, you should try to define the problem in a clear and structured manner. This technique is often called *framing* a problem, because it tries to explain the boundaries and extent of the issue. Here are a few basic questions to ask (and the responses to record):

- When does the problem occur? When did it start, when did it last happen, and does it happen only at certain times or in performing certain operations?

- How does the problem occur? What are the precise steps taken to reproduce it? If it cannot be reproduced, what was done previously and what might be different now? Also, what still works that is in a similar area? (Reminds me of the amusing technical support question, "What did you do before you didn't do anything?")

- What is the extent of the problem? What is affected—is it all or some users, transactions, or enterprise structures?

- What does the problem look like? How is it manifested to the user, and especially what are the exact detail of any errors, warnings, or incorrect results?

- What is the impact of the problem? How and why does this issue cause challenges in completing business tasks? Can the impact of the problem be worked around using alternative steps?

In addition, it's often worth generally discussing the problem with any users who experienced it, since often small throw-away comments can be critical to resolution. For example, occasionally a user will say things such as, "Oh, yeah, I heard others seem to get this type of problem in this area sometimes as well," hinting that some kind of regular combination of factors are to blame. These types of conversations often lead to valuable background information, such as small changes to the system, its data, or its use that are actually outside any formal change management process.

If you have worked with Oracle Support you might have heard of Oracle Diagnostic Methodology (ODM), Oracle's technique for ensuring that key parts of the problem are captured throughout its lifecycle, and this begins with a similar definition step.

**Problem Analysis**     After defining the problem incident, the application manager (and related IT staff such as DBAs and system administrators) can often benefit from a few process-based recommendations. The right approach to problem analysis is frequently more important and leads to faster and better resolution that a mountain of technical expertise that is applied in a haphazard manner. Basic professionalism and quality even in these deeply technical areas help ensure that the health of reactive work is always maintained. A huge number of potential steps can be involved in problem analysis, and although a whole chapter or book could be devoted to this area alone, I'll try to summarize the key points.

Some fundamental techniques can be used in performing detailed analysis. The first step should be to set the *analysis context*. Here each phase of analysis has a clear goal, and each goal aims to take the process one step closer to a resolution. This kind of discrete and progressive approach helps avoid drift and is also exceptionally helpful when handling multiple problems at once.

Having decided upon the context and the associated goals, you can check for the existence of similar issues (and their solutions) and identify potential temporary workarounds, especially when the problem is business critical. Once in the depths of problem investigation, you can ensure that analysis activities are logical, well documented, and continue to build on the results gathered so far; these simple methods can be a huge time-saver, especially when you're working on multiple long-running issues.

A more detailed analysis principle is to ensure that each activity is completed in a systematic, methodical, and thorough manner. All too often, when business users and managers are exerting intense pressure for resolution, some basic steps can get skipped in the rush to perform complex and technical investigations. Figure 11-6 summarizes basic steps that can be applied to most types of analysis.

This model also helps to ensure that each significant piece of information is properly recorded for later use—in my experience, it's not only positive results that qualify as significant information and findings, since negative results are also helpful in creating a picture of a problem. Repeating analysis steps because they were not well documented the first time is a complete waste of time.

The most common and easiest method of technical problem solving is to use questioning techniques, in which the same question is asked repeatedly—commonly five times—and is simply "Why?" Looking at the problem and

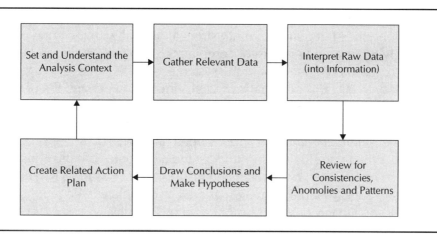

**FIGURE 11-6.** *Basic problem analysis steps*

asking why that is the case gets the analysis moving. For example, "Why does this specific error occur?" might lead to the answer that process X is failing. Then comes another "Why?" and the answer will probably provide more detail about the workings of process X. Another "Why?" is asked, and then perhaps you notice that the problem affects only a small subset of data (users or transactions) that process X uses when it fails; this can be checked and some inconsistencies may be noticed compared to working attempts. Another "Why?" helps pinpoint what it is about the data that causes a problem. The final "Why?" helps clarify the origin and validity of the problematic data based on setups and reference documentation. From here, conclusions can be made on the issue's cause and appropriate solutions can be investigated.

This basic example illustrates how simple practices of *critical thinking* can be applied to technical problem-solving. The adoption (even informally) of a basic process for completing well-reasoned analysis can make the whole process somewhat less stressful because it becomes better organized, and the results are of higher quality for the benefit of everyone involved.

In addition to analytical methods, some basic abilities and work practice traits can help in making reactive technical support more effective and, as a consequence, prompting good application management health. First is the ability to stick with a task doggedly until it's complete. A significant amount of determination, perseverance, and discipline is required to resolve complex issues, especially those that are poorly understood, where supporting resources are thin, and whose occurrence is severe but infrequent and seemingly impossible to replicate upon demand. Coupled with these is motivation, since it requires an inner strength to deal with the grind of a seemingly never-ending stream of complaints, problems, and grumbles from business users (and others) about the system.

It's easy to take this personally as well, since as owner and the person responsible for the enterprise application, you may be blamed for all the problems and issues that come up. In my experience, the best way to handle this is to ensure that communication is open and honest, and most of all, frequent. When one side doesn't understand and appreciate the constraints and efforts of the other, resentment and dissatisfaction sets in. When business users share background information as well as complete issue reports, and the application manager shares his or her efforts, results, and plans, everyone understands why situations are as they are, and more often than not additional positive collaboration ensues.

My final recommendation in terms of attitude and approach is a bit more positive. I have found that by maintaining focus, having an inquisitive nature, and continuously being able to come up with creative solutions to problems brings huge benefits. These attributes apply not just to finding final solutions but also to problem analysis, when trying to determine next actions based on complex, confusing, and even contradictory information requires something extra special.

A few people possess all these traits, and certainly fewer still automatically apply them to every problem, but a partial solution is also at hand. By recognizing the basics when designing the support infrastructure and build in features that embed key steps and approaches the dependency is ingrained automatically. Often, by creating standard processes, procedures, and tooling, you can include most of the key aspects into the flow of work. Two additional aspects that can be readily built in are thoroughness and attention to detail, where tooling in particular can allow commencement and completion of work only when a prior task is completed in a satisfactory way.

A final note on problem analysis: try to keep things simple. As Albert Einstein said, "Make everything as simple as possible, but not simpler," which in this case means that it's vital for you to validate the basic fundamentals of a problem, and to look first at what is the simplest and most likely causes of an issue. Avoiding assumption (such as checking all setups) is important; by doing this, the basic checks will be complete long before you dive into the more complex and time-consuming processes, and often the most simplest of answers is the right one. The analysis of software problems requires a forensic-like approach, and by following the available evidence and studying internal relationships among components, you can piece together one or more investigative threads, each of which can be followed to their logical conclusion.

**Technical Skills**    As shown in Figure 11-6, several key parts of the equation require technical expertise. First is the capture of additional data to help investigate the issue. This requires a good understanding of the process in question, which technical components are involved, and precisely how to execute or configure these to create more information, such as diagnostic output or more detailed log files. Second, taking this additional raw data and transforming it in its raw state into meaningful information requires some basic skills in understanding system outputs and being able to recognize key statements and understand their significance to the issue at hand.

Finally, armed with some new information, you can look for further knowledge to be able to draw conclusions upon applicable next steps. Indeed, simply coming up with the list of potential actions itself requires significant skill, never mind being able to conclude which route will lead to the fastest and most effective solution. Simply knowing precisely how processes and parts of the system work is essential to ensuring that adjustments to configuration settings are effective (such as performance), validating the existence of setup or data issues, or even simply being able to establish valid expectations on what a process should be able to handle.

Although technical knowhow can be learned through training, and the adage "hire for attitude, train for skill" is certainly never as true as it is for enterprise application support, experience will still garner a lot of respect. It's true that many components are brand-new and few people have loads of experience (just like Fusion Applications itself), however many of the underlying concepts and technology underpinnings have been around for years in one form or another, and when you look at application issues, you can call upon your related and equivalent experiences to help direct your progress. Failures often involve core technology concepts (such as Java functions listed in stack traces), or perhaps your experience in working with particular business processes (such as payroll processing, finance period closure, or document approval) helps you formulate some likely potential causes and good avenues to investigate. Experience also helps you interpret potential effects of changes to the application, especially where attempts in the past have left painful memories in the application manager's mind.

**Customer Skills**    In a role external to Oracle, I am an assessor for the U.K. Institute of Customer Service's Professional Awards program, and we teach and validate that the customer-facing staff of our member organizations exhibit what it takes to deliver exceptional customer service. Surprisingly to some, we regard a customer as not only the customers of the products and/ or services that the organization brings to market, but simply as anyone to which a person interacts—colleagues, managers, subordinates, suppliers, partners, or anyone at all. This helps staff focus on what we call the *holistic approach* to customer service, where everyday work practices focus not only on the fee-paying customer but also on interactions with colleagues and others within the organization (and its goals), as well as addressing personal development and growth.

The customer, whoever he or she might be, is the primary focus, and one aspect often overlooked by IT support teams is the fact that the business user often needs a fast solution and is often happy with any kind of temporary adjustment or change. The user simply needs to be able to move forward, no matter how ugly the progress. Being able to understand and keep an eye on what matters most to the customer is an important skill and can work wonders to solidify the ongoing relationship.

In addition, although very closely related, it's crucial that you properly set the expectations of all parties involved as early as possible. Ideally, this would be to provide an ETA for resolution, but that is only rarely possible and as such it's worth regularly spending just a couple of minutes to explain exactly where the resolution process is heading (and why), what actions are currently ongoing, and what actions will follow down the line. Much more respect for the hard and complex work involved in supporting application issues is generally shown where basic details like this are shared.

One final point to make on the subject of customer skills is that everyone loves to deal with someone with a positive, can-do attitude. This can be difficult to maintain, and you need to be careful not to come across as simply annoying or patronizing; by being very clear in communicating plans and approach at every stage of a problem, and involving the customer at least by sharing detailed information, the whole experience tends to be less painful for all involved. Exuding confidence should always be backed up by sharing justified actions and their meaningful results.

**Resourcing and References**    A few tools, when implemented internally, can make a significant difference. The first is the ability to respond and resolve the slew of requests for assistance, especially in the first few months of implementation. The next section looks more at the helpdesks as a layer of triage that should be in place so that a reasonable proportion of problem reports are resolved by a team of front-line staff with basic support training. Without this, the application manager will never get to the items in the Optimization Plan, and even items in the Governance Plan can suffer due to a lack of proper attention. It's also usually a poor and expensive use of valuable resources to tie up the application manager with helpdesk issues.

The second aspect here is making sure that a detailed repository of supporting information exists that can be used to check for known issues and cover many knowledge gaps. It's simply nonsensical to consider for a moment that a single application manager will be able to understand every aspect of something as broad and deep as Fusion Applications, and therefore a reference library of some kind is crucial. These are usually called *knowledge management systems*, but less formal resources, coupled with capabilities available in portals such as My Oracle Support are essential. Without this the application manager can easily be the bottleneck in resolution processing. In these days of information overload, the person who filters and shares key information has the most authority and influence, and the days of holding tight to special knowledge are long gone.

## A Healthy Enterprise Application Helpdesk

Many other resources, such as books, courses, and consultants can help you set up and operate a technical support helpdesk, so this section will make no attempt to go down that road. However, when managing Fusion Applications, you can leverage the tooling and features of the application to integrate into existing helpdesk infrastructures, as well as be used for the creation of new applicable services. Let's start with the diagram in Figure 11-7 and use it to discuss this area further.

Although Figure 11-7 is somewhat oversimplified, let's look at the capabilities, tooling, and flows for each of three main sections. First is the reporting of application problems, which essentially comes in two forms: Problems records (or tickets) can be routed to the helpdesk to indicate a problem that needs resolving. This type may include business user concerns, problems, or questions. For technical-related issues, this may lead to the use of additional diagnostic tools, such as manual DFw incident creation, but most of these types of issues are functional or data related.

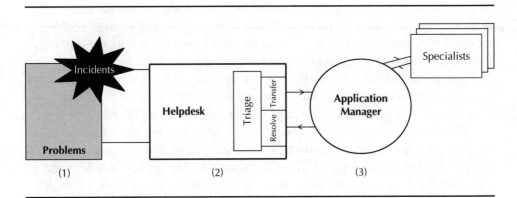

**FIGURE 11-7.** *Incident management*

The second channel is through the in-built incident management process, whereby the system itself catches serious failures and the helpdesk team is alerted to the problem and a problem record (ticket) is created. The incident management system (that is, the Support Workbench and Automatic Diagnostic Repository Command Interpreter [ADRCI]) may also not be something the application manager considers appropriate for helpdesk engineers to use, so the application manager might also control some of the flow of problems. The same might be said for some of the other system monitor tools inside Enterprise Manager, such as performance and availability information mentioned in Chapters 7 and 8 inside Fusion Applications Control and the Database Control. Clearly, however, by limiting access to these tools, the application manager also retains some responsibility for managing and resolving problems and incidents, since handing off issues to the helpdesk can generate a large amount of unnecessary administrative work (especially since many issues will happen again). By providing training and controlling security, a reasonable compromise can be reached so everyone has the tools they need.

So moving on to (2) in the diagram, the helpdesk should be skilled enough to provide basic triage services for most enterprise application issues. This would naturally include functional and technical problems and steps, as well as skills in defining the issue, researching known and similar issues, and perhaps validating configurations and collecting more detailed information such as that in DTF and basic diagnostic logs.

When it comes to in-depth detailed analysis, some extra help might be required and specific actions transferred to the application manager. The volumes coming through the helpdesk will often govern to what extent the staff (or a subset) will specialize in handling enterprise application problems and how far their diagnosis will go. Apart from technical problems, the helpdesk may offer a method to invoke the help of business specialists who can provide guidance on expert use of the applications features. These domain experts can often help resolve problems because the precise features and implementation configuration will be outside the capability of the application manager alone.

By arming the helpdesk with clear processes by which they can get assistance of experts as well as providing steps for involving the application manager, many critical issues can be quickly routed to those with the appropriate skills, while keeping day-to-day non-urgent issues progressing through the standardized and efficient helpdesk process. The third step (3) in the diagram illustrates how the application manager assists in resolving complex problems, by providing discrete inputs and reviews or by taking ownership of some of the most critical types of issues (such as availability). Again, depending on volumes, this connection can also serve as a training flow back into the helpdesk, where experts can share information with the helpdesk team so that they are better prepared to provide more extensive capabilities next time. As indicated at the end of the process, in addition to business domain experts (such as finance experts), technical specialists may be involved in issue resolution, from DBAs, to network administrators, and of course Oracle Support. Again ensuring that these interaction processes are clear allows for speedy resolution of even the most critical and complex problems.

As a final note on this section, in fostering collaboration and efficient process and procedures, thoughts immediately spring back to the ITSM-like models, where expectations and engagements (services) are clearly set out ahead of time. Although full implementation of these models has its challenges (cost, administration, and so on) the underlying principles can be reused by the forward-thinking application manager to ensure that the infrastructure definition includes a healthy reactive support process.

# Eleven Proven Ways to Application Health

Human health is often focused on three aspects: regular exercise, good diet, and emotional balance. Each area is well represented in large numbers of books and magazine articles. Most people use a mixture of what fits along with other desires, responsibilities, and of course using they have learned through experience. Although the health of Fusion Applications (or most enterprise applications) could be reviewed by using the standard categorizations of the lifecycle defined back in Chapter 4, each specific implementation involves its own set of constraints to what can actually be realized. The following tips and tricks represent some useful pieces of advice picked up over the years that may prove helpful in maintaining system health.

# Project Management

In most enterprise application manager positions, the exceptionally high number of diversions and distractions can prevent the timely completion of many non-urgent tasks. By implementing simple project management processes and related tooling, optimization and governance improvement efforts can be initiated, progressed, and monitored with ease. By displaying and reporting on activities, progress, and deadlines, all parties can see into the  IT department, to understand, appreciate, and occasionally contribute to specific efforts.

Another candidate area that benefits from effective project management is customization. Ensuring that customization efforts include appropriate management capabilities requires proper engagement in the right tasks at the right time, from requirements gathering to testing. One aspect that is often poorly understood in customization is precisely where the recommended practices begin and end, and although Oracle has published some advice on implementing customizations in a standardized fashion, it was sometimes hard to follow precisely.

With Fusion Applications comes more extensive support for extensions and customizations although is complemented with more complete documentation on all related capabilities. At a bare minimum this provides some familiarization work for the application manager who should become a crucial contributor to ensure that all changes and extensions comply as intended, and are properly recorded, understood, and managed.

# Reusable Templates and Automation

Successful automation in systems and application management has been measured as providing a 50 percent decrease in upgrade costs and a 100 percent increase in DBA productivity. By simplifying basic tasks through more standardization and automation, frequently used processes become more effective, consistent, and thoroughly completed, leaving more resources available for other important tasks.

Areas to consider include system cloning for managing separate test and production instances, data migration between systems, basic troubleshooting, adjusting configuration, adding capacity, and procedural steps such as invoking the assistance of another expert. Templates and automated can help ensure that off-track nonstandard adjustments are easy to make and that change management processes track all dependencies properly, avoiding conflicts later on.

# Training

Although functional product awareness might be somewhat outside the applications manager's realm, some cross-training process should be available. Effective application managers have often worked on the business side at some point and can fully appreciate the day-to-day interactions required to get business tasks completed. It's tempting for application managers to separate themselves from business operations, but they lose a lot of contextual information, and engaging in training activities can help to reaffirm this. Fusion Applications offers many short, easy-to-consume videos in its online User Assistance library.

Training shouldn't be a one-time event either, and should include regular basic refreshers as well as more expert workshop sessions, something for the application manager to use as optimization opportunities. The application manager's technical skill development plan can also benefit from cross-training with the other specialists, such as DBAs and networking administrators. Training also works both ways, since expert users and other technical staff may benefit from basic overviews of the application management functions so that they can contribute better as well.

# Make It Fun

Fusion Applications is more engaging and rich than its predecessors, so why not try to make the management experience the same? This applies to both the application manager and for the business users. Empowering the application manager with tools such as RUEI gives them extended scope for a deeper involvement with their tasks, as well as the abilities to unearth unprecedented insights, to resolve more issues, improve management quality, and offer new levels to the application provision service.

Creative thinkers often use techniques such as lateral thinking to come up with insights and engaging content and; it takes only a sprinkling of effort to turn drab statistics and technical processes into something much more appealing. Wear your marketing hat for five minutes to see how you can communicate in a much more engaging way.

A similar proactive type attitude can be adopted to the reactive support process, where instead of treating it as a drain on resources, you can mine the resulting information for potential improvement candidates and the cost savings that go with them.

# Learn from Experience

Inertia is not a good enough excuse to ignore the pursuit of excellence. Just because you or your organization has always managed the IT systems in a certain way doesn't mean that's good enough now. One of the core reasons that Fusion Applications was developed is because the business and technology worlds have evolved so far that it requires the reinvention of work practices, process improvement opportunities, and their associated management capabilities. If you think about it, adopting a new enterprise application is a fantastic opportunity to redesign systems, question the old methods, validating assumptions of what must be, and generally trying to simplify, streamline, and optimize.

Talk with colleagues who manage other components to look for similarities and ideas. Discuss with respected individuals and recognized visionaries in management, as often these folks see a bigger, broader picture that can be helpful in making even the smallest infrastructure setup decisions. Look outside your organization, at customers, suppliers, and partners, to learn about what they're doing for clues on best practices and pitfalls. This kind of conversation can help lay some groundwork for future conversations as well. For too many years, heads-down, basement-dwelling system administrators have had to reinvent the wheel over and over again to deliver the same (or similar) set of generic application management services. Those days are over, and the time has come to unleash a creative and insightful management infrastructure.

Apart from technical expertise, experience is usually the main value that outside consultants bring to the table, and this often manifests itself through the application of a cookie-cutter approach to implementation. This is based on generic sets of best practices and is regularly fine-tuned from significant experiences, both bad and good. Although paying to avoid critical mistakes makes perfect sense, lessons are truly learned only when some semblance of the experience is completed. It is perhaps best if this is kept to as few negative experiences as possible by understanding in detail what others did and how that went—learning through the experience of others.

# Channeling Communication

Communication both to and from the application manager is an essential ingredient as business users continue to understand and interact with the software system. Even internally, the alerts, notifications, monitoring interfaces, incident reports, and health dashboards must all work seamlessly and effectively with the single aim of supporting application management. Fusion Applications comes with various components and tools for integrating discrete information sources, such as WebCenter, and by leveraging some creative solutions, you can bring the disparate tooling together and save considerable day-to-day task-switching effort and time.

Inbound communication must also be tightly controlled so that an overload of raw data or requests for action does not distract the application manager from important tasks. It's helpful to schedule regular reviews of what is working and what inputs are not regularly adding any real value (consider the 80/20 rule to help decide). From this, simply fine-tune the processes and tools involved, removing rarely used and low-impact items. It's often difficult to take a step back and have the ruthlessness to ditch items of information that might be useful someday, but when this spring-cleaning is done effectively, it usually pays for itself within only a few days, quickly returning significant time savings and productivity gains.

## Create Knowledge

With a slightly different angle to the training item mentioned earlier, the application manager is faced with a software system so vast in technologies and functionality that it is simply impossible to be a true expert in the whole thing. You need great reference documentation, which can take a couple of forms. First is the record of system information, such as configuration management, implementation designs, service level definitions, and the like. This allows you to find the information you need to analyze and manipulate the system. Lots of basic component information, such as configuration, is built into the management tools such as Enterprise Manager, where you can drill-down into a component on a management dashboard to see its current configuration settings. This information is limited, and a process should be in place to help you quickly find more. This might be a simple shared file system library of standard document types or some kind of purpose-built management repository such as a database application specifically for holding information.

The information storage systems are usually known as a *knowledge management system* or a *knowledgebase*. This is essentially an in-house version of the tool that Oracle maintains and provides within My Oracle Support, itself filled with many thousands of articles and documents to help you use the application, troubleshoot problems, and resolve known issues. The My Oracle Support portal also allows you to publish knowledge articles for the benefit of the whole community. Many organizations still want to operate a knowledge repository of their own, commonly containing information that pertains to their own specific uses and implementation, such as details on configurations, extensions, integrations, and customizations. Overall Knowledge Management is a complex and wide-ranging topic, and should be researched further.

# Using Outsourcing

You can also choose to let someone else worry about the management and health of the application. By choosing to implement one of the ever-increasing range of software-as-a-service (SaaS), cloud-based, or on-demand type services available on the market, you can implement various capabilities of enterprise applications without having to touch or maintain any hardware or software systems. Oracle offers an ever-expanding portfolio of on-demand services to its applications customers, where parts (specific products and features), collections of parts (product families or pillars), or simply the whole set of capabilities are available to be accessed over the network, with the back-end completely managed by Oracle.

You can leverage other types of outsourcing opportunities as well, such as integrating a third-party extension to the standard capabilities to get more efficient or comprehensive features, such as catalog and data management services provided by specific domain experts. Outsourcing management of parts of the technology stack, such as the database, allows regular management tasks to be completed and health checks to be run so that optimizations can be made and operations made as effective as possible. Another common area of outsourcing is the development of extensions and customizations that can be both created and hosted by an entirely external organization.

One thing you will need to maintain is the relationship with the outsourcing supplier (or commonly with several of them), and a well-understood set of delivery requirements and expectations must be in place. Even though outsourcing alleviates many day-to-day tasks, some basic monitoring should still occur, and when things go wrong, the subsequent processes must be smooth, clear, and supported by staff with the appropriate skills from all sides.

# Careful Resourcing

Much of this book is written with a single reader in mind, the person who is responsible for the management of Fusion Applications. It's likely that in reality this will be more than one person, where an existing DBA covers much of the database side, the middleware support team looks after much of the Fusion Application components running in the WebLogic application server, and a few other specialists handle other parts (perhaps Business Intelligence, for example). Overseeing this is an IT manager who assumes ownership as a whole. So assuming this reality, a few points might help the right workload to be assigned to the right place for the best results.

First think about people. With enough people to handle the basic and reactive tasks, potentially more proactive type optimizations can be done. Rarely will there be enough people to cover all possible tasks however, so setting priorities is the best method to ensure the right things get attention. The best way to do this is to redefine the role of those who manage part of the application as an additional task, since the priority of this new task needs setting properly against existing work.

Next comes the resourcing of projects. A key aspect to successful application management is ensuring a solid and sound ongoing management infrastructure is in place from the start, and this is often part of an implementation project that gets dropped off at the end, especially when resources are tight and pressures to complete the implementation are encountered. Ensuring application management is included in the sign-off criteria and mandating a careful hand-over process is an essential tip for success.

Third comes the resourcing and provision of tools. Many tools can bring substantial benefits to the application manager, but they need resourcing, both from an implementation and on-going management perspective. In addition to those discussed, many third-party tooling solutions have proven popular with Oracle Applications over the years and with new technologies involved, even more options will be available. One example would be the System Testing tools, where although adoption has been historically low, surveys report that a high percentage of failures could have been found upon basic well-executed and organized acceptance testing.

Finally comes hardware resourcing, and specifically the suitable provision of capacity for multiple instances of the application. Although clearly adding instances adds management overhead, ensuring that test instances are equivalent to production instances in terms of architecture, dataset, configuration, and capacity can significantly aid in off-line investigation of problems, especially those that require invasive activities such as  enabling logging, tracing, and restarting of key components.

# Getting More from Partners

Few organizations will undertake the implementation of Fusion Applications alone and will instead look to leverage various specialist services from preferred suppliers, such as additional technical expertise, product feature and implementation expertise, or areas such as business process re-engineering. All of these areas involve a close collaboration with the application manager and there are a few tricks to making that as successful as possible.

The first key to success is to set boundaries and expectations, and when possible have enforcement agreements or at least a clear plan on dealing with unsatisfactory results.

Next is not to be satisfied with basic results and to try to push for those little extras that make all the difference as to how practical and usable a solution is. Good examples are business process documentation and training, various custom performance reports, and scripts and utilities for managing technology. This also illustrates the fact that it's important to think about day-to-day solutions as well as the long-term strategy, since all too often the future changes before the strategy is realized and great amounts of time and money were wasted.

Ask questions, and lots of them. An effective consultant should be able to translate and transfer his or her expertise into meaningful information that the application manager can use to keep the system going after the engagement ends. Often the standard deliverables from such engagements need further explanation, since they are often written based on style, content, and structure that is familiar to the consultant but new and unclear to the organization. This simply requires reviewing the material but then making dedicated time to grill consultants for more details and clearer explanations. Remember that every engagement should include quality handover and the desire for positive outcomes and feedback.

In addition, the range of services available from specialist organizations (including Oracle) is evolving all the time, and it's worth the application manager regularly investigating what is on offer since it can sometimes really help resolve particular problems areas, or simply add significant improvements.

Examples might be database health checks and tuning, network and hardware optimization, and business process redesign (especially post acquisition/ merger). Rather than spend hours trawling web sites and service catalogs, simply inform the appropriate partners of your interests and simply get them to summarize new solutions that might fit your needs.

Another recommended practice that can offer useful opportunities to learn from others is to engage in the standalone communities dealing with the Oracle products. The Oracle User Group and its partner the Oracle Applications User Group have regional and international divisions that offer opportunities to engage with and learn from leaders and specialists from within and outside Oracle, and most importantly with experienced Oracle customers, just like you. These opportunities include online services, information and forums, as well as conferences, special interest group meetings, and workshops. In addition, many publications, blogs, and online communities have formed around particular products and sets of products and again can provide some invaluable insights. You can set up and manage a small set of relevant external resources to engage with, as these can provide valuable information and opportunities.

Finally, get support and formal sponsorship from senior management. Although a line-management chain will no doubt exist, for some aspects of application management it can be helpful to have the backing of a senior person. This is especially true in areas of optimization and governance, where special projects (and costs) may be required to implement effective long-term solutions and gain as much support as possible. Also by having regular review sessions with a senior executive sponsor, you can share key ideas and proposals and get some valuable open and honest feedback. Similarly, going through existing projects, summarizing and discussing progress and challenges, can also lead to helpful advice. Clearly, the right sponsor needs to be found and an appropriate relationship established, since this kind of mentoring activity requires some specific skills and is not suitable for everyone. Also the existing line-management must also be supportive, taking care to involve or collaborate with sponsors in any area that encroaches on the day-to-day tasks and responsibilities. With care, and from personal experience, I can say that such communication can make huge differences in the quality (and therefore health) of the overall application management.

# A Fusion Application Manager's Checklist

The application manager needs to consider a few common tasks before and after implementing Fusion Applications. Fusion Applications adoption will likely be gradual, as a piece-by-piece migration of features, capabilities, and products from existing applications to those inside Fusion Applications. As such, some of these tasks may be quite small to start with, but looking through the list you'll see that they apply whether the business users are using just one feature or product, or the whole suite.

Before performing any of these tasks, the application manager needs to understand what is involved in that task and formulate a clear and approved plan for the task. Most of this has been covered to some degree in this book, and together with the additional material listed in the Appendix it should help lay the foundations for creating and maintaining a healthy Fusion Applications environment.

- Reliability Plan

  - Set up and configure diagnostic tools.

  - Set up logging and tracing configurations and guidelines.

  - Set up failure monitoring and alerting infrastructure and tooling.

  - Set up internal helpdesk process for incident and problem management.

  - Set up proactive issue avoidance plan.

- Availability

  - Set up regular maintenance plans and tooling.

  - Set up backup and recovery plan and resources.

  - Set up hardware lifecycle plan, including upgrades, replacements, and so on.

  - Set up emergency plans—contingency, resolution and escalation processes.

  - Set up instance provision plans, including resourcing and usage profiles.

  - Set up systems integration management, both internal and external.

- Performance

  - Set up performance monitoring plan.

  - Set up automated alerting infrastructure and tooling.

  - Set up capacity management plan, including scalability and lifecycle.

- Optimization

  - Set up application management resourcing—people, time, tasks, priorities.

  - Set up configuration management process and tooling (including customization management).

  - Set up improvement reviews of cross-organization stakeholders, content, and frequency.

  - Set up supplier/partner capabilities, engagements, and monitoring.

  - Set up budgetary and cost management plans.

- Governance

  - Set up system security (all aspects, including violation rules and processes).

  - Set up all audit and reporting tooling.

  - Set up patching methodology and tooling.

  - Set up application testing methodology and tooling.

  - Set up application software lifecycle plan (upgrades and so on).

  - Set up change control process and tooling.

  - Set up data management methodology and tooling (cleansing, quality, optimization).

# CHAPTER
## 12

# Planning for the Future

s more and more pioneering organizations use Fusion Applications its management needs will become much clearer, however even now as a new product suite it is still possible to highlight some key areas that the application manager should include as part of their infrastructure and future planning.

This chapter does not uncover any product designs or unpublished plans, however helps create a helpful picture that should allow the development of a management strategy that includes longevity and helps secure an ongoing return on investment.

There are three main sections to this discussion. The first gives some highlights on where the general technologies and architectures used in Fusion Applications are heading. The next section looks directly at Fusion Applications and how its products and features will evolve going forward. And the final section considers Fusion Applications management and how requirements, tooling, and approaches will develop over time.

# Application Architectures

Fusion Applications has been built and launched on the latest version (11$g$) of Oracle's technology products, from Fusion Middleware, Business Intelligence, to the Database. This means it's unlike many other existing applications that must play "technology catch-up" as they are put through certification testing and extension to support the latest platform releases. Although this time lag between technology and application development means that Enterprise Applications are always a little behind the latest technical capabilities, many would say that this is a good thing, because it allows for a sensible stabilization period before the newest technologies are used as part of real business processes and data. The savvy application manager will keep an eye on each new release of the core techstack components, knowing that by being aware of these, he or she can gain a head start on any future adoption into the application stack.

# Client Evolution

The ways in which users engage with web-based applications are constantly, almost weekly, changing—with new browser releases; new user interface paradigms such as Flash, HTMLv5, 3-D graphics, and augmented reality; and even in new client hardware technologies such as tablets and smart phones. This all helps set an application users expectations. Even though we're not surprised that Enterprise Applications are not quite as engaging as our favorite media or games applications, we can easily forget (and cannot readily measure) how software usability directly affects productivity.

Fusion Applications certainly changes things and its streamlined interface sets new standards in user productivity. The application manager also needs to be prepared for requirements for newly appropriate client solutions—be it handheld terminal support, mobile application support, custom portal mash-ups and dashboard-like pages, detailed personalization options, and direct integration with collaboration tools such as e-mail, wikis, blogs, and other social networking capabilities.

# Component Maturity

Some of the components of the Fusion Applications technology stack are very mature, such as WebLogic Server and the Database, but other capabilities are less so, especially when used as part of an Oracle Applications solution. Oracle SOA Server and other Fusion Middleware components such as Enterprise Scheduling Service (ESS), Approval Management Service (AMX), and Oracle Business Rules (OBR) are being applied in much more comprehensive and pivotal positions than ever before and will be pushed by the demands that a true enterprise application will place on them. As such, some capabilities will be extended and built-out in the future to meet the ever-increasing tasks involved in real business operations.

The application manager should be familiar with these areas and have a reasonable appreciation of the capabilities and maturity of the technology stack components. They must know what is available while contributing requirements and enhancements back to Oracle where important capabilities remain unsatisfied or where capability improvements and extensions could be made.

# Business Intelligence and Analytics

Fusion Applications is certainly rich when it comes to its reporting and analytic capabilities, but these will most likely encourage even more desire for reporting features, options, and content. Of course, the better the business management teams can monitor, control, and improve the operations, the happier everyone will be and BI tooling will be an important contributor. Consider for a minute the flexible analysis workbenches and wizard-like report creation tools discussed in the toolbox chapters earlier and how the application manager needs to clearly understand and use each of these, since business operational data will quickly flow into Fusion Applications and these tools and the demands put upon them will be a quickly evolving area that needs support.

All BI components, like those mentioned before, will continue to add features and capabilities, and many of these will be incorporated into Fusion Applications. When used in its standalone deployment mode, BI already provides some interesting potential for advanced multidimensional analysis and predictive business modeling. In the race for competitive advantage and to squeeze every last efficiency from the business operation, these kinds of built-in capabilities will increase in importance going forward.

# Integration Expansion

The coexistence opportunities in version 1.0 already illustrate the integration-ready nature of Fusion Applications; going forward, these opportunities will be expanded, as organizations, their trading partners, and centralized hub-like service providers look to integrate their systems to Fusion Applications.

The savvy application manager will have a good grasp of the resources involved (via OER) and will ensure they are involved in the development and adoption of all integrations to promote the inclusion of supportability and manageability.

# Hardware

It's clear from the computer hardware business that Information Lifecycle Management (ILM), discussed in Chapter 4, is becoming a key management consideration in the search to gain efficiencies from evolving distribution media formats and related network architectures. Splitting the application data and components across specialist hardware resources makes perfect sense for Fusion Applications, since it allows for specialization and a focus on specific capabilities to meet precise needs, while keeping utilization rates high.

The enterprise data center of today leverages both physical and virtualized servers and storage distributed across their networks. This allows them to tailor the hardware provisioning to the needs of their applications. As Fusion Applications implementation experience grows, the application manager can use these capabilities to fine-tune the network topology and it is likely that Oracle's own hardware products (Exadata, Exalogic etc) will be offered in a way that is optimized specifically for running Fusion Applications.

# Fusion Applications

Let's take a brief look at Fusion Applications as a product, how it is likely to evolve, and what the application manager can do to prepare for this.

## Business Processes

With each new release, Fusion Applications will add more functional features with which a wider range of organizations can run more parts of their operation. We already noted in Chapter 1 that areas such as manufacturing, public sector, and budgetary control will be enhanced in future releases, although this is just the tip of the iceberg of what will come. Fusion Applications version 1.0 is intended to support the core business operations that are common to most organizations, thereby forming a stable base upon which more specific features will be built. So although more breadth in terms of features and different business processes is coming, it's also likely we'll see more depth to the existing features as well.

To support wider business processes across different industry sectors and additional global operating regions, new features will include more configuration and setup options to enhance the flexibility of the core parts. In addition, more reporting and analytical options will be available, so the information coming out of the system will be even more applicable to each newly supported business environment.

New features and options mean more implementation-type tasks for the enterprise application manager, including reviewing all related parts of his infrastructure to ensure that everything is covered. This includes special emphasis on capacity planning, since usage profiles may change substantially and new capabilities might need resourcing in new ways.

# Pillar Replication

As mentioned in Chapter 2, it will soon be possible to split the database on which Fusion Applications runs into multiple instances. These separate instances, known as pillars, will have their data (or at least a core subset of it) synchronized so that all applications will have the details they need. This will present some additional options to the application manager in terms of the physical and logical division and location of the datasets they manage.

Related to this, the technical components that facilitate this solution, such as Oracle Data Integrator (ODI), are part of the Fusion technology stack, and with newer capabilities such as those from the acquired GoldenGate toolset comes a potential platform for the distribution of business data across additional boundaries and its use in other systems. This may also be an area of general opportunity for the application manager's attention.

# Business Activity Monitoring

Oracle already offers comprehensive insight into the business processes that are implemented as part of its SOA Suite, via a tool known as Business Activity Monitoring (BAM). Though this is not prepackaged with Fusion Applications, it still represents a significant opportunity for organizations to be able to drill into their business operational processing data and truly measure and analyze it, looking for efficiencies and improvements. Although the manual implementation of BAM can be used now, going forward, this may make a valuable addition to the standard fusion application technology stack and offers both business analysts and the application manager some rich and powerful capabilities.

Similarly, the Oracle Business Process Modeling Suite, may become more integrated into Fusion Applications, and it seems sensible to imagine a method by which significant adjustments can be made in the business process design-time view without the need for invasive customization and coding. With tighter integration to the BPM Suite such changes would be reflected in the runtime application, across the user interface, the application logic, and across all spawned events such as Business Process Execution Language (BPEL) processes and ESS jobs. Although some elements of this are already available, a full end-to-end filtering of declarative changes down into the application components and code would provide a valuable extension.

## Cloud-Based Solutions

The range of outsourcing services for Fusion Applications, both from Oracle and other providers, will continue to grow, based on their practical deployment profiles as well as the market demand. With IT department budgets remaining tight, the consumption of discrete, fit-for-purpose services seems far more reasonable than planning a major replacement of existing application resources. As such, the range of offerings for Fusion Applications will most likely match many similar capabilities that exist in the market today. For those parts of Fusion Applications that are especially well suited to provision in a single or multitenant, on-demand style, a full range of hosted options will likely become available, leveraging the existing building blocks that support integration into back-end on-premise systems.

## Third-Party Services

As with all popular and innovative solutions, a whole host of products and services will evolve around Fusion Applications, whether from the larger integration partners and consultancies or from niche providers of point solutions. Through participating in conferences, forums, and specialist media, the application manager can match business requirements with specific prepackaged products and services on the market. These solutions might be standalone capabilities that can be integrated with minimal effort or form some semblance of a prebuilt customization and extension solution. The application manager should keep an eye on the service offerings available so that potential solutions to existing problems or shortcomings are noticed and investigated.

# Fusion Application Management

Now that we've looked at a few predictions for application architectures and Fusion Applications, let's try and tie the two together by considering how Fusion Application management itself might evolve.

# Implementations

As Fusion Applications is implemented more and more, a wealth of valuable information will become available. This will take various forms, from solutions, recommendations, and advice that gets things working, to direct constructive feedback and improvement suggestions. Inevitably, Oracle (and implementation partners) will respond with adjustments and changes to help meet common challenges. Areas such as Functional Setup Manager (FSM) and the application provisioning process will likely see new information and potential changes resulting from feedback from more real user experiences.

# Enriched Supportability Ecosystem

The frameworks that exist to help support application use will evolve substantially as more experiences lead to more ways of resolving and avoiding issues. The Diagnostic Test Framework (DTF) will become a repository that holds detailed tests to validate a wider range of business processes and objects. Likewise, the proactive support services available in My Oracle Support will evolve, allowing health and patch recommendations to be displayed upon checking each instance against an ever-increasing set of validation routines. Some of these capabilities will not be implemented without the applications manager's consent and active engagement (such as Oracle Configuration Manager collections), so ensuring that systems are updated with the latest tools, tests, and capabilities is essential right from the start.

The incident and problem management capabilities of Fusion Applications will mature by handling many different types of failures. The range diagnostics it collects will expand and fire only those applicable to each failure context. Some automated analysis and resolution capabilities will inevitably be introduced at some point as well.

To support these technical features, the additional experience of implementing incident and problem management within an IT Service Management (ITSM) methodology (such as Information Technology Infrastructure Library) will allow the subsequent processing flows to become standardized, easier and more flexible to implement, and ultimately improve resolution time.

# Coexistence

These prepackaged integrations will evolve as customer need dictates, either laterally crossing additional business processes or by being built out so each one is a more complete flow. Obviously the ultimate vision is that the use of Fusion Applications is extended beyond a small subsection of functionality and transitions to adopt core features, with the final shift being a decommission of the existing legacy applications.

One thing is for certain, the application manager's skills in project contribution and management will be tested to the full. This is why project management was one of the tips mentioned in Chapter 11.

# Configuration and Change Management

Again mentioned in Chapter 11, to manage the complete application configuration (platform, technology stack, and functionality), a hybrid solution is required, merging and extending the different out-of-the-box tools available. The same applies to change management, where some parts of the application (such as the database) may be well equipped while other parts are less so. This represents another opportunity for future instrumentation, where tools such as the Enterprise Manager add-in packs could be used to extend and integrate disparate information into one change management console.

In addition, with Fusion Applications' unparalleled support for incorporating customizations and extensions, it's likely that the leading providers of development services (Oracle included) will offer associated management tooling, and where core features and data are affected, governance capabilities shouldn't be overlooked.

# Patching

In the future, we can expect the near-zero-downtime patching to become true zero-downtime patching. Although currently some restarts may be required for technical reasons, as things evolve these limitations are likely to be minimized or completely removed and online maintenance will become a reality.

In addition, although Fusion Applications represents some significant advancement in patching, it again seems likely that the user interface will move closer to that of the Oracle Universal Installer, offering features such as graphical progress information and time-to-end calculations. The integration of patching information into Enterprise Manager via its Patch Checker and My Oracle Support's Patching Plans shows that things have moved forward quickly, with the addition of not only the list of missing patches but also supporting information such as usage statistics, content information, and dependency analysis. We can expect more of this rich information to come as well, such as more helpful details (and automation) on post-patch testing process flows.

## Deeper Technology Stack Management

Oracle is constantly adding rich technical management capabilities to its product portfolio, and as these products mature, they'll support specific Fusion Applications use cases. One simple example could be the acquired AmberPoint product range, where advanced SOA management tooling would be useful for managing and analyzing the composites within Fusion Applications.

## Seamless Tooling

The tooling around Fusion Applications tends to fit into the channels based on the origin of the resource being managed: Fusion Middleware Control for middleware, Fusion Applications Control for applications, Database Control for database, Weblogic Console for Weblogic Server, Functional Setup Manager for the implementation of product features, the Diagnostic Dashboard for running tests, and so on. Oracle's Enterprise Manager's goal is to run across these silos, and it seems sensible to imagine that going forwards this will come closer to offering the complete applications management view, up and down the technology stack.

## Health Automation

The ultimate panacea is for software applications and systems to be self-healing. When embedded health monitoring begins to detect some changes (ideally before real problem symptoms occur), an intelligent process should be triggered to analyze the change and apply an appropriate corrective action.

Although this is over-simplified, it remains the ultimate aim. So how close are we in Fusion Applications version 1.0? The presence of OCM for automatically capturing and health-checking system information and the Diagnostic Framework (DFw) that triggers various diagnostic test executions upon incident creation and processing both signify huge steps forward on this path.

Going further and outside of Fusion Applications' current capabilities, a few third-party providers already offer predictive learning engines that analyze software applications and try to pinpoint appropriate solutions based on what has proven successful in the past. These artificial intelligence–based solutions not only learn about problems and solutions as they go but also track the pattern of system use. This means that sudden but very short peaks in system activity are not always misconstrued as emergency problems, but should they begin to show reoccurring patterns and repeated problem symptoms, extra capacity can be automatically provisioned.

Looking at problem patterns and signatures can be rather painstaking and laborious work; therefore, using automated routines makes perfect sense, especially where the volume of data is simply too large to ensure reasonable accuracy using manual processing. With organizations entrusting their money-making operation to Fusion Applications' processes, it again seems logical that some related capabilities can be expected in the future. Such tools are exceptionally complex both in how they work and the results they come up with, and inaccurate results can quickly cause a loss of faith in such a tool. As such, related solutions might seem relatively slow to appear.

The automation involved in finding and resolving health issues is especially important in resource and capacity management, since there is little point in having fail-over type features if they are not automatically invoked to avoid serious user impact. Although much of this is already available out-of-the-box in Fusion Applications' high availability options, some clever solutions may be just around the corner. For example, to ensure continuity of business process flows, problematic processes or data could be quarantined, allowing only known-good actions to be available until a solution to the problem is implemented, kind of like a system being run in a safe mode.

The point of learning problem patterns and signatures is to identify matching solutions and apply them implicitly without the involvement of the application manager. This still remains incredibly challenging for various reasons, such as the wide range of potential solutions, incomplete data, and a lack of trust of automation. However, once these exciting capabilities do become part of everyday life, the last consideration will be just what the Fusion Applications Manager will do with all his newly found spare time!

# APPENDIX

## Further Reading and References

hree types of documents are listed here. First is the official Oracle Fusion Applications product material, a must-read that can be easily supplemented by attending a corresponding Oracle Education class. These documents form the application manager's core reference library. The second type of document is more general and covers Oracle's products that are used within Fusion Applications, either to run, manage, or extend it. Finally, complementary documents from the Oracle Press series that, while they do not focus on Fusion Applications specifically, do provide lots of helpful background material.

In addition, as explained in Chapter 1, for all product functionality, the User Assistance system (online help) within Fusion Applications is designed to provide all the content required for using and managing business functionality.

One final note, the availability of specific documents changes frequently, and this list should provide just an outline of topics for which material may be provided.

# Oracle Product Documentation

The following documentation is intended to support Oracle Fusion Applications. Note that these guides frequently reference other material (such as Fusion Middleware), and it's especially prudent to follow the links for a complete picture.

- Oracle Fusion Applications Concepts Guide (E15525-01)
- Oracle Fusion Applications Administrator and Implementer Roadmap (E17329-01)
- Oracle Fusion Applications Enterprise Deployment Guide (E16684-01)
- Oracle Fusion Applications Administrator's Guide (E14496-01)
- Oracle Fusion Applications Installation Guide (E16600-01)
- Oracle Fusion Applications Patching Guide (E16602-01)

- Oracle Fusion Applications Security Guide (E16689-01)

- Oracle Fusion Applications Extensibility Guide (E16691-01)

- Oracle Fusion Applications Developer's Guide (E15524-01)

# Other Oracle Documentation

Upon first glance, you might be thinking this section is a bit short, especially around middleware; however just the top-most documents are listed here with a few examples of where you can find out more:

- Oracle Fusion Middleware - Documentation Library 11*g* (E14571-01)

  - Oracle Fusion Middleware Administrator's Guide 11*g* (E10105-07)

  - Developer's Guide for Oracle Application Development Framework 11*g* (B31974-03)

  - Introducing Web Services 11*g* (E14294-03)

  - Developing Web Applications, Servlets, and JSPs for Oracle WebLogic Server 11*g* (E13712-02)

  - Developer's Guide for Oracle Enterprise Scheduler 11*g* (E10142-01)

  - Using Clusters for Oracle WebLogic Server 11*g* (E13709-02)

  - Modelling and Implementation Guide for Oracle Business Process Management 11g (E15176-01)

  - Developer's Guide for Oracle SOA Suite 11*g* (E10224-03)

  - Developer's Guide for Oracle WebCenter 11*g* (E10148-04)

  - User's Guide for Oracle Business Activity Monitoring 11*g* (E10230-01)

- Oracle Database Concepts 11*g* (E10713-05)

- Oracle Database Administrator's Guide 11*g* (E10595-07)

- Oracle Database Performance Tuning Guide (E10821-05)

# Oracle Press Series

Following are selections from Oracle Press:

- *Oracle Fusion Developer Guide: Building Rich Internet Applications with Oracle ADF Business Components and Oracle ADF Faces*, by F. Nimphius and L. Munsinger

- *Quick Start Guide to Oracle Fusion Development: Oracle JDeveloper and Oracle ADF*, by G. Ronald

- *Oracle JDeveloper 11g Handbook: A Guide to Fusion Web Development*, by D. Mills, P. Koletzke, and A. Roy-Faderman

- *Oracle SOA Suite 11g Handbook*, by L. Jellema

- *Enterprise Grid Computing with Oracle*, by B. Goyal and S. Lawande

- *Oracle Business Intelligence Suite Developer's Guide*, by M. Rittman

# Online Resources

In addition to (and including) the material highlighted here, each product is released with detailed online content that is easily searchable and downloadable. Visit oracle.com/documentation to get started.

The Oracle Technology Network (oracle.com/otn) also contains many tutorials, case studies, examples, and white papers on all topics and is fantastic for putting a practical spin on the product documentation.

Finally, My Oracle Support provides detailed knowledgebase articles that build upon the standard documentation with specific content dealing with known problem solutions, advice on completing non-standard tasks, and on sharing recommendations and best practices. This content is constantly being expanded and is organized in a way the application manager can readily use, whether it's for learning, troubleshooting a specific problem, or simply managing a part of the application lifecycle.

# Index

Functional Setup Manager
    application setup
        optimization, 182
    business process
        governance, 198
    business process reliability,
        116–117
    future evolution of, 282
    overview of, 12–13
    proactive configuration
        management, 249
functional testing, 202
Fusion Applications Control,
    143–144, 164
Fusion Applications, future evolution
    of, 279–285
Fusion Applications Taxonomy, 29
Fusion Middleware. *See* FMw
    (Fusion Middleware)
future plans
    advantages of success, 87
    application architectures,
        276–279
    Business Activity
        Monitoring, 280
    business processes, 279
    cloud-based solutions, 281
    management, 281–285
    managing for optimization, 78
    overview of, 276
    pillar replication, 280
    third-party services, 281

### G

Generation-Y workforce
    benefits of sharing information,
        228–229
    expectations of application
        usability, 19

generic lifecycles
    Application Lifecycle
        Model, 94
    benefits and limitations of,
        98–99
    example of IT, 90–91
    Information Lifecycle, 94–95
    IT Service Management,
        95–98
    Rapid Application
        Development, 93
    software development, 92–93
global area, layout, 19
governance
    of change management. *See*
        change management
    of data cleansing, 80–82
    enterprise application
        manager checklist for, 274
    enterprise application
        manager role, 59
    healthy, 227
    impacts of failure, 87
    information gatekeepers
        and, 82
    overview of, 78
    of security, 79–80
    of SOA performance, 163
Governance, Risk, and
    Compliance. *See* GRC
    (Governance, Risk, and
    Compliance)
governance tools
    applications technology,
        201–204
    business processes, 198–201
    GRC products, 196–197
    platform layer, 205–208
    structure of, 108–109
    testing, 248

# GET YOUR FREE SUBSCRIPTION
# TO *ORACLE MAGAZINE*

*Oracle Magazine* is essential gear for today's information technology professionals. Stay informed and increase your productivity with every issue of *Oracle Magazine*. Inside each free bimonthly issue you'll get:

- Up-to-date information on Oracle Database, Oracle Application Server, Web development, enterprise grid computing, database technology, and business trends
- Third-party news and announcements
- Technical articles on Oracle and partner products, technologies, and operating environments
- Development and administration tips
- Real-world customer stories

If there are other Oracle users at your location who would like to receive their own subscription to *Oracle Magazine*, please photocopy this form and pass it along.

## Three easy ways to subscribe:

**① Web**
Visit our Web site at **oracle.com/oraclemagazine**
You'll find a subscription form there, plus much more

**② Fax**
Complete the questionnaire on the back of this card
and fax the questionnaire side only to **+1.847.763.9638**

**③ Mail**
Complete the questionnaire on the back of this card
and mail it to **P.O. Box 1263, Skokie, IL 60076-8263**

ORACLE®

# Want your own FREE subscription?

To receive a free subscription to *Oracle Magazine*, you must fill out the entire card, sign it, and date it (incomplete cards cannot be processed or acknowledged). You can also fax your application to **+1.847.763.9638. Or subscribe at our Web site at oracle.com/oraclemagazine**

○ **Yes, please send me a FREE subscription** *Oracle Magazine*.    ○ No.

○ From time to time, Oracle Publishing allows our partners exclusive access to our e-mail addresses for special promotions and announcements. To be included in this program, please check this circle. If you do not wish to be included, you will only receive notices about your subscription via e-mail.

○ Oracle Publishing allows sharing of our postal mailing list with selected third parties. If you prefer your mailing address not to be included in this program, please check this circle.

If at any time you would like to be removed from either mailing list, please contact Customer Service at +1.847.763.9635 or send an e-mail to oracle@halldata.com. If you opt in to the sharing of information, Oracle may also provide you with e-mail related to Oracle products, services, and events. If you want to completely unsubscribe from any e-mail communication from Oracle, please send an e-mail to: unsubscribe@oracle-mail.com with the following in the subject line: REMOVE [your e-mail address]. For complete information on Oracle Publishing's privacy practices, please visit oracle.com/html/privacy/html

**X** _____
signature (required)                              date

name                                              title

company                                           e-mail address

street/p.o. box

city/state/zip or postal code                     telephone

country                                           fax

**Would you like to receive your free subscription in digital format instead of print if it becomes available?** ○ Yes  ○ No

---

## YOU MUST ANSWER ALL 10 QUESTIONS BELOW.

**① WHAT IS THE PRIMARY BUSINESS ACTIVITY OF YOUR FIRM AT THIS LOCATION? (check one only)**
- □ 01 Aerospace and Defense Manufacturing
- □ 02 Application Service Provider
- □ 03 Automotive Manufacturing
- □ 04 Chemicals
- □ 05 Media and Entertainment
- □ 06 Construction/Engineering
- □ 07 Consumer Sector/Consumer Packaged Goods
- □ 08 Education
- □ 09 Financial Services/Insurance
- □ 10 Health Care
- □ 11 High Technology Manufacturing, OEM
- □ 12 Industrial Manufacturing
- □ 13 Independent Software Vendor
- □ 14 Life Sciences (biotech, pharmaceuticals)
- □ 15 Natural Resources
- □ 16 Oil and Gas
- □ 17 Professional Services
- □ 18 Public Sector (government)
- □ 19 Research
- □ 20 Retail/Wholesale/Distribution
- □ 21 Systems Integrator, VAR/VAD
- □ 22 Telecommunications
- □ 23 Travel and Transportation
- □ 24 Utilities (electric, gas, sanitation, water)
- □ 98 Other Business and Services _____

**② WHICH OF THE FOLLOWING BEST DESCRIBES YOUR PRIMARY JOB FUNCTION? (check one only)**

CORPORATE MANAGEMENT/STAFF
- □ 01 Executive Management (President, Chair, CEO, CFO, Owner, Partner, Principal)
- □ 02 Finance/Administrative Management (VP/Director/ Manager/Controller, Purchasing, Administration)
- □ 03 Sales/Marketing Management (VP/Director/Manager)
- □ 04 Computer Systems/Operations Management (CIO/VP/Director/Manager MIS/IS/IT, Ops)

IS/IT STAFF
- □ 05 Application Development/Programming Management
- □ 06 Application Development/Programming Staff
- □ 07 Consulting
- □ 08 DBA/Systems Administrator
- □ 09 Education/Training
- □ 10 Technical Support Director/Manager
- □ 11 Other Technical Management/Staff
- □ 98 Other

**③ WHAT IS YOUR CURRENT PRIMARY OPERATING PLATFORM (check all that apply)**
- □ 01 Digital Equipment Corp UNIX/VAX/VMS
- □ 02 HP UNIX
- □ 03 IBM AIX
- □ 04 IBM UNIX
- □ 05 Linux (Red Hat)
- □ 06 Linux (SUSE)
- □ 07 Linux (Oracle Enterprise)
- □ 08 Linux (other)
- □ 09 Macintosh
- □ 10 MVS
- □ 11 Netware
- □ 12 Network Computing
- □ 13 SCO UNIX
- □ 14 Sun Solaris/SunOS
- □ 15 Windows
- □ 16 Other UNIX
- □ 98 Other
- 99 □ None of the Above

**④ DO YOU EVALUATE, SPECIFY, RECOMMEND, OR AUTHORIZE THE PURCHASE OF ANY OF THE FOLLOWING? (check all that apply)**
- □ 01 Hardware
- □ 02 Business Applications (ERP, CRM, etc.)
- □ 03 Application Development Tools
- □ 04 Database Products
- □ 05 Internet or Intranet Products
- □ 06 Other Software
- □ 07 Middleware Products
- 99 □ None of the Above

**⑤ IN YOUR JOB, DO YOU USE OR PLAN TO PURCHASE ANY OF THE FOLLOWING PRODUCTS? (check all that apply)**

SOFTWARE
- □ 01 CAD/CAE/CAM
- □ 02 Collaboration Software
- □ 03 Communications
- □ 04 Database Management
- □ 05 File Management
- □ 06 Finance
- □ 07 Java
- □ 08 Multimedia Authoring
- □ 09 Networking
- □ 10 Programming
- □ 11 Project Management
- □ 12 Scientific and Engineering
- □ 13 Systems Management
- □ 14 Workflow

HARDWARE
- □ 15 Macintosh
- □ 16 Mainframe
- □ 17 Massively Parallel Processing
- □ 18 Minicomputer
- □ 19 Intel x86(32)
- □ 20 Intel x86(64)
- □ 21 Network Computer
- □ 22 Symmetric Multiprocessing
- □ 23 Workstation Services

SERVICES
- □ 24 Consulting
- □ 25 Education/Training
- □ 26 Maintenance
- □ 27 Online Database
- □ 28 Support
- □ 29 Technology-Based Training
- □ 30 Other
- 99 □ None of the Above

**⑥ WHAT IS YOUR COMPANY'S SIZE? (check one only)**
- □ 01 More than 25,000 Employees
- □ 02 10,001 to 25,000 Employees
- □ 03 5,001 to 10,000 Employees
- □ 04 1,001 to 5,000 Employees
- □ 05 101 to 1,000 Employees
- □ 06 Fewer than 100 Employees

**⑦ DURING THE NEXT 12 MONTHS, HOW MUCH DO YOU ANTICIPATE YOUR ORGANIZATION WILL SPEND ON COMPUTER HARDWARE, SOFTWARE, PERIPHERALS, AND SERVICES FOR YOUR LOCATION? (check one only)**
- □ 01 Less than $10,000
- □ 02 $10,000 to $49,999
- □ 03 $50,000 to $99,999
- □ 04 $100,000 to $499,999
- □ 05 $500,000 to $999,999
- □ 06 $1,000,000 and Over

**⑧ WHAT IS YOUR COMPANY'S YEARLY SALES REVENUE? (check one only)**
- □ 01 $500, 000, 000 and above
- □ 02 $100, 000, 000 to $500, 000, 000
- □ 03 $50, 000, 000 to $100, 000, 000
- □ 04 $5, 000, 000 to $50, 000, 000
- □ 05 $1, 000, 000 to $5, 000, 000

**⑨ WHAT LANGUAGES AND FRAMEWORKS DO YOU USE? (check all that apply)**
- □ 01 Ajax
- □ 02 C
- □ 03 C++
- □ 04 C#
- □ 05 Hibernate
- □ 06 J++/J#
- □ 07 Java
- □ 08 JSP
- □ 09 .NET
- □ 10 Perl
- □ 11 PHP
- □ 12 PL/SQL
- □ 13 Python
- □ 14 Ruby/Rails
- □ 15 Spring
- □ 16 Struts
- □ 17 SQL
- □ 18 Visual Basic
- □ 98 Other

**⑩ WHAT ORACLE PRODUCTS ARE IN USE AT YOUR SITE? (check all that apply)**

ORACLE DATABASE
- □ 01 Oracle Database 11*g*
- □ 02 Oracle Database 10*g*
- □ 03 Oracle9*i* Database
- □ 04 Oracle Embedded Database (Oracle Lite, Times Ten, Berkeley DB)
- □ 05 Other Oracle Database Release

ORACLE FUSION MIDDLEWARE
- □ 06 Oracle Application Server
- □ 07 Oracle Portal
- □ 08 Oracle Enterprise Manager
- □ 09 Oracle BPEL Process Manager
- □ 10 Oracle Identity Management
- □ 11 Oracle SOA Suite
- □ 12 Oracle Data Hubs

ORACLE DEVELOPMENT TOOLS
- □ 13 Oracle JDeveloper
- □ 14 Oracle Forms
- □ 15 Oracle Reports
- □ 16 Oracle Designer
- □ 17 Oracle Discoverer
- □ 18 Oracle BI Beans
- □ 19 Oracle Warehouse Builder
- □ 20 Oracle WebCenter
- □ 21 Oracle Application Express

ORACLE APPLICATIONS
- □ 22 Oracle E-Business Suite
- □ 23 PeopleSoft Enterprise
- □ 24 JD Edwards EnterpriseOne
- □ 25 JD Edwards World
- □ 26 Oracle Fusion
- □ 27 Hyperion
- □ 28 Siebel CRM

ORACLE SERVICES
- □ 28 Oracle E-Business Suite On Demand
- □ 29 Oracle Technology On Demand
- □ 30 Siebel CRM On Demand
- □ 31 Oracle Consulting
- □ 32 Oracle Education
- □ 33 Oracle Support
- □ 98 Other
- 99 □ None of the Above